AUTHORIZED
HERITAGE

AUTHORIZED HERITAGE

PLACE, MEMORY, AND HISTORIC SITES IN PRAIRIE CANADA

ROBERT COUTTS

UNIVERSITY OF MANITOBA PRESS

University of Manitoba Press
Winnipeg, Manitoba, Canada
Treaty 1 Territory
uofmpress.ca

Cataloguing data available from Library and Archives Canada
ISBN 978-0-88755-926-6 (PAPER)
ISBN 978-0-88755-930-3 (PDF)
ISBN 978-0-88755-928-0 (EPUB)
ISBN 978-0-88755-932-7 (BOUND)

Interior design by Karen Armstrong
Cover design by Marvin Harder
Cover image: Prince of Wales Fort, Churchill,
courtesy of Parks Canada

Printed in Canada

This book has been published with the help of a grant from the Federation for the Humanities and Social Sciences, through the Awards to Scholarly Publications Program, using funds provided by the Social Sciences and Humanities Research Council of Canada.

The University of Manitoba Press acknowledges the financial support for its publication program provided by the Government of Canada through the Canada Book Fund, the Canada Council for the Arts, the Manitoba Department of Sport, Culture, and Heritage, the Manitoba Arts Council, and the Manitoba Book Publishing Tax Credit.

Funded by the Government of Canada | Canada

To my wife, Catherine, who can see from a great distance what I cannot see close.
And to Margot and Hugh.

CONTENTS

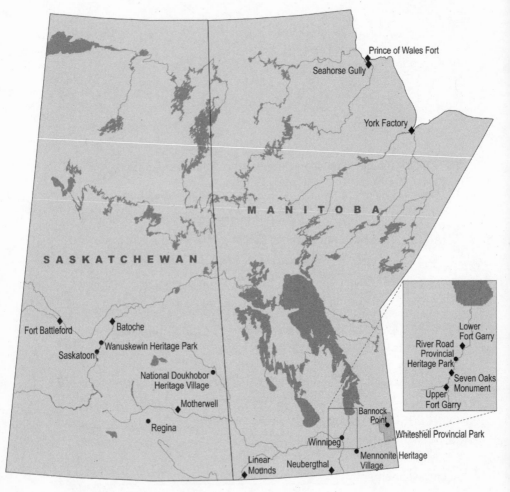

Map 1. Heritage places discussed in this book.

Within the map:

PRINCE OF WALES FORT
Seahorse Gully
York Factory
MANITOBA
SASKATCHEWAN
Fort Battleford
Batoche
Wanuskewin Heritage Park
Saskatoon
National Doukhobor Heritage Village
Motherwell
Regina
Bannock Point
Winnipeg
Whiteshell Provincial Park
Linear Mounds
Neubergthal
Mennonite Heritage Village

Inset:

Lower Fort Garry
River Road Provincial Heritage Park
Seven Oaks Monument
Upper Fort Garry

♦ National Historic Sites

Landscapes of Memory in Prairie Canada

Landscapes are culture before they are nature; constructs of the imagination projected onto wood and water and rock.

Simon Schama, *Landscape and Memory*

Landscape as culture. It is a concept that at first glance seems peculiar. Upon reflection, however, we realize that our Western view of landscape is the result of shared values and shared culture, a culture assembled from a rich accumulation of myths, folklores, events, and memories. Such landscapes of memory are cultural memories, and we all experience place and memory in different ways. One of my own encounters came from historical interest rather than personal familiarity. It was in August of 1983 that I found myself with a small group of people in a boat heading to Hudson Bay. We were travelling on the Hayes River in northern Manitoba, bound for York Factory, the once great trading post and entrepôt of the Hudson's Bay Company. Leaving from the junction of the Fox and Hayes rivers about 120 kilometres southwest of Hudson Bay, we travelled the river in the warm summer sunshine as the topography of the lowlands became flatter, the riverbank grew steeper, and the fir trees appeared smaller and stunted, bent low by the winter winds off the bay. We travelled for hours and the wilderness around us seemed interminable. But as the river grew wider, a last bend revealed a remarkable sight; the massive, gleaming white Depot Building of York Factory appeared as if an apparition, its presence startling in the vastness of the surrounding wilderness. I had read much about this place and its history, but I found it exhilarating to finally experience it in person.

I thought about the Indigenous peoples who witnessed this same sight over centuries, though they journeyed from far greater distances and of course without the modern motorized transport that made our trip so comfortable. Although it is colonial space (even if I had not thought of it that way in 1983), York Factory remains a place of becoming, of memory both local and beyond, and a representation of place and community that embodies the persistence of the past in the present. Whether "the most respectable place in the territory"[1] according to one nineteenth-century observer, or "a monstrous blot on a swampy spot"[2] to another, less generous writer, York today remains a place of cultural memory that is central to the traditions of the Muskego Cree community in northern Manitoba. But unlike York Factory and so many other striking and meaningful locations in the West, not all places of significance are necessarily monumental or old or even aesthetically pleasing. They are places that do not have inherent value or convey a meaning that is innate. For those who have lived in or near these landscapes, or for those who might come to a particular place with a different appreciation, it is historical reference—associative, personal, or imagined—that makes them physically symbolic and meaningful.

▲ ▲ ▲

In her 2006 book *Uses of Heritage*, the Australian writer and archaeologist Laurajane Smith described her meeting with a group of Indigenous women from the Waanyi community on the banks of the Gregory River in Boodjamulla National Park in northern Queensland. The women, according to Smith, had come from some distance away to meet and fish at this traditional Indigenous site. In attempting to, as she writes, "pester people with maps, site recording forms and tape measures," Smith soon realized that for these Waanyi women, the act of fishing was more than simply catching dinner; it was an opportunity to savour simply being in a place that was important to them. It was, as she comments, "heritage work" being in this place, renewing memories and sharing experiences with friends and family members to strengthen present and future social and family relations.[3] Smith describes how the Elders related stories of the Gregory River location to younger Waanyi women and about the traditional events associated with that place. Their conversations, she comments, reminded her of her own heritage, of the family stories she had inherited and how she would transmit them to her own children. In such a process of receiving and passing on memories, a certain fluidity of meaning is understood, becoming characteristic of both personal and community heritage in much the same way that it informs our perceptions of place. The significance that Smith drew from her own stories, the uses she made of them, and the places that resonated with her would, she wrote, "be different to the meanings and uses the generation both before and after me had and would construct."[4]

My own experience with community memory and the meaning and significance of place was somewhat similar to Smith's. A number of trips after my first visit to York Factory in 1983, while conducting ethnohistorical research at York Factory in northern Manitoba as a historian with Parks Canada in 2002, I met with a number of Muskego Cree Elders who had flown there for a reunion and with whom I had arranged informal interviews. The conversation was relaxed as we talked about the history of the place and the Elders' experiences growing up at York. In these conversations I noticed that their memories often began with some reference to place, to a geographical entity or location that became the reference point for a story, a memory, a cultural observation, or even a joke. I realized that for these York Factory people, their history, their heritage, was more than just about the past or about physical things but was an act of engagement and a process of finding meaning that resonated in the present. And it was about place and the layers of memory and meaning we attribute to it. It was at such site visits that I first began to think about landscape, place, and memory, how history plays out on the ground, how the social construction of heritage is established and commemorated, and how the meaning of place is often contested. Most often one has to actually be at these sites and walk these spaces. Like the historian Simon Schama, I have also drawn upon my own "archive of the feet" (as he calls it) and how it has informed much of the way I view the concept of heritage.[5]

The goal of *Authorized Heritage*, while at one level concerned with memory and place, is also to ask critical questions related to how and why certain heritage places were selected over others as significant. Do these perceptions of importance by governments, communities, and individuals change over time and, if so, how? I explore each of these questions within the thematic framework outlined in the various chapters and in the representation of different types of historic sites within a larger heritage context. It is my contention that most historic sites chosen by government relate to an authorized heritage discourse that is almost always based on those conventional messages that are part of national narratives and colonialist views of the past. I also explore the challenges over what is presented, the struggles of the marginalized regarding whose voice prevails, and how communities can form distinct and alternative perspectives on specific places. If an authorized heritage can still dominate and still influence those places we consider to be important, their significance is also affected by community perceptions and the emergence and persistence of social memory. Yet, often the two approaches are conflated, as a local perception that is no longer moored to social memory might simply echo the dominant discourse. It is then that an authorized heritage and a community perception become effectively one and the same.

The historic places chosen for this study are part of a larger space, a space we have come to know as the "prairie West" or the modern-day provinces of Manitoba and Saskatchewan. But in a greater sense the concept of the West as a region might suggest, at a physical level, a certain unity of landscape, setting, and geography. Of course, the West as a distinctive territory is made up of multiple geographies that include the topographies and ecologies of prairie, of parkland, and of boreal forest, and even of the western Hudson Bay lowlands. As a modern administrative construction it might refer to the region we now call the "Prairie Provinces," a modern and clearly bordered territory. In a historical construction, however, a more vague and indeterminate region comes to mind, one that includes the historic borderlands of the old "Northwest" as well as the broadly imagined West of culture, commerce, colonialism, literature, and social movement. At the political level I deal with a selection of historic places in what is now Manitoba and Saskatchewan, but in terms of geography these places cover the wide range of topographies and landscapes mentioned above.

In his 1999 book *The West: Regional Ambitions, National Debates, Global Age*, Gerald Friesen cites the geographer Cole Harris's description of Canada as a country made up of regions "having only fuzzy locational meanings," yet part of our spatial ambition (and resentment).[6] If Harris is right that regions may be only indistinctly grasped, the various environments that constitute "the West" do have an impact on the way history and culture are established—most particularly with the sorts of places discussed in this book. How these places, born of particular geographic, environmental, cultural, or political realities, have come to be known in a global digital age as "heritage places" brings a new dimension to any discussion of their past. It suggests that it is not purely landscape that defines the West. Rather it is the spirit of places and spaces that distinguishes this region, that tells sanctioned stories that are both conventional and unconventional, sometimes unified by perception and perspective and sometimes fragmented by history and culture, yet continuing to tell the individual and distinctive narratives of province, region, and community. In large part this book focuses on the way the interpretation of historic place in the West came to define attachment to the soil as private property, to the creation of capitalist labour markets, to the ascendency of individualism, and to the view that the territories occupied by Indigenous nations were empty lands.

The sorts of historic sites in this work range from the local to the national and represent, I believe, effective illustrations of important themes in prairie history. While the bulk of the research for this study came from government records, along with archival and published sources, the overarching themes that inform my writing are influenced by my individual experience with historic places throughout western Canada and abroad. I link my many personal experiences at places in western Canada with the enormous documentation that records the establishment, the values, the physical settings, and the interpretation of specific historic sites in Manitoba and Saskatchewan, and then contextualizing these realities and perspectives within the growing national and international literature on place, heritage, and memory. Within the broad themes of each chapter I provide brief histories of the selected places, but I have included them only to help set the context for their later designation and their modern-day roles as historic sites. I offer no detailed or exhaustive history of these places.

It is important to note as well that the list of historic sites chosen for this book is not intended in any way to be comprehensive or all-inclusive in regard to the particular themes they might represent. For instance, my discussion of pre-contact Indigenous sites in Chapter 1 or fur trade sites in Chapter 2 highlights a handful of sites in Manitoba and Saskatchewan that I am familiar with through visitation and research and that more importantly are examples of heritage designation and commemoration. These chapters and others do not attempt to cover *all* places of historical significance in the West—clearly an impossible task. Moreover, this book is not intended to provide any kind of comprehensive history of Indigenous cultural sites, or fur trade sites, settler sites, places of resistance, or places related to gender and sexuality in the West but rather to examine how and why these places were commemorated by government, how they are interpreted, and how that interpretation might have changed over time. Therefore, a certain process of selection was required, and I have chosen particular places that best fit the themes of the book. If other authors were to tackle this topic, they would no doubt have alternative sites in mind, but the places discussed in this book are ones I had become familiar with over the course of my career as a historian with Parks Canada.

The other question to be addressed is why I focus on Manitoba and Saskatchewan and not Alberta, even though the term "Prairie Canada" is used in my subtitle. As mentioned above, in choosing themes and sites, a certain process of selection is required, and the topics that were chosen are well represented by a variety of historic sites in Manitoba and Saskatchewan. The other reason is much more prosaic: my work did not involve Alberta sites (other than some brief research related to Rocky Mountain House, a designated fur trade site in west-central Alberta). I thought it best to not write about places I had never visited. I can add that because I use the term "prairie Canada" to mean the modern provinces of Manitoba and Saskatchewan, I have included northern sites such as York Factory, Seahorse Gully, and others in my analysis. I effectively view the two provinces as bordered territories of current governmental construction.

Apart from my direct experience with historic places and the mean-ings they convey, to some degree the inspiration for this study has come from the writings of Laurajane Smith, whose book *Uses of Heritage* got me to think about the concept she labels the "authorized heritage discourse." Of course, this is not a new idea, though it is a new label. It has been discussed over the years in a variety of forms by a variety of writers. I suppose, like my Parks Canada colleagues, I was aware that the history I was writing was a sanctioned undertaking—like a good civil servant I followed the directions of my managers—although also like my colleagues I often attempted new (and sometimes naive) in-terpretations and innovative perspectives. Although in truth we might not have thought a great deal about the differences between the two, we generally believed we were writing "history" while leaving "heritage" for park managers, site interpreters, and park planners. Of course, that separation was often blurred, as the hoped-for goal of historical writing in an agency such as Parks Canada is to have it applied to the practicalities of conservation, programming, and the realities of on-the-ground interpretation. That was frequently not the case.

But it is Smith's work that effectively situates these concepts within the larger discussions around heritage: heritage as a cultural (and bureaucratic) process, the authenticating institutions of heritage, and the culture and discourse of the heritage narrative. "Heritage," although variously understood, is seemingly ubiquitous. At one time the concern of only a minority of devotees, broadly speaking, heritage is now widely valued in most cultures. How this process occurred, how factors such as style, age, monumentality, aesthetics, tourism, and political imperative came to naturalize selected narratives about place, privilege expert knowledge, and indeed confer historic significance provides the theoretical basis for the following discussions about particular themes and places that form part of the history of prairie Canada. Over the last half-century federal, provincial, and municipal strategies fill many thousands of pages of policy direction in the selection, designation, definition, quantification, and management of heritage. I discuss the impact of these policies on the development and interpretation of historic places, and on heritage in general, in western Canada in the following chapters, and the impact of the more distinct and vernacular narratives of community-based heritage.

Generally, "heritage" is viewed as a process that characterizes places, spaces, people, events, practices, histories, objects, or ideas as a legacy from the past. Such legacies, according to cultural scholars Susan L.T. Ashley and Andrea Terry, are culturally produced, signified, and reproduced as heritage.[7] Heritage can function as both a process of engagement with place and as an act of communication that helps to create worth in and for the present. It is a subjective and political mediation of memory and identity. Cultural memory and the idea of a collective past can advance and endorse consensus versions of history (usually by the cultural institutions of the state and its elites) to control and standardize modern social and cultural life or what might be called the "dominant heritage discourse." I would argue that perceptions of place and memory are often related directly to those places in prairie Canada that we consider heritage. How does our view of the past influence the way we perceive authorized historic places and, conversely, how do these places affect our broad view of the past and the present, if in fact they do at all?

Understanding and unpacking the significance of a particular place is more easily done if one is actually there, and I have visited, usually multiple times, each of the sites discussed. To this last point the historian Simon Schama has written, "Historians are supposed to reach the past always through texts, occasionally through images, things that are safely caught up in the bell jar of academic convention; look but don't touch."[8] The places that we call "heritage" suggest a nuanced and often complex view of the past, but they do require a sense of touch that allows us to see history not just as a "thing" but rather as a cultural and social process. They suggest acts of remembering that are sometimes personal and sometimes official, the authoritative and imposing views of the past that are often created outside of the cultural identities shaped by personal attachment to place. Landscapes can have an aesthetic attraction for some and/or a cultural meaning for others, becoming sites of memory where an absence has become a presence.

Fittingly for this book, my first project for Parks Canada involved the writing of a landscape history of Batoche National Historic Site (NHS) in Saskatchewan, an attempt to research how the site landscape of the 1885 battlefield had changed over the roughly 100 years since the end of the Northwest Resistance. It was somewhat of a naive undertaking as I earnestly went about analyzing early descriptions of the battlefield, studied period photographs, and walked the area with the idea that Parks Canada would then alter the twentieth-century landscape to recreate for visitors what the battlefield looked like in May of 1885. It was a time, after all, of large heritage expectations and ambitions and even larger budgets. In the end, we discovered, unintentionally, that the history of that place included its evolution as a community and cultural landscape; that indeed change was part of its heritage. Suffice to say that the hoped-for manipulation of the battlefield landscape—clearing acres of brush and planting new trees elsewhere at a place that had witnessed a century of farming—did not occur except in the artistic renderings contained in site brochures. Nevertheless, it allowed me to employ, to some extent, the "archive of the feet."

Yet, my Batoche experience was an introduction for me to the significance of place as a social construct and the understanding of how history has played out or materialized upon the land. When one looked beyond the cultivated fields at Batoche, it was the shallow depressions of long-ago rifle pits and the vaguely discernable cart tracks of the old Carlton Trail that allowed the landscape to speak to another time and another reality.

Later, in my role as the historian for fur trade and Indigenous sites (places I would now call "sites of colonization"), I travelled to national historic sites in northern Manitoba, in Saskatchewan and Alberta, and eventually to the western Arctic. I was also very much involved in the interpretation programs at Lower Fort Garry, The Forks, Churchill, York Factory, and places such as the River Road Heritage Parkway just north of Winnipeg. While the work involved considerable research in various archives, just as importantly it entailed walking the length and breadth of these places, sometimes with site interpreters and visitors, often with archaeologists, and occasionally alone. Although I, like my Parks Canada colleagues, certainly subscribed to the Western idea that heritage can be studied, mapped, protected, conserved, and managed through government policy and legislation, we realized that the places we thought important were also social constructions that at one level reflected official versions of history. The long list of national and international agreements, from the Athens Charter to the Venice Charter, and heritage organizations such as ICOMOS (International Council on Monuments and Sites) and UNESCO (United Nations Education, Scientific and Cultural Organization), as well as a variety of supranational cultural resource management strategies, all speak to this "scientific" view of heritage. At the same time, heritage is a concept that can challenge received beliefs where the significance and meaning of place can be contested. The work of my former colleague Diane Payment on the Métis people of Batoche certainly speaks to this latter interpretation.[9]

Of course, historic sites differ widely. Some, like Lower Fort Garry, embody a heavily manipulated landscape, its buildings, lawns, and gardens in many ways contrived to meet visitor anticipations and comforts. If, at its most superficial level, the past at the Lower Fort is presented as different from the present, at a deeper level it reproduces not the past in the present but more a manufactured attraction and movie set of fur trade entertainments than a place of meaning. As a "living history" site it displays little of what heritage professionals might call "authenticity," a vague and imprecise concept that can be understood at different levels. At one level there is the physical and curatorial authenticity of buildings, rooms, landscapes, costumes, and the other choreographed material trappings and artifice of living history. At another there is the authenticity of voice: who is speaking and for whom. What meanings are conveyed? Are they contrived for visitor recognition, or do they communicate different voices and different narratives? Do they challenge perceptions, or do they simply reinforce them? It is most often at living history sites that the constitutive performance experience of a heritage place engages with contemporary identities, revealing how heritage can legitimize national narratives and hierarchies.[10] They are what the American historian Lisbeth Haas has called "aestheticized spaces" or the imagined pasts of heritage construction.[11]

Writing about the concept of "authenticity," Laurajane Smith argues that the search for cultural authenticity can paradoxically drive the heritage tourism experience at the same time as it constructs cultural experiences that in effect undermine it. She describes how tourists may comprehend authenticity quite differently from the way that it has traditionally been described, with its emphasis upon essentially material qualities. Tourism literature, she argues, invariably frames the complex issue of authenticity in marketing and consumer or consumption language, a language generally viewed as simplistic within those humanities that deal with ideas of heritage.[12]

However, other places, such as York Factory National Historic Site and the historic sites in the vicinity of Churchill in northern Manitoba, might, for example, represent a different dynamic.[13] The historic sites near Churchill include Seahorse Gully and Eskimo Point, a 4,000-year-old Pre-Dorset, Dorset, and Inuit site of almost continuous occupation, and the eighteenth-century European sites of Prince of Wales Fort, Sloop Cove, and Cape Merry. These places do not signify performance, and they do not attempt to freeze a moment or manipulate the sensory experience. They are just there. While protected, and to some degree conserved, such places present landscapes that have evolved over time and continue to evolve.[14] They have different meanings, and although to some degree they are part of the dominant discourse, they present storyscapes that feel real. And it is just these multi-layered meanings that support what philosopher Michel

Foucault has called "counter-memory"—that is, the individual's ability to resist official versions of historical continuity.[15]

▲ ▲ ▲

With collective memory so vital to pre-modern and modern Western culture, society has long articulated a version of the past that is enshrined at historic sites, in museums, in protected buildings and landscapes, in objects, and even in roadside plaques. Commemoration of such objects and spaces is a process that links societal views of history with memory and identity, promoting perceptions that are often authorized and accepted as unchanging or fixed in time. Memory and identity are frequently characterized as material things; memory is "kept alive" and identity, either in the collective or personal sense, can be lost and found.[16]

The memories and identities that shape concepts of heritage are socially constructed representations of reality and mould the cultivated pasts that help define contemporary notions of identity and belonging. "Heritage" can be defined as a range of associations with the past. These associations are usually marked by an attachment to places, objects, and practices that, as a culture, we believe connect with the past in some way. As the American historian Rodney Harrison has noted, the word "heritage" is used to describe everything from the solid (buildings to bone fragments) to the intangible (songs, festivals, and language).[17] Moreover, what is often labelled as "heritage"—living history sites are consistently an example—represent a creation of the past in the present, while more genuine heritage places and landscapes demonstrate a persistence of the past in the present. Exploring the dynamics of what is considered heritage and what is not, particularly in regard to place, reveals stories of hegemony and challenge, struggles over contested space, and even the eclipse of memory. These are the critical distinctions relating to how "heritage" is defined and used that I will explore throughout this book.

By examining the commemorative and interpretive history of some representative sites in Manitoba and Saskatchewan, I address such questions as how, as a culture, we determine which memories survive and become the authorized discourse, which are ignored or forgotten, which underpin traditional perspectives, and which challenge these perspectives; and specifically, how and why the meaning of place is often disputed. The dissonance between history and heritage—the idea that historic places are not inherently valuable but are the product of modern and cultural processes of meaning—can contest the authorized, challenge accepted notions of progress, and undermine traditional Western perceptions of history and history making. At the same time, regional, national, and even international heritage narratives can fuel official views that are heteronormative or can often exclude or marginalize women, the working class, particular ethnic groups, and Indigenous peoples. The historic sites discussed in this work—from pre-contact Indigenous landscapes to settler sites and places of resistance—illustrate how at one level some heritage places reinforce the authorized discourse while at another level they can be interpreted as a challenge to that discourse.

Place provides an important touchstone for culturally constructed heritage and those spaces that a society considers historically significant. Designation, according to this model, is often an act of faith where places we consider to be heritage can give physicality to the values that reaffirm a community's view of itself. It is where places are given meaning and where we often speak of the "cultural landscapes" that can resonate with individuals, with communities, and with nations, and even at an international level. I tend to use the word "place" more so than "site" because, in my experience working in the federal historic sites program, "site" can be a restrictive term that invokes a sense of mapped boundaries, tightly defined and circumscribed landscapes, and a built heritage that often stands disconnected from its surroundings. "Place" has a broader connotation and suggests socially formed and culturally relevant and meaningful spaces of memory that are often steeped in local and multiple constructions.

Geographer Yi-Fu Tuan has argued that "place" can be created from "space" and it is in fact the localities that mark the historically and culturally defined pauses in a wider expanse. "Place is security, space is freedom," he writes, "where we are attached to one and long for the other."[18] Space is an open arena of action and movement, Tuan suggests, while place is about stopping and resting and becoming involved. For Tuan, place is also a type of object and embodies the lived experience where whole landscapes and cityscapes can be seen as sculpted meaningful spaces.[19] He believes that our sense of place has emerged from such concepts as rootedness, memory, veneration of the past, and nostalgia. Place is constructed from space when an event or larger value is attached to a space that historically has little or no significance. It can be defined by the spiritual, cultural, or ecological significance of a landscape or by direct human intervention through architecture and other examples of human engineering. Continuing in the humanist tradition, Canadian geographer Edward Relph views place as integral to human "being," with space and place a measure that links abstraction (space) with experience (place). Employing phenomenology, an approach that focuses upon the study of consciousness and the objects of direct experience, Relph suggests that understanding the self comes only with understanding the self in place; to be human is to exist "in place."[20]

In a more broadly relational vein, Tim Cresswell, in studying the concept of place in Western thought, links common understandings of place and identity, mobility, memory, and belonging with the more speculative discussions that have arisen, particularly in the field of geography, around place (and space) as ways of comprehending the world in almost epistemological ways.[21] Cresswell highlights what he calls the "genealogy of place," where significance is defined according to a variety of disciplines such as history, anthropology, geography, literature, and urban planning. For Cresswell, "place memory" describes the ability of a specific place to make the past come to life and thus contribute to the production and reproduction of social memory.[22]

Between the polarities represented by geographers Tuan, Relph, and Cresswell is a vast and multi-faceted articulation of place that has moved into other disciplines such as history. For instance, Ian McKay's and Robin Bates's *In the Province of History: The Making of the Public Past in Twentieth-Century Nova Scotia* looks at how place is manipulated by a tourism industry to create a mythology that effectively misrepresents regional history to create an antimodernist past where "all the world was safe and happy" and where racial identities and class conflicts are discounted.[23] Building upon McKay's earlier work *Quest of the Folk: Antimodernism and Cultural Selection in Twentieth-Century Nova Scotia*, their analysis looks at how governments and cultural figures cooperated to create "tourism history." McKay's work on the creation of the oftentimes mythical pasts of public presentation and consumption (to an extent related to Eric Hobsbawm's and Terence Ranger's *The Invention of Tradition*) resonates with this study of authorized heritage, memory, and landscapes, especially in my analysis of heritage presentation and the tourism of place at fur trade and pioneer historic sites. However, McKay's study of antimodernism in twentieth-century Nova Scotia casts a wider net, going beyond my focus on how heritage is created and maintained and how it comes to support "founding father" narratives and national and regional mythologies. The various historical contributions to James Opp's and John Walsh's *Placing Memory and Remembering Place in Canada* underscore how "place memories and memory places" must, as Opp and Walsh indicate, "accommodate differences, acknowledge injustice and ... share authority over 'the past.'"[24]

"Place" and "site" have a familial relationship. Arguably, "site" is a further refinement of "place" in which significance—real or imagined—is further detailed and defined, whether by perceptions of history and heritage or by current uses and more contemporary applications of meaning. Like Simon Schama's ideas around memory, "place memory" evokes a sense of the past in the present and thus adds to the production and reproduction of social or collective memory.[25] With place, we see the establishment of meaning that reflects the significance of human intervention on the landscape in all its forms, from the less visually evident spiritual and cultural landscape to the more obvious intrusion of the built environment. The various chapters in this book look at the way place is realized within different forms of historical landscapes. From pre-contact Indigenous spaces to the heavily manipulated topographies of settler society, each impacts our collective memory and the broad narratives that we use to define the past.

"Settler society" and "settler colonialism" are two terms I use in this book, especially in Chapter 3. They are both recent terms that have gained traction in describing the impact of colonial economies and cultures in the West. Of course, such terminology has a much broader usage outside prairie Canada and can be defined as an ongoing system of power that creates and perpetuates the repression of Indigenous peoples and cultures. In both historical and contemporary times, settler colonialism and settler society entail an oppression based on racism, patriarchy, and capitalism. Authoritative in its scope toward Indigenous peoples, settler colonialism is together assimilatory and exclusionary as it exploits lands and resources to which Indigenous peoples have age-old relationships. It is not an event but a process that

over time characterizes settler society as "original," in effect indigeniz-
ing and naturalizing newcomer status as it obscures the conditions of
settler invasion.[26] In the context of this study, the normalizing of settler
societies is often realized through the celebration of settler heritage
and the commemoration of those places, events, and people that mark
a continuous settlement tradition. While pervasive throughout the
topics with which this book engages, this tradition is most evident in
the establishment and commemoration of the settler culture described
in Chapter 3 and in how an "authorized heritage" has endeavoured to
construct tradition and authenticity.

Just as the significance of heritage place is cultural, it is a process
that is also relevant to ecological places, the significance of a particular
geographical feature or natural landscape also being a public construct.[27]
The American historian David Glassberg comments that "a sense of
history and a sense of place are inextricably intertwined; we attach
histories to places, and the environmental value we attach to place
comes largely through the historical association we have with it."[28]
Following Glassberg's lead, I use the phrase "a sense of place" often
in this study. For me, it represents how and why an individual or a
community instills a particular location with meaning and resonance.
It is conceptually bordered and perceived as different from the space
that surrounds it. Of course, a sense of place does not always relate to
heritage—natural landscapes can evoke the same sensations although
they become cultural by virtue of their distinctiveness and identity. Yet,
finding meaning in a "sense of place" can be at times ephemeral; places
can have meaning(s) for some people that little resonate with others.

Landscapes are cultural because they evoke both meaning and
memory. Heritage places in prairie Canada are not inherently valuable,
and neither do they carry meaning that is natural but are the product of
traditional and present-day processes, activities, and perceptions. Such
a view is not, of course, uniform around the world, as different cultures
and traditions look upon the concept of heritage, whether in relation
to places, objects, or the less tangible examples of cultural significance,
in different ways.

With modern Western concepts of heritage, a prevailing physicality
makes it in effect quantifiable; heritage can be designated, mapped,
studied, collected, preserved, and managed while being subject to
national and international legislation. The long history of international

conventions—from the Society of Ancient Buildings Manifesto (a product of late Victorian England); the Athens, Venice, and Burra charters of the twentieth century; to the founding of UNESCO in 1947 and the establishment of the ICOMOS in 1965—speaks to the long history of heritage management over the last few centuries. It has led to the establishment of a heritage industry, as community and cultural groups, as well as governments at all levels, have embarked upon what David Lowenthal has conspicuously called "the heritage crusade."[29] Canada has held its own in this crusade: the heritage industry has thrived in this country (at least until recent years) as it has in most Western jurisdictions, creating sizable bureaucracies to research, designate, develop, and manage all that is deemed to be the critical components of its history.

All of this designation and quantification has helped to establish a hegemonic discourse about heritage, a more or less official approach that influences the way societies think about history and heritage, about what is important and what is not, about what should be preserved and what should be ignored, and about the stories that form the national narrative. Which historical discourses do we commemorate at a national, provincial, or community level and which do we relegate to antiquarian obscurity? And when we talk about "the past," are we talking about one past (the use of the definite article might suppose so), or do we see various pasts, different voices that contest Smith's "authorized heritage discourse"?[30] Such a discourse determines who speaks for the past, at least in the places that are commemorated, and, according to Smith, "continually creates and recreates a range of social relations, values, and meanings about both the past and the present."[31] At the same time things such as personal and community memory also shape our perception of place and our views of the past. To what degree they influence this discourse might vary from place to place, although they arguably remain an important part of the heritage dialogue.

For the most part a product of the mid- to late nineteenth century, this dominant heritage narrative has come to be associated with what might be described as the treatment or management of the material past, a past that includes place. As I discuss in Chapter 4, how does official heritage—if such a term can be used—deal with contested views of the past, especially as they relate to the significance of place? An authorized heritage discourse very often focuses upon the aesthetically pleasing places, landscapes, and material objects that the present generation *must* preserve so that they may be passed to future generations so as to create a shared identity with the past.[32] Contested places, however, frequently challenge such common identities, and the ways we confront cultural authority can present alternative interpretations that sometimes push aside the dominant narrative. Similarly, a community-based sense of heritage, again largely related to place, can present different views of the past or at least pasts that do not fit tidily within an authorized discourse.

Despite my earlier caveat regarding the use of terms such as "site" and "place," heritage as broadly understood in Western societies tends to focus on "site"; in Canada, for instance, we have official historic sites, not historic places, even if international charters tend toward a broader use of the latter term. That being said, in more recent years in Canada, public heritage agencies have gone some little way in broadening the traditional narrow configurations of site to be more inclusive of ideas around place. To a large degree this change has moved designation away from some earlier proscriptions concerning site and what public heritage agencies have described as "commemorative intent." For Parks Canada, a Statement of Commemorative Intent (or the acronym SOCI for short) provides an answer to the question: Why was this place designated as a national historic site?[33] It is part of a larger concept for national historic sites developed by Parks Canada in 1990 that they called "commemorative integrity," which refers to the condition or state of a national historic site when it is what the agency refers to as "healthy and whole."[34] Commemorative integrity (or CI) exists when the resources that relate to the reasons for site designation are not impaired or under threat, when the reasons for the site's national historic significance are effectively communicated, and when the site's heritage values are respected by all whose decisions or actions affect the site. The SOCI for a particular site relates to the second part of the definition of CI, or the Commemorative Integrity Statement (CIS).

The traditional dominance of site in relation to heritage was arguably the result of the physicality of heritage and the authority of such disciplines as archaeology and architecture in defining and managing the material culture of heritage. Historically, it is architecture that has played the principal role in the designation of heritage in Western culture, as protection of the built environment, from forts to stately homes, was most often the focus of a modernist perspective and a conservation ethic.[35] The heritage value of historic architecture, however, is often reduced to a specific footprint rather than a broader landscape of meaning and representation. In prairie Canada it can also distort our understanding of settlement history and settler culture, as it is the more substantial architecture of the prosperous that tends to survive rather than the modest typicality of the built environment of the past. In Manitoba, for instance, the nineteenth-century Red River parish of St. Andrew's has often been interpreted as the home of well-to-do landowners, since it is the handful of their large stone houses that remain. However, the modest Red River frame homes of the vast majority of the parish's inhabitants—the poor hunters and farmers—have long ago disappeared.[36] Through a physical absence their stories become less well known, less understood, and less a part of the heritage of that place. Canadian historian Cecilia Morgan also notes that it is often the buildings and material culture of the elites that benefit from historic preservation, partly because they are the structures to have survived and often because influential individuals or organizations have lobbied for their preservation.[37]

On a larger scale one can claim that the forces of globalization have diminished the local; that, in fact, it is the very processes of heritage commemoration that can weaken the language of place, comprehending its significance only within a broader narrative of historic themes and topics often organized with bureaucratic efficiency, fulfilling bureaucratic goals. Yet, are these approaches necessarily discordant? Can we consider both concepts simultaneously? Has the reality of globalization changed the way we think of place, or can we acknowledge it and take measure of its impact at the same time that we retain the value of the vernacular in our consciousness, in our history, and in our memory? Is there dissonance, or do we reflexively understand the language of place as something to be laboured over, reinterpreted and reimagined on an ongoing basis? Do larger forces—globalization being only one—alter our perceptions of heritage place, or can we fit cultural changes and new perceptions of gender, class, race, sexuality, and modernity into the traditional stories and interpretations that often accompany the heritage of place? As Opp and Walsh have argued, "we must accept that places and memories are always in a state of becoming, of being worked on, struggled over, celebrated, mourned, and even, it bears repeating, ignored."[38]

Not surprisingly, social change and evolving perspectives also bring new places of significance, some meaningful at a local or community level, others at a national and even international level, some at all three. The Tenement Museum located in New York City's Lower East Side is paradigmatic of the house museum that can relate alternative narratives and diverse stories of everyday life in the urban culture of an earlier time. Home to hundreds of working-class immigrants for over more than a century, the apartment depicts urban immigrant home life in New York in the early twentieth century, in the process reimagining the role of the house museum in how stories can be told. Another might be The Barracks, a gay bathhouse in Toronto, the site (along with other area bathhouses) of a 1981 massive police raid known as "Operation Soap" that resulted in the arrest of more than 300 men. While lives and reputations were destroyed, the raids galvanized Toronto's gay community and ultimately led to a strong, well-organized, and ongoing fight for rights and arguably the beginning of the gay rights movement in Canada.[39] A third could include Gadsden's Wharf, now a museum and city park adjacent to the harbour in Charleston, South Carolina, where approximately 100,000 slaves were brought to the original Thirteen Colonies between 1783 and 1808. Facetiously called "the Ellis Island for African Americans," the wharf, soon-to-be-opened museum, and nearby park space, where once stood the warehouses that held the captives sometimes for months at a time, are a historic space that can bring home the terrible legacy of slavery more than any book or movie.[40] Yet, the interpretation of place today, even those places associated with slavery, can have contrasting perspectives. On a 2020 visit to Louisiana, I toured the Whitney and Oak Alley sugar plantations. While the former provides the visitor with a grim picture of the realities of slavery, the latter tour portrays the antebellum South as if taken from *Gone with the Wind*. Curiously, of the numerous plantations that are now historic sites in that region, the Whitney promotes itself as "Louisiana's only plantation solely dedicated to promoting an understanding of slavery."

Such diverse examples demonstrate a heritage and language of place that resonate at local and national levels and represent new places of cultural and social significance. Not all historians, of course, agree with such an approach. Lowenthal, for instance, speculates that, while history is still written mostly by the winners, heritage increasingly belongs to the "losers" in what he calls "the cult of the victim."[41] But if some might dismiss heritage as the enemy of truth, it is alternative narratives that can highlight the many voices of history. In these examples the history of class, race, and sexuality is interpreted through place memory, a heritage that can challenge the conservatism of commemoration by recognizing injustice and displaying a willingness to share authority over the past.

These and many other examples reveal heritage place as potentially more than a static concept, or what historian Steven High calls "an empty container where things happen." More accurately, the concept of heritage place should be recognized as a social and spatial process experiencing constant change. Place is contingent, fluid, and multiple.[42] Although many people are receptive to the idea that history is open to revision, the same might not be said for the idea of heritage, especially at a number of historic sites in prairie Canada where interpretation often remains static, single voiced, and less than fluid. It is not just those visitors to heritage places who remain conventional in their thinking but also the agencies that present the past as product and an interpretation that is commodified and rigid. Heritage organizations can engage in what sociologists John Urry and Jonas Larsen call "the tourist gaze," reflecting back to visitors their expectations of place and people and authenticating what the organizations believe the visitor wants to see in the sometimes imagined past of heritage.[43] The fabrication of an artificial environment can appear in many forms. In Manitoba, The Forks, located at the confluence of the Red and Assiniboine rivers, is a heritage place and shopping area that enhances its commercial prospects by promoting the tourist potential of the site with a multi-millennium and spiritually significant Indigenous past, much of it embroidered under the brand of "meeting place," and at Lower Fort Garry reconstruction work is passed off as original. In these examples—ones that are not necessarily typical—heritage place displays a constructed approximation of the past, or what cultural scholar Rodney Harrison labels the "polished patina of the past."[44]

"Authenticity" and a "polished patina" are constituent parts of the history/heritage dichotomy, presuming one exists. As noted earlier, I use the term "authenticity" in two ways: at a basic physical level to describe buildings, artifacts, and material things in general; and in a more esoteric, arcane, and non-physical way of describing how historic sites attempt to communicate the past to a modern audience. Lowenthal tells us that history and heritage transmit different things to different audiences. History, he writes, is about what happened and how things came to be as they are (an artless definition, perhaps, but useful for his distinction). Heritage, on the other hand, passes on exclusive myths of origin and continuance—and one might add myths of power, control, and influence—imparting prestige and common purpose to select groups. He adds that history is for all, while heritage is for ourselves alone; we treat the past as our own age.[45] This view gives rise to his well-known aphorism: "Viewed as history, the past is a foreign country; viewed as heritage, it is highly familiar."[46] In sum, he writes, "We use heritage to improve the past, making it better (or worse) by modern lights. We do so by hyping its glories . . . by divesting its examples of current anathemas (slaveholders, smokers), by banning demeaning clichés (watermelons), by fig-leafing (everywhere) and by improvising former splendour or squalor."[47] Lowenthal's conclusions about heritage and history can be insightful, if somewhat cynical. While we often construct heritage in pleasing and entertaining ways, such a view describes only those heritage places that are contrived and arbitrary, where a cultural and custodial intervention has conflated the past with the present. Many historic sites—including sites in prairie Canada—fit this category. (See, for instance, the discussion of Mennonite Heritage Village in Manitoba in Chapter 3.) At the same time, the true heritage and language of place do not try to simulate or replicate a version of the past; they do not always strive for contrived "authenticity" but remain, rather, a part of it. As discussed earlier, heritage is not an imagined replication of the past in the present but a persistence of the past (or at least some elements of it) in the present.

Determining what is historic place and what is heritage is not a passive process of preservation. It is a conscious and purposeful act of assembling places, objects, and practices that represent a set of values that we want to carry with us into the future. It is, or can be, an authorized heritage that shapes the way we think of the past, the way we think of ourselves in the present, and how we project forward. Here, the term "authorized" refers to the processes involved in researching, categorizing, and managing the past, and what Harrison refers to as the "rapid and all pervasive piling up of the past in our quotidian worlds."[48] In Canada this description speaks to the bureaucratic approaches of the heritage establishment where, over the last four or five decades, research, designation, regulation, definition, cataloguing, and management have become complex and idiosyncratic. We analyze, we parse, and we categorize the definition of what is heritage and what is not using an almost scientific terminology of proof and evidence in the establishment of a largely artificial assessment of "good" heritage and "bad" heritage.

Critical to understanding heritage and place, especially as they relate to historic sites in prairie Canada, is to identify time frames. The twentieth century, especially the latter half of the century, witnessed the growth of a state control of heritage, the establishment of regulatory processes, modernist bureaucratic planning, and an increased and centralized administration of the local. As the state increasingly exercised control over heritage commemoration and preservation, it also redefined it, enlarging its influence over a growing range of objects, buildings, and landscapes.[49] One example is Canada's Historic Places Initiative, a 1999 partnership program between the federal government and each of the provinces and territories, providing users with information about the Canadian Register of Historic Places and the standards and guidelines for their conservation. The initiative is intended to provide the lead in building an enhanced culture of conservation across the country—primarily focused upon historic architecture—with the federal government assuming the principal role. The conservation of heritage place is presented as imperative, as, according to the program guide, "Historic places capture the soul and spirit of our country. From the covered bridges in rural New Brunswick," it reads, "to the cobblestone streets of Quebec City, from the industrial heritage in Ontario to the warehouse district in downtown Winnipeg, and from the trading posts in western Canada to Victoria's Fan Tan Alley—historic places make our communities more interesting places to live."[50] (That historic place makes a community more interesting is, of course, a value judgment that is seldom questioned.) The initiative describes the growth of expertise and identifies the expansion in heritage conservation across the country. The guide goes on to lament the loss of pre-1920 heritage places to demolition, "a threat to the distinctiveness of our communities and to our understanding of our history."[51] Conservation guidelines developed by the federal government outline the approaches to the conservation of historic places in Canada. In keeping with international standards, these strategies are generally proscriptive. According to the guidelines, preservation is always the first treatment recommended, although its use depends on the condition of the historic place. Rehabilitation is a less permissive treatment involving modifications or additions related to a new use. It allows for contemporary interventions as long as they are compatible with, and respectful of, the place. Rehabilitation is the most common treatment, especially in programs for the revitalization of historic districts such as the Exchange District in downtown Winnipeg and to a lesser extent at The Forks site. Less utilized is restoration as a treatment, which, according to the federal conservation guidelines, "is appropriate [only] when the representation of a particular period of the building can be justified, although it may lead to the disappearance of certain existing elements. It must be based on adequate and accurate documentation."[52]

Although the Historic Places Initiative is seemingly a worthwhile program, like similar programs in other Western countries (for example, the Heritage Action Zone program in England), it can begin to fetishize place and object, or at least escalate their bureaucratization.[53] There is "designated place" (strictly determined), while historic objects are "cultural resources," the term "cultural" used to imbue a particular entity with public significance. With archaeological investigation, for instance, the found object is given significance on a scale that is related to a predetermined theme or set of themes. Parks Canada's Cultural Resource Management Policy defines "level one" and "level two" resources with firmly determined criteria for each as well as strict guidelines regarding planning, research, conservation, and presentation. With such exacting norms the ultimate result is the absence of an attempt to work this found heritage into a historical narrative or a broader story. Through the increasing bureaucratization of heritage, the assembly of objects—the collection—is considered the final goal of the work. Its mere existence, often devoid of context, is its value. Frequently archaeological reports become little more than ranked lists of objects with no attempt to weave their significance into a broader history.

Heritage, Memory, and Place

Writers have described memory and place as playing key roles in our understanding of heritage. As noted above, "heritage" is a word with diverse meanings but perhaps most commonly comprehended as a set of relationships with, or attitudes toward, the past. These relationships are usually characterized by a collection of meanings or attachments to the objects, ideas, and places that are associated with history and history making. Yet, today, heritage can be understood more broadly. These attachments to the past are articulated in the present or represent a production of the past in the present.[54] Although history often explores a past grown opaque over time, heritage is the profession of faith in a past tailored to present purpose.[55] Heritage is often a form of historical representation that creates a history that both sustains and even invents the present.

As noted previously, heritage values are not self-evident and historic places are not documented, commemorated, and preserved because they are seen to have intrinsic significance. Heritage value is not inherently part of specific physical places. However, by being socially constructed, heritage places can create an identity that conforms to publicly acceptable, authoritative, and official perceptions of historical significance.

The cultural construction of place often evolves from collective memory or the shared knowledge and information in the memories of a social or community group, for many people a lived history rather than a learned history. Much of the early work on collective memory was carried out by the philosopher and sociologist Maurice Halbwachs, whose book *La Mémoire Collective* examined a form of social memory that is passed from generation to generation, a memory that can be shared, preserved, modified, and transformed. Collective memory is a communal representation, a language of the past that is collectively comprehended, revealing identity, a view of the past and present, and a vision for the future. Specific landscapes, streetscapes, monuments, and architecture even in vestigial state can evoke symbolic associations with past events, with people, and with one's own personal past. And they can evoke connections to much wider stories and events that can be generational.

Employing the concept of collective memory, Eric Hobsbawm's and Terence Ranger's *The Invention of Tradition* examines the way the state and governing classes "invent" traditions in order to socialize and situate populations into an established order. For Hobsbawm, symbolic rules and rituals are repeated to reinforce the behavioural norms that support continuity with the past (including an imagined past), the authority of tradition, and a conforming and adaptable public.[56] The past, according to Hobsbawm and Ranger, is shaped to suit the dominant interests of the present. Rituals are invented in part to create new political and cultural realities in what we refer to as "heritage."[57] It can be argued, however, that if modern societies are witnessing the expansion of individual choice, it becomes difficult to construct a cohesive and common public memory. Conversely, a decline in knowledge of the past through the diminished role of history in modern education, or the decline of folk memory, might in fact make it easier for whole populations to accept one view of history—"our heritage," so to speak—with little questioning.

If collective memory is one portal to the past, it is also subjective. It can, for instance, explain the way we think of complex class and gender relations that influence what is remembered or forgotten, who remembers or forgets, and for what end. As mentioned earlier, Michel Foucault's ideas around counter-memory describe the resistance against official versions of historical continuity. He views history as an incomplete story of the past, a discipline that comes into conflict with memory, which in turn creates a system of signs, symbols, and practices to help identify and recognize what has come before. As with other authors, Foucault notes how some of our past is forgotten, some is given significance, and some emerges only after long periods of concealment or suppression.[58] Yet, the present certainly informs the past, or at least the way we think about the past. In his 1852 extended essay *The Eighteenth Brumaire of Louis Bonaparte,* Karl Marx argued that "man makes his own history, but he does not make it out of the whole cloth; he does not make it out of conditions chosen by himself, but out of such that he finds close at hand."[59] The present in the past informs our memory, and, for Marx, the past is made from circumstances and environments that are familiar and recognizable.

What, then, is the relationship between collective memory and the heritage value of place? Heritage value is a cultural instrument that nations, communities, and individuals use to construct a sense of identity and meaning, and where the power of memory associated with place—both personal and collective memory—provides the reality to expression and experience.[60] As Newfoundland artist Marlene Creates has suggested, when we recall events associated with place, the landscape becomes a centre of meaning, not an abstract physical location but a geography charged with personal significance that shapes the image we have of ourselves.[61] This construction of identity through place, of social and cultural belonging, is usually produced through the perception of some shared past, and one that can be manipulated to promote a national and overarching heritage narrative. Our awareness of historic place, or what French historian Pierre Nora has described as *lieu de mémoire*, also builds upon Halbwachs's ideas around collective memory.[62] Nora defines *lieu de mémoire* as any significant entity, either material or non-material in nature, that through human will has become a symbolic element in the commemorated heritage of a community. For Nora, sites of memory are where cultural recollection is shaped and can broadly be defined to include not just places such as historic sites, museums, and archives but also the intangible heritage of cultural practice and ritual. All, in fact, cache memory in ideas, places, and landscapes that can resonate in the human psyche. He contends that memory and history are not synonymous. Memory, he says, is in permanent evolution, open to the dialectic of remembering and forgetting, and a bond that ties us to the present. History, on the other hand, is a universalizing representation of the past as distinct from the present, an intellectual analysis that, he claims, attempts to suppress and destroy memory.[63] Nora is firm on this last point when he writes that urbanization, industrialization, and the rise of both secularism and the nation-state (and one can add the professionalization of history) have put history in fundamental opposition to memory. Nora even argues that in the last half of the twentieth century, we have witnessed the "eradication of memory by history." "Memory," he claims, "is by nature multiple and yet specific; collective, plural, and yet individual. History, on the other hand, belongs to everyone and to no one, whence its claim to universal authority."[64] Where memory, especially collective memory, might best describe how small community populations conceptualize the past, history belongs to a modernist urban era of written linear texts, evidence, analysis, and abstraction.

But as Opp and Walsh contend, Nora's *lieux de mémoire* has little resonance with the spaces and places it represents, appearing "inert" in the face of the "assault of history in the modern era."[65] Although memory is not always defined by physical place, it is often shaped by landscapes and topographies.[66] Yet, Nora's oppositional categories are overly simplistic. Memory can still inform perceptions of history and heritage, especially at the local and community levels where a national narrative often fails to gain traction. For instance, American historian

Susan Crane has discussed that while much of Nora's thinking is based upon the work of Maurice Halbwachs and his concept of collective memory, Halbwachs, unlike Nora, saw the implicit possibility of re-combining historical and collective memory. Crane proposes relocating the collective back in the individual, "the individual who disappeared in the occlusion of personal historical consciousness by the culture of preservation."[67]

To transfer this to the Canadian context, one could argue that at the same time that Canadians are influenced by central narratives, they might also remain loyal to their neighbourhood and community heritage or to organic oral traditions that have survived generations. Published local histories, once pervasive throughout prairie Canada, rely upon such traditional vehicles as genealogy, family memory, kinship networks, and the shared experiences of homogeneous populations. Of course, that such histories are often contextualized within an overarching narrative of the past might still inform historical writing at its most local level.

A growing confidence in oral history—its evolution in recent decades has become significant and institutional, and oral history centres have been widely established—suggests that memory still informs our view of history as well as our view of heritage. As increasingly the courts in Canada incorporate concepts such as traditional knowledge (both cultural and ecological) into Indigenous land claim settlements, these initiatives indicate that oral history is not simply equal to history but is history itself.

A Shared Past?

In unpacking how the concept of a shared past has come to influence "professional" heritage practices in Canada, there is at one level an of-ficial, if sometimes nuanced, articulation of the way we engage with history. Yet, at another, heritage is often a process of contestation where our views of the past and its meaning are often contradictory or at least ambiguous. The very significance of place, broadly defined and cross-disciplinary in nature, can often be challenged, as, for example, the way Indigenous perspectives can dispute conventional non-Indigenous views of the past, or how refocusing through the lenses of gender and class can yield new places of commemoration and new perceptions of existing places that help to expand the broader heritage narrative.

Modernity, or more particularly late modernity, has been critical to the invention of heritage and the way our society views itself, not just in relation to the past but to the present as well and indeed to the future. The view that heritage reflects a linear view of time with an emphasis on progress has helped to create the traditional view of the past as a kind of passage from darkness to light and the present as an improvement upon the past. Yet, like Hobsbawm, some maintain that what we refer to as "tradition" is little more than the elite and powerful using cultural production to normalize and consolidate their authority. Contemporary views of settler colonialism would support such an interpretation.

In shaping our official narratives of heritage and place, we tend to emphasize material authenticity and a preservationist desire to freeze the moment as heritage and to conserve it as an unchanging monument to the past. Some have even facetiously referred to this as "freeze-dried history." And in this sense, monuments themselves are meant to last unchanged, becoming the most conservative of commemorations, a phenomenon that Friedrich Nietzsche referred to as "monumentalism" (or a "monumental view of the past") and a protest against the change of generations. In his essay "On the Utility and Liability of History for Life," Nietzsche characterizes the permanence of the monument as a dissention from transition, an attempt, he argues, to almost stop time.[68] While one could claim that the erection of monuments, at least in Canada, no longer enjoys the popularity it once did, it has been in recent times that the former Conservative government of Stephen Harper initiated its controversial plans to build a Memorial to the Victims of Communism adjacent to the Supreme Court in Ottawa. Later, Liberal Minister of Canadian Heritage Mélanie Joly announced that a scaled-down victims memorial would be moved to the Garden of the Provinces and Territories. A winning design was approved in May of 2017 and will be completed in 2020. Evidently, "monumentalism" still exists, as, according to Joly, monuments "play a key role in reflecting the character, identity, history and values of Canadians. They should be places of reflection, inspiration and learning, not shrouded in controversy."[69] In fact, monuments, at least traditional monuments, rarely evoke inspiration and learning, and arguably represent the victor and only occasionally the victim, most without inspiration or reflection. In the U.S., and to some degree in Canada, traditional monuments have aroused the ire of those who see many of these older statues as monuments to racism. Recent events in both countries would certainly bear out this view of monuments as objects of debate. On occasion, however, "controversial" monuments like the Vietnam War Memorial in Washington do inspire contemplation.[70] Completed in 1982, the design of the memorial by twenty-one-year-old undergraduate student Maya Lin was criticized by many. Today, however, it is seen as almost a shrine. A German example that evokes Foucault's ideas around counter-memory might be called the "counter-monument." In 1995 a competition for a national memorial to the Holocaust in Berlin drew one entry that proposed that the city's Brandenburg Gate be blown up, ground into dust, and then sprinkled over the memorial area and covered with granite plates. The artist, Horst Hoheisel, argued that a destroyed people should be remembered and commemorated by a destroyed monument; a newly opened space in the heart of Berlin would memorialize the void left by a murdered people.[71] Memorials, whether three-dimensional or "negative-form," as Hoheisel's work was described, remain paradigmatic of how governments use history to reflect particular ideologies. Traditional statues of particular historic figures present a specific type of monument as well as a view of the past that is often different from the present view, and while I do not wish to enter into the long and controversial discussions around the removal of certain statues, the conversation in recent years regarding removal has been contentious.

Arguably, our view of the past is continually evolving, although the discourse of official heritage can often act as a check upon reimagining the narrative of place to incorporate new interpretations and new associations. The idea of historic place suggests not just a physical act of preservation but also an emotional and/or spiritual comprehension of meaning and significance. In this way heritage and place can function at different levels, at times coexisting and at others competing for space in the consciousness of the visitor. And it is these competing narratives that can act as subversive ideologies that by their nature challenge accepted wisdom.[72]

In Manitoba and Saskatchewan a contested history can be explored within the broad themes and places that commemorate Indigenous life, fur trade economies, and settler colonialism. It can also be used to examine how class, gender, and sexuality often remain apart from the heritage discourse. Within this paradigm, government-designated heritage, or authorized heritage, can also be compared with widespread perceptions of community, region, and nation. We can explore how heritage, as broadly understood throughout western Canada, is part of the authorized heritage discourse that emerged in a modernist time of historical commemoration of space in the West and how and why certain narratives were left untold. And we can learn how official agencies such as the Dominion Parks Branch (later Parks Canada) and various provincial agencies such as the Manitoba Heritage Council or Saskatchewan Heritage became the mediators of what was heritage and, just as notably, what was not.

In Canada, as with a number of other Western countries, the first half of the twentieth century witnessed the growth of the heritage movement. Architectural historian Shannon Ricketts has described how it was the years between the two world wars that shaped not only the direction of the federal commemorative program in Canada but also the public's image of the country's past. As heritage activity increased, especially in regard to site commemoration, alternative scholarly approaches appeared as historians continued to rely on textual records, while the emerging field of architectural history focused on the country's built heritage and archaeologists searched for cultural resources below ground.[73] Academic approaches diversified in the interwar years, but national historic sites continued to present a particular vision of Canadian history, one that was intimately associated with colonial expansion and a military legacy increasingly "leavened" by the architectural interests of an Anglo-Canadian elite.[74]

It was the beginning of a critical component of the heritage process in Canada that by the 1960s governments began to assume control over heritage. We began to see research on historic sites migrate from the academy to the largely government-based heritage professional—the public historian, archaeologist, curator, and conservator who (along with the Historic Sites and Monuments Board of Canada or HSMBC) helped shape the public's view of which places, events, and individuals were significant in their country's history and why. These professionals would eventually introduce new voices and new narratives, a development not always well received by politicians and the newly minted officialdom of heritage managers.

Places of commemoration in Manitoba and Saskatchewan that focus upon traditional Indigenous cultural sites, the fur trade, settler colonialism, the contested spaces of Indigenous resistance, and the heritage of class, sexuality, and gender are examples of heritage narratives that can be considered from the perspectives of historical significance and meaning, authenticity, community memory, and commemorative policy. Across the West these heritage narratives are multi-layered, some represented unevenly, if at all, while others are often contested within the changing perspectives of historical interpretation. But as Frances Swyripa has argued, these narratives have also created a heritage that is "constantly invented and reinvented, always subjective and selective," especially at the community and ethnocultural level, where individuals and groups left their mark on the landscape.[75] In *Storied Landscapes*, Swyripa examines how early prairie immigrants formed a connection with place through the "Christianization of the landscape" by building churches and cemeteries or by erecting crosses and shrines. In turn, their descendants erected monuments and settler shrines and created the "founding father" narratives of not only the physical places of settler society but the places of the mind that focus on what she calls an "imagined past."[76]

Historic Place and Commemorative Intent

In the world of heritage the concept of commemorative intent is an important one. The concept describes how and why particular places are considered historically significant or how they become "authorized heritage" in the public sense, and who actually confirms that mantle of significance. On the federal scene it is a crucial part of the way agencies such as Parks Canada determine the significance of heritage place. At the provincial and even municipal levels, it is commemorative intent that establishes for those themes, perspectives, and resources that determine why certain places are considered to be historically significant.

Nationally, the commemorative intent of a particular place is signalled by the HSMBC when determining those sites that are significant and those that are not. According to federal documentation, "the reasons for designation should be expressed using the words and phrases in the HSMBC minutes and approved plaque texts in a way which remains faithful to the HSMBC's intent."[77] The process of establishing commemorative intent is one way that governments mediate the meaning of what is heritage and what is not. Through such bureaucratic processes an authorized heritage asserts and affirms identities and values. By definition, it characterizes history as objective, as the subject of professional research and classification, and, as Laurajane Smith argues, it renders heritage as a "tangible and immutable 'thing'" and therefore self-evident and effectively not open to challenge.[78]

A Note on Sources

The enormous number of national and international works relating to heritage, place, and memory are broad, comprehensive, and multi-dimensional. Their perspectives and analyses, which cover topics from around the world, are important to this current enquiry. However, of particular relevance here are the more specific studies of Canadian and western Canadian heritage places.

A number of Canadian texts, though not all specifically about prairie Canada, are relevant to the topic and some, by authors such as Frances Swyripa, Cecilia Morgan, Ian McKay, C.J. Taylor, and James Opp and John Walsh, have been cited above and/or are discussed in more detail within the various chapters of this work. Some of the more important works on heritage, memory, and place include Opp's and Walsh's *Placing Memory and Remembering Place in Canada*, an edited collection of articles that focus on regional and local commemorations and the recovery of places of memory, including (among others) the significance of place and the displaced worker in a deindustrializing community, the memoryscapes of Japanese internment camps, and the social memory of queer places in Cold War Ottawa. Other Canadian works worth noting are Cecilia Morgan's *Commemorating Canada: History, Heritage, and Memory, 1850s–1990s*, which takes a broad approach to public history in Canada, looking at early commemorations, heritage, and education, as well as museums, monuments, and tourism. Morgan's introductory text builds upon her earlier work *Creating Colonial Pasts: History, Memory, and Commemoration in Southern Ontario, 1860–1980*. Ian McKay's and Robin Bates's *In the Province of History: The Making of the Public Past in Twentieth-Century Nova Scotia* (along with McKay's earlier work *Quest of the Folk: Antimodernism and Cultural Selection in Twentieth-Century Nova Scotia*) provides an in-depth analysis of that province's tourism industry and how the marketing of history has helped to fashion modern perceptions of culture and the "public past" in a maritime province. Alan Gordon's recent book *Time Travel: Tourism*

and the Rise of the Living History Museum in Mid-Twentieth-Century
Canada* focuses on living history and relates in part to my subject area.
Nature, Place, and Story: Rethinking Historic Sites in Canada, published
in 2017 by Claire Elizabeth Campbell, takes an environmental history
approach to the interpretation of national historic sites in Canada,
only one of which (The Forks) is relevant to this study and then only
marginally. Campbell's goal of rewriting the public history of heritage
places as environmental history is not my intent, although my study
of the role of place within a broader historical context does suggest
some overlap. Along with Gordon's focus on living history sites is
Laura Peers's book *Playing Ourselves: Interpreting Native Histories at
Historic Reconstructions*, a useful work not only because it relates to two
themes of my study (fur trade and Indigenous sites) but because it also
provides a thorough analysis of how the complexities of living history
representations can at some times expand cultural awareness while at
others can reinforce traditional cultural stereotypes. Other Canadian
works of note include Henry Vivian Nelles's *The Art of Nation-Building:
Pageantry and Spectacle at Quebec's Tercentenary*, and Chris Andersen's
article "More than the Sum of Our Rebellions: Métis Histories Beyond
Batoche."

This is only an overview of some of the major Canadian works
in the field or at the periphery of the field. Previously I cited some
international studies, especially those related to place, memory, and
heritage, as important to my work. Some historians, such as Lowenthal,
Harrison, Hobsbawm, Roy Rosenzweig, and Dolores Hayden, are
well known in these areas, while others, such as the Australian scholar
Laurajane Smith, are not, although her work, especially her analysis
of the "authorized heritage discourse," has begun to influence the way
some now think about heritage and commemoration. Although the
library of geographic texts on place is immense, the works of a handful of these scholars, especially Tuan, Cresswell, and Relph, have been
useful in helping me to understand this vast literature and how I might
begin to relate those geographical perspectives to historic places in
prairie Canada.

Looking beyond the published literature, the most critical component of my research has involved the archival and government sources
that trace the development of commemoration and interpretation in
western Canada. Also important, though perhaps to a lesser degree,

are current government and community websites that communicate the most up-to-date information about specific historic sites. All these primary sources are integral to an analysis of the language of heritage place and its commemoration and interpretation over time.

In particular with national historic sites in prairie Canada, the records of the Historic Sites and Monuments Board of Canada, along with the Parks Canada records contained at Library and Archives Canada, were critical not only to documenting the history of commemoration and designation but also for tracing the community- and government-based correspondence and documentation around the discussion of various site selections. In many cases the submission of a particular site involved a long and winding road toward commemoration, the product of much private lobbying, bureaucratic wrangling, and political influence. These documents, from decades of Board minutes to the development of commemorative intent statements and the impact of resource management policies, provide a fascinating history of heritage narratives and the construction of memory. In Winnipeg, materials at Library and Archives Canada's Government Records Office were useful, especially for the more recent history of heritage place in the West. The Archives of Manitoba and the Legislative Library of Manitoba contain a wealth of information pertaining to historic sites such as Mennonite Heritage Village, River Road Provincial Park, and the ancient petroforms of Whiteshell Provincial Park.

Of particular importance for this study is the roomful of records filed in the Parks Canada office in Winnipeg. Known as the "Parks Canada Historical Collection," this informal and considerable collection of files, research notes, and published and unpublished government reports provided me with a great deal of information on the research, development, and interpretation of national historic sites across the West. The collection is not open to the public, and I would like to thank Parks Canada for permission to spend weeks ensconced in their file room reviewing the detailed shape and process of heritage development. Although it is a collection that contains the commonplace, often tracing the minutiae of government decision making, it also includes some very useful materials—important internal reports, a considerable collection of "miscellaneous" research files, and straightforward staff memos—that sometimes challenged the accepted policies of the time. The Archives of Saskatchewan in Regina was useful for research on sites in that province, including the Doukhobor settlement at Veregin, Wanuskewin Heritage Park, and the places associated with the Northwest Resistance of 1885. And, as I discussed at the beginning of this chapter, my own first-hand experiences with these sites have influenced my analysis and critique of how a sense of place is or is not realized and how heritage is conceived.

I approach the study of designation and interpretation of heritage in Manitoba and Saskatchewan by examining select places through the broad thematic lens of social and cultural history. This contributes in part to what I think is the originality of this study by exploring such places within sometimes challenging historical contexts different from earlier interpretations. These include Indigenous cultural landscapes, the landscapes of fur trade commemoration, the designation and interpretation of sites associated with Indigenous resistance, and the commemoration of settler colonial sites. How the "authorized" interpretation of such places fits into a larger heritage narrative in western Canada and how our understanding of each might have evolved over the years forms the core of my investigation. In Chapter 5 I take a bit of a departure by focusing on heritage and place in relation to the broad topics of gender, class, and sexuality, yet still relating those themes to designated historic sites in prairie Canada.

Notions of a collective past can advance consensus versions of history that promote a dominant heritage discourse. Yet, the existence of such traditional perceptions does not preclude challenge. In a post-colonial world (although forms of colonial authority continue to pervade social and political culture) classed, gendered, and racialized populations, most often operating outside the dominant power structure, can still provide the driving force for changing views of the past. These narratives of collective memory frequently underscore the distinctions between government narratives and those of the non-government actors found in heritage and community groups, academia, and Indigenous publics. For example, Indigenous perceptions of the past have often challenged the conventions of settler colonial history, just as fluid cultural viewpoints and historiographies can alter the shifting perspective of heritage place.

Attempts to construct authenticity in prairie Canada are not based on meanings that are intrinsic or elemental. Rather, it is modern cultural processes and contemporary views that often define or redefine history and heritage at many historic sites. My argument is that such places are often examples of an imagined past, a heritage defined by modern perceptions, and a landscape fashioned as aestheticized space. I contend that the mapping of the changing interpretations of selected heritage places in the West, how views of the past are challenged and defended, how narratives are broadened (or narrowed), and how memory and history connect or disconnect are the factors that have come to define the way we think about historic place in the prairie West. In terms of Indigenous sites discussed in this book, whether they are pre- or post-contact, my goal is not to provide a comprehensive perspective of Indigenous views of cultural places—and neither would I ever attempt such a challenging undertaking. While I do provide a limited overview of traditional Indigenous pespectives regarding cultural landscapes, my intent is to analyze the way government has viewed these landscapes in regard to commemoration—the "authorized heritage" of my title—and how these interpretations might have changed over time. The broader questions I consider are who decides what is heritage, who claims authority and why, and ultimately how perceptions of place memory are effectively reproduced.

CHAPTER 1

Memory Hooks: Commemorating Indigenous Cultural Landscapes

Any landscape is composed not only of what lies before our eyes but what lies within our heads.

D.W. Meinig, "The Beholding Eye:
Ten Versions of the Same Scene"

Writing about Dene oral traditions in Canada's North, archaeologists Thomas Andrews and John Zoe suggest that traditional places for Indigenous peoples serve as "memory hooks" upon which they hang the cultural fabric of a narrative tradition.[1] Through an almost mnemonic approach, the places of physical geography become a social and cultural landscape where traditional meanings and topography are symbolically fused. Rather than traditional Western notions of history as a (usually written) record, narrative, and interpretation, Indigenous histories often tell stories that are rooted in terrestrial meaning and contextualized in a terminology that is spatial-temporal. These traditions become part of a loosely mapped cultural landscape where events are entwined with place and memory and people use locations in space to speak about events in time.

Here causality, as anthropologist Christopher Hanks has argued, does not necessarily follow a linear time sequence, especially as understood by archaeology. Writing about the Dene peoples of the Mackenzie Basin, Hanks comments that "the events that spawned Native creation myths may, from a Western perspective, be spread over thousands of years and are therefore not easily causally related. In the Mackenzie drainage, geomorphology provides some clues that have allowed events alluded to in traditional narratives to be tentatively ordered in a manner that

Western educated minds can understand." For Hanks, such a link can be seen in the draining of the great postglacial lakes and volcanic eruptions of the region as they provide a chronological structure that links both archaeological and traditional Indigenous interpretations.[2] Time-honoured Indigenous narratives record such spaces as the locations of sacred sites that carry cosmological significance, the places of cultural and historical importance associated with customary economic and resource use, and geographical locations where the story is in fact the guiding map. Unlike much of non-Indigenous heritage, where the significance of place is often separated from the significance of events and people, Indigenous history sees unity in place, culture, customs, events, and traditions.

The use of Western traditional approaches to commemoration, where linear (and written) concepts of history often prevail, has histori-cally constrained public heritage agencies from fully comprehending Indigenous cultural landscapes. This tradition has been part of a larger ignorance of oral culture. Literate people have often been dismissive of societies that are non-literate, and, as geographer Patrick Nunn has argued, literacy itself can be tyrannical, "for it encourages us to under-value our pasts—the knowledge amassed by those countless ancestors of ours who could neither read nor write." "Literacy," Nunn suggests, "spawns arrogance."[3] However, in recent decades Canadian agencies such as the Historic Sites and Monuments Board of Canada and Parks Canada have begun to move away from conventional historical and anthropological frameworks and the traditional criteria used to as-sess the national historic significance of place.[4] To a degree, they have recognized that their predictable criteria and frameworks for evalua-tion do not adequately respond to the values inherent in the history of Indigenous peoples. In response, federal and provincial heritage agencies have increasingly used designation to provide a framework that could encompass traditional Indigenous views, including spiritual perspectives toward the natural world, associative values in the land, and the history of resource use over millennia. At the same time, how-ever, these agencies endeavoured to make such traditional knowledge comprehensible to those predominantly non-Indigenous persons who decide significance and whose world view is typically based in Western historical scholarship.[5]

For both Indigenous and non-Indigenous peoples, cultural landscapes have been described in generic terms as geographical areas that have been modified, affected, or given distinct or unique cultural meanings by people. More specifically, in the 1996 *Report of the Royal Commission on Aboriginal Peoples,* Indigenous cultural landscapes were defined as "land [that] is deeply intertwined with identity . . . [where] concepts of territory, traditions, and customs are not divisible."[6] To some degree the contemporary commemoration of Indigenous cultural landscapes by heritage agencies emerged from the early pioneering work of the International Council on Monuments and Sites (ICOMOS) and the 1971 report of its International Scientific Committee on Cultural Landscapes (ISCCL). The aim of the committee was to develop approaches to conserving natural and cultural heritage while developing holistic conservation approaches to landscapes. Ultimately, ICOMOS Canada recognized the need to address Indigenous views on cultural heritage.

More recently, the 2015 final report of the Truth and Reconciliation Commission of Canada (TRC) outlined a number of paths to recognizing and preserving Indigenous cultural heritage. These included the overarching goal to first articulate an Indigenous perspective on the meaning and significance of cultural heritage. Regarding place, the stated goal is to move towards an understanding of the relationship between environmental conservation and cultural identity. In order to accomplish this, the TRC saw the need for systemic changes in the way that Indigenous heritage is identified and commemorated, including practical organizational strategies regarding the mechanisms of commemoration. Of the ninety-four "Calls to Action" made by the commission, article 79 states:

> We call upon the federal government, in collaboration with Survivors, Aboriginal organizations, and the arts community, to develop a reconciliation framework for Canadian heritage and commemoration. This would include, but not be limited to:
>
> Amending the Historic Sites and Monuments Act to include First Nations, Inuit, and Métis representation on the Historic Sites and Monuments Board of Canada and its Secretariat.

Revising the policies, criteria, and practices of the National
Program of Historical Commemoration to integrate
Indigenous history, heritage values, and memory practices
into Canada's national heritage and history.

Developing and implementing a national heritage plan and
strategy for commemorating residential school sites, the history and legacy of residential schools, and the contributions
of Aboriginal peoples to Canada's history.[7]

These particular recommendations of the TRC have their roots in
reasonably recent international and national initiatives regarding the
heritage of Indigenous peoples and place. However, the specific recommendations by the TRC regarding the makeup of the HSMBC, the
incorporation of Indigenous heritage values in commemoration, and
the specific recommendation in regard to residential school sites place
these initiatives on a more solid and practical footing.

In Canada, government attempts to define Indigenous cultural
landscapes predate the TRC and, as noted above, can be traced back
to the early work of ICOMOS and the ISCCL. Based upon the development of international standards regarding cultural landscapes,
along with Canadian research in the late 1990s, and most importantly
consultation with Indigenous scholars and Elders,[8] the federal government in 2008 came up with the following definition of an Indigenous
cultural landscape: "An Aboriginal cultural landscape is a place valued
by an Aboriginal group (or groups) because of their long and complex
relationship with that land. It expresses their unity with the natural and
spiritual environment. It embodies their traditional knowledge of spirits, places, land uses, and ecology. Material remains of the association
may be prominent, but will often be minimal or absent."[9] This statement
recognizes an intimate knowledge by Indigenous peoples of the natural
resources and ecosystems of their areas, "developed," as scholar Ellen
Lee states, "through long and sustained contact and their respect for
the spirits which inhabit these places, [and that] moulded their life on
the land."[10] It is traditional knowledge, narrative, place naming, and
ecological insight, passed via oral tradition from generation to generation, that embody and preserve an Indigenous relationship to the land
and indigeneity in general. Association with Indigenous cosmology
creates sacred sites. They are respected as places of power, approached

through ritual and codes of conduct, becoming places of mystical and spiritual status. At the same time, Indigenous cultural landscapes can include important resource areas such as age-old localities for hunting, fishing, gathering, and settlement.

And they can have great consequence for modern discussions around land and sovereignty. As a result of formal and informal consultations held during 1990–91, it was apparent that any framework for addressing Indigenous history had to conform to emerging prescriptions in successive northern land claims regarding heritage and cultural sites. The 1997 Delgamuukw decision in British Columbia reinforced the significance of oral history in the establishment of land claims, a turning point in Canadian law and Indigenous sovereignty.[11] The Delgamuukw judgment originated with a 1984 case introduced by the hereditary chiefs of the Gitxsan and Wet'suwet'en First Nations in British Columbia, who took the provincial government to court to establish jurisdiction over 58,000 square kilometres of land and water in northwest British Columbia. Oral history played a major role in establishing Indigenous claim and in the final federal Supreme Court decision.

Indigenous world views are encapsulated in the enduring relationship between people and the land.[12] To achieve this encapsulation in commemoration, heritage agencies must recognize that what distinguishes Indigenous peoples' understanding from that of non-Indigenous peoples is the extent to which the human relationship with place has ethical, cultural, medicinal, and spiritual elements that are interwoven with patterns of economic use. Thus, the goal of commemoration is not simply the protection of these places as key to the long-term survival of their stories but a greater understanding of Indigenous concepts of place within a wider non-Indigenous culture. Over recent decades federal and provincial heritage agencies have, through a series of thematic and site-specific studies, come to consider how effectively the values of Indigenous peoples can define national historic significance and identify places that represent that significance.

Historically, many traditional Indigenous cultural landscapes throughout the world have been identified and documented largely in scientific terms, and mostly through archaeology. In 1990 Australian archaeologist Isabel McBryde observed that all Indigenous heritage sites in that country listed on the World Heritage List were commemorated

in purely scientific terms rather than as cultural or spiritual landscapes
or as representative of Indigenous cultural continuity.[13] However, in
more recent years in North America, in Australia, and in New Zealand,
these spaces have been increasingly recognized and documented because of the continuity of Indigenous culture where the land reflects a
long-standing interaction that is symbolic and religious or more overtly
economic. In Canada federal and provincial commemoration has moved
from a focus on Western scientific knowledge to a greater emphasis on
local and regional traditional knowledge where places are designated
for their spiritual and cultural significance as well as their historic and
economic importance.

Arguably, the expansion in recognizing and commemorating
Indigenous cultural places in western Canada has become more nuanced and increasingly multi-dimensional. Traditionally it has been
non-Indigenous scholars and designating bodies like the HSMBC
that have explored the significance of these sites, if only in the scholarly
literature. More recently, however, Indigenous scholars and Elders have
provided a more contextualized and more comprehensive perspective,
not only on the diverse meanings of such places but in regard to their
protection as well, a trend that has become increasingly persistent across
western Canada. Elders, or knowledge keepers, such as the late Narcisse
Blood, a Blackfoot from the Kainai First Nation in Alberta, have written extensively about the repatriation of threatened Blackfoot sites
in that province.[14] Landscapes are storied places, according to Blood,
and the land itself is animate. Stories, songs, and ceremonies have kept
knowledge of the land alive for the Siksikaitapiiksi (Blackfoot) people,
writes Blood, and all places are significant. Some mark events or artifacts or are markers, such as vision quests, human and animal effigies,
offerings sites, rock cairns, and battle sites. Places of significance also
relate to resource use such as buffalo jumps and pounds, berry-picking
spots, campsites, teepee rings, trails, and river crossings. Religious
places of significance include creation sites and places related to spirit
beings and the origin of medicine bundles and spiritual societies.[15] For
the Siksikaitapiiksi, such places, Blood writes, are "not simply piles of
rocks, cliffs, or glacial erratics; they are places imbued with meaning and
history . . . the equivalent of books, encyclopedias, libraries, archives,
crypts, monuments, historical markers, and grottos."[16] Protecting these
sites in Alberta has been difficult because of resource development

in the oil and gas industry as well as suburban and exurban sprawl, although the former has decelerated in recent times as the price of oil has declined. The Alberta government has implemented policies that involve the Siksikaitapiiksi in helping to protect significant places of traditional knowledge. To better conserve these sites, the people have been involved in finding unprotected locations, gathering traditional knowledge about these places, and gaining Siksikaitapiiksi perspectives on how to best protect traditional resource, community, and spiritual sites in Blackfoot territories.

In an approach similar to the protection of Siksikaitapiiksi sites in Alberta, in this chapter I also look at the designation, protection, and interpretation of some traditional Indigenous cultural landscapes in Manitoba and Saskatchewan. These include the sacred petroforms of Whiteshell Provincial Park, the ancient burial spaces of Linear Mounds National Historic Site in southern Manitoba, the pre- and post-contact Dorset and Inuit remains of Seahorse Gully National Historic Site located on the Churchill west peninsula, and Wanuskewin Heritage Park in Saskatchewan, the site of a multi-millennia meeting place for the Indigenous peoples of the northern plains. Each of these sites represents a version of traditional cultural landscapes; some are spiritual, others are cultural, and one relates to customary resource use and settlement activities carried out over an extended period of time.

Despite the fact that the sites mentioned above have been commemorated based upon their significance to Indigenous peoples in a pre-contact era, it is perhaps self-evident to state that the creation of Indigenous cultural landscapes did not end with the arrival of the fur trade and settler culture in the West. Such landscapes and places are not historically static; they exist in the post-contact era and continue to exist as places of great significance. As localities associated with the fur trade, as reserves, as contested terrains, and as lands removed, such places retain a cultural significance that remain as much a part of the Indigenous story in the West as the ancient places of spirituality and settlement.

In the Land of the North Wind

In the summer of 1966 a fire burned through a three-kilometre-long ridge on the Churchill west peninsula, a treeless headland located across the river from the modern town of Churchill, Manitoba. The summer-long fire denuded the thick tundra layer of heath and lichen that covered the area, leaving bare the stratum of gravel and sand that had once supported the vegetation of the region. While out hunting not long after the fire burned out, Joe Bighead, a local Dene man, discovered a treasure trove of ancient artifacts left exposed on the subsoil.[17]

The artifacts discovered by Bighead consisted primarily of stone tools, many the small, delicately fashioned implements associated with the circumpolar designation that archaeologists refer to as the "Arctic Small Tool Tradition." These chipped or polished stone tools were fashioned as cutting blades, hide scrapers, arrow points, and engraving tools known as burins.[18] The Pre-Dorset and Dorset cultures that made up this small tool tradition were called the "Tunit" by the later Inuit, and inhabited almost all of arctic Canada in a west-to-east Paleo-Eskimo migration from Alaska that started over 4,000 years ago. The Churchill River region represents their most southerly occupation, although minor Pre-Dorset sites can be found further inland in northern Manitoba. While the Seahorse Gully site retains evidence of cultural settlement over 4,000 years, evidence of smaller Pre-Dorset sites have been found inland near Shamattawa and South Indian Lake. Generally, Pre-Dorset and Dorset cultures extended from the High Arctic down the west and east coasts of Hudson Bay, taking advantage of the marine resources found there. The Tunit sites on the west peninsula date from approximately 2500 BCE to 700 CE (Pre-Dorset) and 700 CE to 1000 CE (Dorset). The Tunit were replaced by the Thule, the ancestors of the modern Inuit. The Thule and later Inuit, with their superior technology, were ultimately able to overwhelm the Tunit peoples. An ancient Inuit account comments: "The Tunit were a strong people, and yet they were driven from their villages by others who were more numerous, by many people of great ancestors; but so greatly did they love their country that when they were leaving Uglit there was a man who, out of desperate love for his village, harpooned the rocks . . . and made the stone fly about like bits of ice."[19]

Pre-Dorset peoples lived in coastal areas like the Churchill west peninsula (at the time a series of islands prior to post-glacial isostatic rebound) as well as on the interior tundra. Here they lived in snow houses in winter and skin-covered, semi-subterranean houses in summer, and hunted caribou and birds. In coastal areas they used skin boats in a seasonal marine-based economy, with harpoons to hunt ringed seal and fish. For much of the year Pre-Dorset families lived in small groups, although in spring and summer the west peninsula would see larger communal

Figure 1. Pre-Dorset house remains, Seahorse Gully National Historic Sites, n.d. Credit: Parks Canada.

gatherings. Fall and winter were spent inland. The later Dorset people also lived in snow houses in winter and skin tents in the summer months. Although they primarily pursued a marine-based economy, even in winter when they hunted for seals, the Dorset peoples also hunted caribou in summer.[20] Their culture was marked by a different technology from that of the Pre-Dorset people and the presence of art pieces comprised of small carvings of bone, antler, and ivory. The later Thule and Inuit hunted whales and used dogsleds.[21] As part of their technological advances, Thule peoples also developed harpoon heads and stone assemblages superior to their Dorset predecessors', facilitating their maritime economy in general and whale hunting in particular.[22] A large number of Pre-Dorset, Dorset, Thule, and Inuit sites have been excavated at the Seahorse Gully and Ridge sites, as well as at adjacent locations on the peninsula.

The Seahorse Gully site was recognized of national significance by the HSMBC in October of 1969. The site is adjacent to the northernmost segment of the bedrock Seahorse Ridge and runs 1.8 kilometres along the length of the ridge. The commemoration includes the Dorset Cove site on the western side of the peninsula near Button Bay. The "heritage value" of the site as listed by the federal government notes that it "contains one of the larger Dorset and Pre-Dorset assemblages in Canada."[23] Its character-defining elements consist of its location

Figure 2. Kayak rest remains, Seahorse Gully National Historic Site, n.d. Credit: Parks Canada.

overlooking Hudson Bay (including the surviving viewscapes), its setting below a ridge, the remains of twenty-four Pre-Dorset dwellings—rings of stone in their original placement—and the integrity of the surviving archaeological resources including hunting tools and domestic artifacts.[24] Archaeological research in the 1960s uncovered the rough outline of the site, and further research in the 1980s and 1990s revealed the existence of more dwellings and more artifacts. Remains of harpoon heads and the bones of seals have been found at the site along with lithic materials such as chert that was used to fashion scrapers, adze blades, and chisels.

The commemoration of Seahorse Gully identifies the earliest human use of the Churchill west peninsula. However, the existence of a large number of sites in the immediate area related to post-1000 BCE Thule and Inuit cultures provides the region with a continuity of occupation almost unmatched in northern Canada. Numerous tent rings that date from ancient times to the early twentieth century, along with graves, cache sites, and kayak rests, indicate Indigenous use over millennia and the west peninsula as an important resource and settlement area at the southern edge of the Arctic. Having hiked this area myself a number of times, first with archaeologists and later with Indigenous people, including John Arnalukjuaq, a spry septuagenarian Inuit man from Arviat, I could not help but feel impressed by the breadth of human history on the peninsula and by the ancient adaptability of northern peoples to a harsh climate and landscape.[25]

Unlike the traditional Indigenous spaces discussed later in this chapter, the Seahorse Gully site and nearby sites of Inuit occupation do not appear to be sacred places that carry cosmological significance; at least, we do not have evidence that they do. While there are surviving grave remains associated with places of later occupation—most likely post-contact—there are no surviving oral traditions or physical evidence at this site that relate to metaphysical views of the natural world, or associative values related to the spiritual, mystical, or medicinal, although their existence cannot be precluded, as these oral traditions might have been lost over time. Most likely the west peninsula is a long-used place of occupation and cultural practice, and a landscape that reveals settlement and resource use over millennia.

From a heritage perspective, these sites, when partnered with the post-contact Euro-Canadian historic sites in the immediate area, present an almost unrivalled cultural landscape. Here one can read a language of place that spans thousands of years of history and use. The eighteenth-century stone fortress called Prince of Wales Fort (a national historic site) sits imposingly only a few kilometres away on Eskimo Point, as does nearby Sloop Cove, where the Hudson's Bay Company (HBC) moored its coastal vessels. The location of Fort Churchill, also a national historic site, is located a short distance upriver. Fort Churchill (1783 to 1930) was built by the Hudson's Bay Company approximately five kilometres from the mouth of the Churchill River and was originally the 1619–20 wintering site of Danish explorer Jens Munk. It was also the location of a short-lived HBC post and whale fishery in 1689, and the site of the Churchill River post between 1717 and 1740. Colony Creek, a few kilometres farther upriver, was the 1813 wintering site of the second group of Selkirk Settlers, many of whom arrived infected with typhus. The following spring they walked overland to York Factory and then travelled by York boat to Red River. The west peninsula also contains the remnants of the North West Mounted Police post built in the late nineteenth century and closed in 1930 when the town of Churchill was established on the east side of the river.

The Churchill west peninsula is an area of such rich cultural history spanning many centuries that in the 1990s the Government of Manitoba considered nominating it as a UNESCO World Heritage Site. (That nomination never went forward as UNESCO felt more nominations were required from non-Western countries.) Yet, there remained the opportunity to recognize nationally the whole area as primarily an Indigenous cultural landscape. Unfortunately, at the time Parks Canada had grown wary of the evolving and expanding cultural narratives around many national historic sites, including a changing focus from "site" to "place" and the broader interpretations that went with it. By introducing the policy of commemorative intent across the country, the agency restricted its interpretive focus to original Board recommendations. At the west peninsula this resulted in an emphasis almost entirely upon Prince of Wales Fort National Historic Site and its eighteenth-century role in French-English colonial rivalry, the theme of the Board's 1920 commemoration.[26] The failure to take a wider, more inclusive view by locating places such as Seahorse Gully and Prince of Wales Fort in a broader historical context where the European timeline would be but a small part of a comprehensive human history squandered the chance to interpret a broad sweep of history, and especially the heritage of place and memory. Cultural landscapes such as Seahorse Gully, along with the other ancient Indigenous sites of the area, communicate the integrity of heritage as place and not the contrived representations of heritage as tourism. It is history on the ground, a cultural landscape, and not the tradition of invention (with apologies to Eric Hobsbawm) that often passes for heritage in Canada.[27] More importantly, cultural landscapes show how our history and our heritage can be more than simply affirmative depictions of settler culture.

Spiritual Landscapes and Mortuary Sites

Linear Mounds National Historic Site is located on a plain above the Antler River in southwest Manitoba not far from the Souris River and about seventeen kilometres south of the town of Melita. The mounds consist of two earthen embankments almost 200 metres in length, each terminating in circular mounds.[28] One mound runs north-south while the adjoining mound is an east-west configuration. These are burial mounds, one of the best-preserved examples of the ancient mound-building cultures associated with the Devils Lake-Sourisford Burial Complex, which extends from southeastern North Dakota, through southwestern Manitoba, to southeastern Saskatchewan. Approximately 200 burial mounds exist in southern Manitoba with roughly a third of these located in the Souris region.[29] The linear mounds near Melita are mortuary mounds dating from 900 to 1400 CE and are complex constructions of soil, bone, and other materials.[30] As part of the Sourisford Complex, Linear Mounds was constructed by ancient Indigenous cultures that had developed extensive trading networks as far as the west coast of Canada, east to the Great Lakes, and as far south as the Gulf of Mexico. Beads, quarried copper, and decorated pendants and gorgets (throat and chest coverings) from these mortuary mounds had their origins in these far-off places.

Since their "discovery" by relic hunters in the middle of the nineteenth century and by archaeologists in the early part of the twentieth century, the burial mounds have been partly excavated and a great many artifacts removed. Investigations by the Royal Ontario Museum in 1907, 1913, and 1914 resulted in the removal of human remains as well as many cultural artifacts to this museum, where they remain today.[31] No archaeology has taken place at the site since then. Occasional

Figure 3. Linear Mounds National Historic Site, 2012. Credit: Gordon Goldsborough.

monitoring continues, and in 2004 and 2005 Parks Canada conducted a two-year ground-penetrating radar survey.[32]

Linear Mounds was declared of national significance in 1973 and has remained as a sixteen-hectare protected land reserve since the property was acquired by Parks Canada from private owners in 1978. At the time of commemoration and acquisition, no consultation with local Indigenous groups was undertaken. Today there are no visitor facilities at the site or promotion by Parks Canada. A later Statement of Commemorative Intent reads: "The site contains some of the best-preserved examples of Aboriginal Mounds of the Devils Lake-Sourisford Burial Complex that exist in Canada. It was built and used between AD 900 and 1400."[33] Despite reluctance by Parks Canada to expose the site to potential vandalism (there is only periodic monitoring), the local municipality developed a road to the site and built a parking lot and an interpretive kiosk. Community representatives have hoped to develop tourism opportunities at the site, but its federal status as a land reserve has frustrated attempts at local marketing.[34] Parks Canada has, however, developed an ongoing relationship with the nearby Canupawakpa Dakota First Nation to potentially develop a sensitive interpretation plan, although the First Nation remains skeptical of tourism at a spiritual site like Linear Mounds. The goals of the most recent federal management plan (October, 2007) remain modest and simply state, "A meaningful and long-term relationship with a local First Nation will contribute to management decisions for Linear Mounds. Interested partners, stakeholders and Parks Canada will work together in safeguarding the values of the site while presenting site messages to all Canadians."[35] In 2008 the Canupawakpa Dakota First Nation asked for the return of human remains and artifacts from the Royal Ontario Museum. In response the museum asked the First Nation to gather support for this idea from all Indigenous communities that could claim descent from early Siouan people who built the mounds. The repatriation efforts involved contacting other Dakota First Nations in Manitoba as well as Indigenous communities in North Dakota.[36]

As a cultural landscape, Linear Mounds unites the spiritual and the terrestrial, at the same time revealing the early involvement of the ancestors of the Dakota in a continent-wide trading network. As mortuary mounds and as earthen mausoleums honouring the dead, they signify the prominence of the former, while their elevations, shapes, slopes, and geometry mark them as distinctive features on the prairie landscape. Traditional narratives describe the locations of sacred sites such as Linear Mounds with knowledge passed orally from generation to generation through instructional travel, descriptive images, and metaphorical tales of place. Located in a prairie farmer's field, the mounds are not a site of rustic Arcadian simplicity but a place of power and respect where the heritage of locality is treated as a whole, where place, events, and people are considered as one. It is a view of "place" that goes beyond a material focus and imbues that site with spiritual and transcendent significance. The spirit world unites with the material as beings traverse from the physical to the spiritual and the landscape communicates meaning. Thus, the continued protection and survival of the mounds and their sacred significance is essential to expressing how place can so critically represent the link between the distant past and present and the union between two worlds.

Spirit Stones

Petroforms, sometimes referred to as "boulder mosaics," describe the historic, perhaps ancient, placement of stones on open ground, creating the outline of a figure in usually an animal, human, or geometric configuration.[37] Placed by Indigenous groups throughout much of the northern Great Plains, including Canada's Prairie provinces, it is the animal, human, and geometric outlines that characterize the western edge of the southern Shield. Geometric shapes in the form of medicine wheels can be found in the western grasslands.[38] Whiteshell Provincial Park, located in southeastern Manitoba, contains a great number of these petroforms, approximately 200 sites scattered throughout the park that include rock images of snakes and turtles, humans, and geometric shapes. They are generally laid out on tablerock and vary in complexity and size from a few metres to hundreds of metres. Their age is unknown although they may represent the ritualistic actions of Algonkian speakers in the pre-contact period. The presumption (mostly among non-archaeologists) that the petroform builders were Algonkian speakers is based largely on the historical and current occupation of the area by the Anishinaabe Ojibwa peoples. However, there appears to be no regional oral history associated with the Whiteshell petroforms, and if the Ojibwa were the petroform builders, then their construction would have to postdate the mid- to later eighteenth century, when this group moved into the region on a western migration that originated in the eastern Lake Superior area. Some literature has associated the Whiteshell petroforms with the Midewiwin and the traditional rituals of the Ojibwa Grand Medicine Society.[39]

Dating the Whiteshell petroforms has been problematic, hence the uncertainty regarding which Indigenous groups actually constructed the sites. Difficulties with traditional dating techniques such as radio-carbon dating, cross-dating, and lichenometry, all apparently due to the physical nature of the sites, have left the petroform chronology less than certain. However, within the scholarly community, specifically the work of Dr. Jack Steinbring, it is felt that the petroform sites in the park are much older than Ojibwa occupation.[40] The largest site in the park, the 3.6-hectare Tie Creek site, or at least some of its elements, is thought to be upwards of 3,000 years old, while other components are estimated to have been constructed around 1200 CE.[41] The age of the sites is also unknown to modern Indigenous informants, which also suggests a pre-Ojibwa origin, although their crucial role as spiritual sites is generally agreed upon by all parties. For adherents of the Midewiwin, the petroforms represent Manito Ahbee, the place where God sits. It is considered the place of origin of the Anishinaabe, a people lowered from the sky to the ground by the Creator. While archaeologists might consider the first people to use the petroforms as unidentifiable, these stones are not just relics of past rituals of unknown people. Their importance to the

Anishinaabe continues to this day. However, the specific role these sites might have played in particular religious ceremonies remains undetermined. Some historians have speculated that the alignment of many of the petroforms might suggest an astronomical role as well.

Like many forms of Indigenous spirituality, what Western cultures might consider simply art can have a meaning related to ritual performance as well. These rituals, like ceremonial song and dance, can also include petroglyphs, pictographs, and petroforms. They are cultural, sacred, and ritualistic, helping to define and reinforce the relationship between the physical world and the spiritual. Today these sites continue their ceremonial roles, as Indigenous religious observances are occasionally held at the various petroform locations.[42] Unfortunately, the Bannock Point site, the most accessible petroform location in the park, has witnessed vandalism over the years—stones moved or removed completely and figures rearranged by visitors and campers.[43]

In 1959 Bannock Point was commemorated by the Province of Manitoba's Heritage Council and an interpretive kiosk and provincial plaque were erected nearby. Bannock Point has become increasingly well known, and guided tours are now offered. Other sites in the park, such as those at Tie Creek and Malloy Lake, are not designated by the province, except for the implicit exemptions from development specified under the heritage land-use restrictions of the Manitoba Provincial Parks Act and the general protections offered by the 1986 Manitoba Heritage Resources Act.[44] Neither are national historic sites; their greatest protection comes from their isolation and anonymity. It is unfortunate that a more robust legislative protection for these irreplaceable sites is not in place since it would not only enhance protection but promote the Whiteshell petroforms as significant heritage places in the province, placing them at the same level as the almost exhaustive list of public buildings, churches, and settler homesteads that dominate designated sites in the province.

Such boulder mosaic locations outside the park should also be extended the same level of protection, although Manitoba's track record of putting comprehensive conservation measures in place has been less than effective. For instance, the province's Heritage Resources Act, while being comprehensive, including significant prohibitions against the damage or destruction of historic resources, is rarely invoked against those who impair Manitoba's cultural heritage.[45]

As one long-time heritage advocate in Manitoba, who has done extensive research and writing on a wide variety of provincial resources, commented to me: "I would characterize the provincial government as toothless with respect to enforcement of heritage-related transgressions. However strident the legislation may be, they have committed no resources to it, with the result that the [Heritage Resources] Act is essentially a sad joke."[46]

Interwoven with the sacred significance of the petroforms of southeastern Manitoba is a culturally constructed heritage where the language of place communicates a setting of power. Such boulder mosaics, as British archaeologist Nicholas Saunders suggests, are "sacred landscapes [that represent] the manifestation of world-views which populate a geographical area with a distinctive array of mythical, religious, or spiritual beings or essences."[47] While we might know little of the original intent of petroform construction, just as the original meaning(s) of neolithic stone monuments elsewhere might remain mysterious, we do realize that they are places of power. As such, they are cultural landscapes that are to be respected through customs, rituals, ceremonies, and rules of conduct. They can resonate with individuals and with cultural communities. And, to return to an earlier discussion, the Whiteshell petroforms conform to the meaningful space of memory and the multiple constructions of historic "place" and not the sometimes contrived restrictions of heritage "site."

"Seeking Peace of Mind": The Topography of Cultural Identity

Indigenous cultural landscapes in North America are often ancillary—they "fly under the radar," at least for non-Indigenous people who might view a cultural landscape as a form of nature that has been human engineered, often in a significant way. As spiritual places, as topographies of cultural identity, or natural landscapes possessed of cultural meaning, they can remain unseen to settler culture due to the particular nature of the site itself or to its isolation, to social and historical marginalization, or perhaps to all of these factors.

The use of the land, either in a physical or spiritual sense, is critical, sometimes hidden from obvious view and sometimes overtly recognizable. An example of the latter might be the spectacular cliff dwellings of the Anasazi, the ancestors of the present-day Pueblo peoples, who lived in the American Southwest from about 900 CE to 1450 CE.

Figure 4. Wanuskewin Heritage Park and National Historic Site, 1988. Located on the banks of the South Saskatchewan River just north of Saskatoon, the park has applied for UNESCO World Heritage status. Credit: Patrick McCloskey.

These complex, masonry-walled communal habitations found in the box canyons of present-day New Mexico, Arizona, and Colorado are built into high cliffs, most likely as protection against the elements as well as enemies.[48] Some of the best examples of this ancient architecture can be found at Mesa Verde National Park (declared a World Heritage Site in 1978) and Yucca House National Monument in Colorado, as well as at the Canyon de Chelly National Monument in Arizona. An ancient cultural site closer to home is Head-Smashed-In Buffalo Jump. Located near present-day Fort Macleod in Alberta, the site is almost 6,000 years old and was designated a national historic site in 1968 and a UNESCO World Heritage Site in 1981.

In Saskatchewan, a cultural landscape not immediately identifiable, at least prior to its development as a historic place, is Wanuskewin National Historic Site, located fifteen kilometres north of Saskatoon. Wanuskewin, a modern Cree term meaning "peace of mind," is located in the broad Opimihaw Creek valley near the South Saskatchewan River. The 56.7-hectare site contains archaeological and physical evidence of some of the most significant pre-contact Indigenous habitation and resource use sites on the Northern Plains. Nineteen archaeological sites have been identified to date and include a medicine wheel, multi-component habitation sites, buffalo kill sites, and ceremonial locations. Over many centuries the Opimihaw Creek valley drew Indigenous plains peoples to this sheltered and relatively confined place, and archaeological work since 1982 by the University of Saskatchewan has uncovered evidence of a large number of cultural levels indicating continuous occupation over 6,000 years.[49] Cultural levels at Wanuskewin describe various occupations of the area over hundreds of generations, their distinctiveness determined through the analysis of lithic deposits and faunal remains, as well as arrowheads and projectile points. Some of the historic locations in the park include the Tipperary Creek site and its fourteen levels of occupation; the late pre-contact Tipperary Creek Medicine Wheel; the 4,000-year-old Mosquito Habitation site; the nine 2,000-year-old teepee rings of the Sunburn site; the Meewasin Creek site; a buffalo jump, pound, and bison processing centre; and the multi-level, multi-millennia habitation sites at Red Tail, Amisk, Juniper Flats Cathedral Park, Buena Vista, Cut Arm, Dog Child, Thundercloud, and Wolf Willow.

Archaeology in the park has also uncovered the remains of a few early homesteader sites.[50] Although developed initially as a provincial site under the auspices of the Meewasin Valley Development Authority, Wanuskewin was declared a national historic site in June of 1986. The Canadian Register of Historic Places lists the Statement of Significance for the site in its description of historic place as: "Wanuskewin National Historic Site of Canada is located in the Tipperary [now Opimihaw] Creek Wanuskewin Conservation Area on the South Saskatchewan River, in Saskatchewan. The archaeological sites contained within the 57-hectare (140 acre) conservation area represent nearly 6000 years of cultural history relating to the Northern Plains First Nations people. There are several kinds of remains in the deep coulees along the river-banks of the site including a medicine wheel, camps, tipi rings, and stone cairns. Official recognition refers to the present limits of Wanuskewin Heritage Park."[51] According to the minutes of the HSMBC in June 1986, Wanuskewin was designated a national historic site because "its archaeological features represent all the major time periods in Northern Plains pre-contact history . . . its archaeological sites representing 6000 years of cultural history."[52] Here the statement is amplified to mention the clarity of land use at Wanuskewin, the functional relationship

Figure 5. Interpretive Centre at Wanuskewin Heritage Park, 1988. Credit: Wanuskewin Heritage Park.

between many of the locations including surface features such as teepee sites and medicine wheels, and a number of major bison kill and processing sites.[53] All are located within a relatively small area of pre-contact settlement and use.

The recognition, commemoration, planning, and development of Wanuskewin as a place of Indigenous pre-contact heritage is an interesting story. While oral evidence had long suggested the importance of the Opimihaw Creek valley, ethnographic and archaeological interest in the site began only in the 1920s. Despite the significance of the oral history of the region, as late as the 1980s park planners continued to look upon traditional oral history at Wanuskewin with some suspicion. A November 1986 study of the development of visitor services at the site by Kanata Heritage Research recommended that ongoing archaeological, ethnographic, and natural science research should continue to play a major part in telling the Wanuskewin story. This type of information, the study concluded, "provide[s] the first knowledge not dependent on the hazards of oral transmission."[54]

The Saskatoon Archaeological Society directed the first limited archaeological excavations in the area between 1930 and 1932.[55] However, it was not until 1982 that a systematic archaeological program under the direction of Dr. Ernest Walker at the University of Saskatchewan began to uncover the rich history of the area. The Vitkowski family originally owned this land along the South Saskatchewan River, although they left the property uncultivated. In 1982 they sold the land to the City of Saskatoon, who sold it the following year to the Meewasin Valley Authority, a conservation agency created in 1979 to protect the cultural and natural resources of the South Saskatchewan River valley. Meewasin began preliminary planning for the park in 1979 and launched a five-year development plan in 1982. The archaeological program was initiated that same year. In 1983 Saskatchewan declared the then named Tipperary Creek location a provincial heritage site. In 1985 an Elders Advisory Committee (later changed to the Wanuskewin Indian Planning and Development Committee) was created and in 1986 they passed a resolution on Spiritual Values. That same year the HSMBC declared the site to be of national historic significance.

In 1987 the Cree word *Wanuskewin* was chosen for the park development, and the HSMBC, recognizing the importance of the site beyond simple commemoration via a plaque, recommended to the federal minister that "enhanced" involvement from the federal government be considered. According to then HSMBC chair Thomas Symons, "The site contains the richest known concentration of resources associated with the whole spectrum of pre-historic activity on the northern plains." Symons added that "if Parks Canada is convinced that the long-term preservation of the in-situ cultural resources at Wanuskewin is assured and that its *special sense of place* [italics mine] will be protected from unsympathetic intrusions, the Program should enter into discussions with the Meewasin Valley Authority and other interested parties with a view to determining an appropriate role for itself to play in the co-operative development of the site."[56] Not surprisingly, Symons was cautious regarding the nature of development at Wanuskewin. Although federal policies such as cultural resource management were still in the future, the program was concerned about inauthentic development at the site. Initially, federal investment in the project centred on research; in 1984 Ottawa committed $260,000 for a five-year program.[57] In 1988, after federal involvement was confirmed, Ottawa provided $3 million for site development to be overseen by the Saskatchewan Department of Economic Development and Tourism, the Department of Parks, the Saskatoon Archaeological Society, Recreation and Culture, and the Meewasin Valley Authority.[58] The City of Saskatoon provided $300,000 in operational funding.[59]

Evidently Wanuskewin had been on the cultural and development radar for some time, both from an archaeological perspective and with various levels of government, including the Meewasin Valley Authority that had originally purchased the site in the early 1980s. Aside from designation, a variety of master development plans, site development plans, cost-benefit studies, marketing plans, tourism research reports, and interpretive plans were carried out over roughly a decade, so clearly there was considerable "buy-in" from government, Indigenous organizations, and non-governmental agencies. If the 1960s and 1970s had witnessed the development of major fur trade and settler colonial heritage sites in Canada, the 1980s and 1990s would see a greater focus on Indigenous heritage with the development of Métis sites like Batoche along the South Saskatchewan River at the same time that Wanuskewin and Head-Smashed-In Buffalo Jump in Alberta were becoming the poster sites for pre-contact heritage.

Wanuskewin would soon take the lead in other ways as well. On 1 September 1989 the Wanuskewin Heritage Park Act (WHPA) was proclaimed, making the site not a federal, provincial, or municipal park but an independent entity under the administration of a board of directors appointed from the federal, provincial, and municipal governments, the University of Saskatchewan, the Meewasin Valley Authority, the Federation of Saskatchewan Indian Nations, and Wanuskewin Indian Heritage Incorporated. An earlier draft of the Act was called the "Wanuskewin Provincial Heritage Park Act" and did not mention the Indigenous community, the City of Saskatoon, or the Meewasin Valley Authority. In March of 1989 Fred Heal of the Meewasin Valley Authority, in a letter to Tom Young of the provincial Department of Economic Development and Tourism, protested the absence of these critical entities from this early draft.[60] The province then amended the text of the Act to include these stakeholders prior to its official launch the following September.

The first board chair of the WHPA was Grand Chief Cyrus Standing of the Dakota First Nations of Canada. The goal of the Act was to establish Wanuskewin as a world-recognized heritage park and tourist attraction that would increase awareness and understanding of the cultural legacy of the Indigenous peoples of the Northern Plains. By protecting the site's artifacts and spiritual character, Wanuskewin would provide a focus for this cultural heritage as well as afford opportunities for spiritual ceremonies and other cultural celebrations.[61] Wanuskewin Indian Heritage Incorporated (WIHI) is a corporation "established to review all planning for development and operations at Wanuskewin Heritage Park. WIHI ensures that the needs of the Indian people are met and an authentic and unique experience is provided for all visitors to the park."[62] The goals of this Indigenous organization included their "active partnership in the planning and development of Wanuskewin Heritage Park ... that Indian culture is reflected accurately and sensitively, . . . to hold traditional Indian ceremonies in private areas of the park [and] to develop business opportunities at the park for Indian people especially in the operation of the restaurant and gift shop." Economic spinoffs, it was argued, should include employment for Indigenous people, job training, career planning, and the development of managerial skills.[63] In line with this thinking, the Meewasin Valley Authority stated its hope that the project would reflect "Indian values and traditions" and that the park development would benefit Indigenous people through the ownership and leasing of facilities for the operation of commercial enterprises on the site.[64]

Phase 1 of design and construction began in 1989, commencing with a $1 million grant from Western Economic Diversification and another $1 million from a tourism agreement between the province and the federal department of Industry, Science and Technology Canada. The construction design included a visitor reception centre, a system of trails and outdoor interpretive stations, and an outdoor activity area. Projected costs in 1980s dollars amounted to over $6 million, $2.5 million of which was earmarked for the visitor centre and its functional infrastructure including meeting areas, a restaurant, and gift shop. Scenic walks and trails leading to the many outdoor sites were budgeted at $1.5 million. The balance of the project costs would go towards planning, architectural, and interpretive consultants; interpretive displays; a slide show; and signage.[65] Phase 1 completion was scheduled for 1992, with the site projected to attract between 110,000 and 150,000 people per year.[66]

Today, the park's trail system is over six kilometres long and takes visitors past bison kill sites, teepee rings, medicine wheels, and ancient settlement areas. Called the "Path of the People," the main trail descends into the valley where interpretive signage tells the broad story of the valley, the prairies, and the first peoples to visit and use the area. Other trails branch off from the main pathway, including the "Trail of Discovery" that leads north and emphasizes how archaeology reveals the past lives of Indigenous peoples. Archaeologists from the University of Saskatchewan continue their excavations in this area. The "Trail of the Buffalo" leads up onto the east prairie and offers visitors a view of the valley and the South Saskatchewan River. The "Circle of Harmony" trail leads onto the south prairie and past teepee rings and the medicine wheel site.

My own visits to the park in the early to mid-2000s (twice in summer and once for a winter meeting) were enjoyable and rewarding; the trails are not difficult to negotiate, the information provided is useful, and the views are remarkable. Guided tours are offered by Indigenous staff, who are not in any kind of period costume, a refreshing change from the experience one finds at "living history" sites. Corporate sponsorship signage at rest stops can be off-putting but no doubt are a reality of funding for modern heritage sites. The current exhibits in the visitor centre are excellent although a bit dated, and art exhibitions are staged on a regular basis. The site's website as of July 2019 indicates that future expansion of the galleries is being planned, as is the relocation of a bison herd to the site.[67] The theatre slide show entitled "What Does Wanuskewin Mean to You" dates to the early 1990s. Special programming around Indigenous themes is a regular part of site offerings all year round, including productions of visual and performance art by contemporary and traditional artists and theme-related lectures and talks. In this way, the site hopes to keep its programming fresh rather than relying solely on the more static offerings of traditional exhibitry. Wanuskewin's proximity to Saskatoon allows its meeting rooms to be used regularly for conferences, talks, and seminars.

While the visitor centre is stimulating, it is on the trails that visitors can gain the greatest insight into the ancient life of the valley. The site's original Visitor Services Plan underscored the importance of the "sensory experiences of the landscape ... the experience of separateness [and] ... stepping outside the visitor centre away from the modern world into a 'time warp.'"[68] Although this is no doubt "consultant talk," visitors do, I believe, want to experience and interact with the heritage of the natural environment, and less so with the pedagogical yet varied programming of the visitor centre. As a historian who worked for many years on multiple exhibits at historic sites and national parks throughout western and northern Canada, I have some difficulty in acknowledging this. However, allowing the visitor to see the site as "place" is crucial to understanding the relationship between heritage and history. It is what separates authentic historic sites from contrived heritage theme parks and historic sites from museums.

The current interpretation program at Wanuskewin was developed with the assistance of various consultants and Indigenous Elders and board members. The results of the extensive archaeological program carried out at the site over many years, a program still undertaken by students from the University of Saskatchewan, has formed much of the historical basis for the permanent programming at Wanuskewin. To that has been added the contributions of Indigenous oral history and spiritual teachings, as well as cultural programming and education.

In 1989 the design company Aldrich Pears led a series of Indigenous focus groups to aid Wanuskewin planners in the development of interpretive media and messages. The media favoured by these groups—audiovisual presentations, exhibits, guided and self-guided tours, storytelling, trail signage, archaeological interpretation, and activity nodes—followed the usual pattern of historic site interpretation (although they also stressed the importance of protecting the land). It was in their discussion of storyline messages, however, where the groups struck off in new directions. According to the Aldrich Pears summary, Indigenous respondents "described their current accomplishments and their outlook on the future." The report went on to note that respondents wanted to see "references ... made to problems originating at the time of contact, but only to provide context for the actions and achievements of Indians today in the arts, education, the economy, the political realm and the revival of culture."[69] Despite the fact that these focus group comments shifted away from the messages inherent in the ancient story of Wanuskewin, they do underscore Indigenous desires to portray not just the stories of their distant past but an exploration of their culture in contemporary ways and in contemporary contexts. However, in the margin of the Aldrich Pears summary of focus group comments, a handwritten note observes the "absence of reference to treaties, depopulation due to disease, enforced farming, residential schools, banning of ceremonies, reserve system, discrimination." Did that marginalia refer to historical topics mentioned by the groups that were not part of the planned site interpretation or were they actually considered as part of the overall message? Regardless, the note then goes on to comment: "May wish to minimize to 1500 years B.P."[70] This last statement might suggest that the original organizers wished to restrict historical interpretation to topics related to ancient occupation and away from more recent issues surrounding Indigenous life in western Canada. It appears that some tension existed early on between Indigenous advisory groups and interpretive consultants regarding the potential focus of the site.

Wanuskewin Heritage Park officially opened in June of 1992. Today the trails and site exhibits deal principally with the ancient history of Wanuskewin. It is with the site's ongoing programming, however, that many contemporary themes are introduced. For instance, one recent exhibition was entitled "The Next 150: Visions of Canada's Future," where Indigenous artists explored what the relationship might be in the future between Canada and Indigenous peoples. Another recent exhibition featured a talk and display entitled "An Eloquence of Women" by Indigenous and well-known historian and arts and curatorial expert Sherry Farrell-Racette.[71] Clearly, at Wanuskewin, traditional concepts of historic place are merged with contemporary interpretations of Indigenous life in the modern world, where unity in place, culture, customs, events, and traditions is reinforced.

Since 2012, a comprehensive renewal strategy for Wanuskewin has been under way, involving a business and marketing analysis that resulted in a new Visitor Experience Master Development Plan. In the spring of 2018 the site management board initiated a capital campaign called "Thundering Ahead" for renewal at Wanuskewin, which will encompass new construction at the visitor centre, including innovative exhibits and a large-scale immersive audiovideo production. This renewal has been planned since 2005. Revitalization of the building infrastructure is also under way.[72] In December of 2017 Wanuskewin Heritage Park was added to Canada's list of submissions for UNESCO World Heritage status.[73]

Wanuskewin Heritage Park is a unique historic place in western Canada. It successfully combines those elements and discoveries that make up a remarkable cultural landscape—one that fuses the natural environment with the human—at the same time providing visitors with a wide range of alternative and changing cultural and historic programming. Most importantly, it does not portray Indigenous heritage as existing only in the past but considers the cultural, social, and political influence of Indigeneity in a modern world. Yet, at its core, one sees history at Wanuskewin on the ground, the realization of a narrative heritage.

▲ ▲ ▲

Many Indigenous cultural landscapes have historically been identified, documented, and commemorated by governments in scientific terms, primarily through archaeology. Although this is largely true with the sites described in this chapter, their interpretation in more recent decades has been increasingly understood in multi-dimensional terms where the landscape can reflect meanings that are at once symbolic, spiritual, and economic. Today these spaces are not relics but living landscapes that focus upon complex relationships with the land. These relationships can be religious and mythological, economic and cultural, or an amalgam of all four. They can reveal religious ritual or the seasonal and day-to-day activities of living on the land. Traditional Indigenous knowledge connects these associations to the land through narratives, place names, sacred sites, rituals, and long-established resource use. Commemorating and interpreting Indigenous cultural landscapes must recognize the extent to which place is deeply bound up with identity, and where territory, traditions, and customs are not viewed in isolation but are "memory hooks" upon which hangs the cultural foundation of a narrative tradition. For the most part Indigenous cultural landscapes remain traditional places less manipulated by the artifice of the aestheticized spaces that often accompany views of a colonialist past. And they are expansive narratives that are defined by long stretches of time and articulated through views of an ancient past.

CHAPTER 2

National Dreams: Commemorating the Fur Trade in Manitoba

Now if the young are not receiving lessons about the fur trade, just how long will it take a Communist fifth column to overcome us without the use of missiles?

Barbara Johnstone, Superintendent, Lower Fort Garry, 1959

In the conclusion to her book *Playing Ourselves: Interpreting Native Histories at Historic Reconstructions*, historian Laura Peers writes about how at historic sites we give meaning to the past in the present and how we select from the past those narratives that make sense to modern visitors.[1] At the historic places that commemorate the fur trade, visitors are asked to engage with the past—engagements that commonly focus on material culture—while their encounters with Indigenous interpreters take place in the present (both physically and metaphorically) and can address cultural topics around indigeneity. At times these conversations can go beyond the commonplace ("What kind of fur is that?", "Were these teepees cold in the winter?", "What do you eat?") and address things such as cultural stereotyping and traditional racist perspectives regarding Indigenous people in history. From time to time interpreters may use their interactions with visitors to address contemporary issues such as land claims, self-government, and the continuing significance of treaties, although these types of exchanges are usually rare and are, of course, dependent upon the interest and knowledge of the visitor and the interpreter. Yet, such interactions, when they do occur, are interesting on a number of levels. At one level there is a communication by the interpreter of post-colonial Indigenous cultural sensibilities at the same time that, as a people, they are placed in historical context amidst the search for some form of authenticity, however that is defined. At another level it is difficult, especially at historic sites that commemorate the fur trade, to portray post-colonial histories at places that were built on the assumptions of colonialism.[2]

Regardless, in western Canada it was the commemoration of fur trade places that provided the cornerstone for a growing interest in heritage and the founding myths of assimilation and nation building. Recognition of the history of the fur trade and, more importantly, recognition of the actual places associated with this resource economy, played a vital role in the creation of the Historic Sites and Monuments Board of Canada in 1919.[3] As key parts in the colonialist iconography of progress, fur trade forts in the West (in conjunction with the "drum and bugle" military sites of central and eastern Canada) used the commemoration of heritage place to establish a nation-building narrative that provided the necessary link in a modernist era between the "savage"wilderness of Indigenous histories and the "civilization" of later agricultural and urban settlement. In considering the commemoration of the fur trade in Manitoba, one begins to see how the politics of heritage—and more particularly the politics of fur trade heritage—contributed to contemporary perceptions of Canadian territorial expansion and colonialism, the production of staples, and the perceived decline of Indigenous cultures.

Many of the commemorated forts in Manitoba reveal the kinds of iconic characteristics that are the mark of a larger colonial history in western Canada. Log palisades (and sometimes stone walls), Red River carts, York boats, metal traps, and all of the other paraphernalia of fur trade interpretation provide a backdrop for the larger issues of social and cultural change, ethnogenesis, and the racialization of Indigenous peoples that have been instrumental in understanding the trade and its commemoration. Of course, the most important legacy of the trade, and a critical part of its post-colonial heritage, is not its material culture but the establishment of a new mode of production that incorporated the Indigenous economies of western Canada into an international market of trade and production, making Indigenous cultures part of a global economy based upon a trans-imperial exploitation of resources.

Beginning in the early decades of the twentieth century, the commemoration of fur trade sites demonstrated how as a culture we attach layers of meaning to authoritative views of the past. Early assessments of the role of the trade generally followed the lead of historian Harold Innis, whose well-known statement that Canada "emerged not in spite of geography, but because of it" was followed by his lesser-known remark that "the significance of the fur trade consisted in its determination of this geographic framework."[4] This early awareness of fur trade history in prairie Canada is most evident in the selection of heritage sites by the HSMBC throughout the 1920s. Most of the Board's earliest commemorations, at least in the West, involved the fur trade. Two very early sites were Fort Langley in British Columbia and Prince of Wales Fort at Churchill.[5] A host of other commemorations soon followed, including Upper Fort Garry, York Factory, Rocky Mountain House, Fort Edmonton, and various others.[6] Although many of these designations were indicated by simple plaques and markers, others saw additional investments in infrastructure, restoration, and even reconstruction. The designation of these early sites by the Board marked more than simply the recognition of the history of the fur trade. The expansion of outsider non-Indigenous settlement, the political extension of the Canadian nation-state, and the growth of a resource-based economy in the West to facilitate the development of manufacturing in central Canada were also key themes in the recognition of the fur trade as a prelude to the implementation of a national policy.

In Manitoba, places like Lower Fort Garry (also known historically as the "stone fort" or the "lower fort"), once a Hudson's Bay Company (HBC) trading post and trans-shipment centre, along with York Factory, the company's major depot in Rupert's Land, and Prince of Wales Fort, the eighteenth-century stone fortress on Hudson Bay, were chosen by the Board to help define fur trade geography and place. Somewhat of an outlier to this list, Lower Fort Garry was initially designated as nationally significant in 1925, not for its role in the fur trade but as the location for the signing of Treaty 1 in 1871. At the time Lower Fort Garry was cited, along with Fort Qu'Appelle in Saskatchewan and Blackfoot Crossing in Alberta, as being the places where Treaties 1, 4, and 7 were made.[7] It was not until the 1950s and the passing of the ownership of the fort and the surrounding grounds to the federal government that the fur trade history of the site became the focus of commemoration and interpretation.[8] The designation, restoration, and development of Lower Fort Garry has for decades been the foremost heritage development in western Canada.

Today, all are important places in the federal system of national historic sites. The HMSBC, since its inception in 1919, has designated a number of fur trade sites in Manitoba, but it is Lower Fort Garry, York Factory, and Prince of Wales Fort that garnered the most investment in terms of research, conservation, reconstruction, and interpretive development.

Tourism and the Heritage Narrative at the Stone Fort

A 1931 article in the *Winnipeg Evening Tribune* described how at Lower Fort Garry in the winter of 1911, "a northern dog team driver cracked his whip and with a loud 'marche', swung his huskies for the last time round the crescent inside the fort to the saleshop. There, meeting a company trader, he re-enacted a scene which had taken place inside the fort for eighty years and so trading ended at Lower Fort Garry."[9] The fort, constructed under the guidance of George Simpson in the 1830s, had long supplied the lower Red River parishes with goods, had participated in the trans-shipment of furs via York boat to York Factory, and for a brief period served as the district administrative headquarters of the HBC until supplanted by the establishment in the late 1830s of Upper Fort Garry at the forks of the Red and Assiniboine rivers. It was also the site of the signing of Treaty 1 in August of 1871 between the Crown and the Anishinaabe and Cree peoples of southern Manitoba. Shortly after the fort's closing, the company approached the federal government's recently established Parks Branch to purchase the fort. The Dominion Parks Branch, which had been founded in 1911 under the Department of the Interior, was the first national parks service in the world. It was renamed a number of times: in 1930 as the "National Parks Branch"; in 1973 as "Parks Canada"; in 1984 as the "Canadian Parks Service"; and in 1998 as the "Parks Canada Agency."[10] The HBC offered to sell the fort and the surrounding acreage for a price of $60,000. The government rejected the offer to create a "national reserve," as the federal initiative to commemorate historic sites had yet to be formalized.

In 1911, recognizing the historical significance of the fur trade and taking ownership of the accompanying physical resources were not high on the list of government priorities. At the time it was central Canadian sites associated with the Loyalist tradition and the battlefields from the War of 1812 that occupied the attention of heritage groups such as the Historic Landmarks Association, a precursor to the HSMBC

Figure 6. "Delivering fur to the Hudson's Bay Company at Lower Fort Garry, 1904." Credit: Archives of Manitoba.

and for the most part Anglo-British in their composition. Interest in such central Canadian sites was largely based upon their role in extending British-Canadian colonialism, including their culture and institutions. Historian C.J. Taylor describes how the disparate groups and organizations that made up early heritage advocacy in Canada tended to focus on local contexts and regional biases, although they shared similar cultural and ethnic backgrounds. Despite that cultural cohesion, Taylor contends, there existed numerous conflicting views, and early on the Historic Landmarks Association had to steer away from nationalist ideologies in order to avoid conflict. This tension between the local and the national would characterize historic site commemoration and interpretation for decades to come, and arguably continues to this day.[11]

After failing to interest the federal government in acquiring the fort and its extant stone buildings, the HBC in 1913 leased the site to the Motor Country Club (MCC) for an annual rent of one dollar. The MCC, one of the earliest automobile clubs in Canada (and founded by the Winnipeg Automobile Club), was established by well-off Winnipeg gentry "to hold, organize and establish from time to time, automobile tours or endurance contests." In fact, that facet of the club's purpose would take a minor role as the MCC soon evolved into a more traditional private country club with a golf course, tennis courts, and a members' lounge located in the Big House, the large, central, stone building constructed for George Simpson in 1838. The MCC occupied the fort until the end of 1962 and over this fifty-year period it made a number of changes at the site, including the "modernizing" of various buildings (although the work was done with some regard to historical character), planting trees, and the development of gardens inside the walls.[12] In 1951 the HBC deeded the fort to the federal government, although the MCC lease continued for another twelve years.[13] During that time those interested in visiting the old fort could tour the grounds, although they were not allowed inside the club's buildings. As visitation swelled throughout the 1950s, some conflicts occurred between club members and visitors and complaints about lack of access appeared in Winnipeg newspapers.[14] Noting the growing popularity of the site, the federal government ended the MCC lease and took over the fort as a historic site at the beginning of 1963.[15]

As mentioned above, the lower fort was the location for the signing of Treaty 1 in 1871, which was the reason for its commemoration by the HSMBC in 1925. Designated among other treaty sites across the West, Lower Fort Garry was cited "as being [one of] the places where treaties were made whereby the Indians renounced their possessory rights in these provinces."[16] A plaque was unveiled at the site in 1929, yet no Indigenous leaders were asked to speak at the ceremony. C.H. French of the HBC, however, did give a talk on "the Indian and his habits of life."[17] The text of this original 1920s plaque read: "Here on 3rd August, 1871 this treaty was made between Wemyss M. Simpson, representing the Crown and the Chippewa [the traditional American designation for the Anishinaabe] and Swampy Cree Indians whereby those tribes surrendered their rights to the lands comprised within the boundaries of Manitoba as then existing. The agreement ended the restlessness of the Natives and left the way open for peaceful settlement."[18] This original text, especially the references to "ending the restlessness of the Natives" and leaving "the way open for peaceful settlement," leaves bare the attitudes of the time toward Canadian expansionism in the West and the fate of Indigenous peoples within its boundaries. Indigenous peoples were viewed as a threat to white settlement in 1871, and their dispossession was considered worthy of historical commemoration almost six decades later. In the 1970s the plaque was replaced. The new wording reads: "To promote peaceful settlement of the newly acquired western territories after 1870, Canada negotiated a series of treaties with the native peoples. Here on 3 August, 1871 the first of these treaties was signed by Mis-kee-ke-new, Ka-ke-ka-penais, Na-sha-ka-penais, Na-na-wa-nanan, Ke-we-tay-ask, Wa-ko-wush, Oo-za-we-kwun representing the Ojibwa and Swampy Cree people of Manitoba and Wemyss Simpson on behalf of the Crown. In return for services and the promise of annuity payments, livestock and farming implements, the Indians ceded the land comprising the original portion of Manitoba."[19]

Although this more recent text does mention the names of the Indigenous leaders who signed the treaty, it still leaves out a number of critical issues. These include mention of the outside verbal promises (some of which were added to the treaty in 1875), the failure of the federal government to live up to many of the guarantees such as the provision of agricultural implements, the later removal of hunting and fishing rights through conservation measures introduced by the Manitoba government, and most importantly the question as to whether the treaty entailed land "surrender" or "shared use."[20] In the early 2000s the Board and Parks Canada attempted to work with southern Manitoba Indigenous groups through the Assembly of Manitoba Chiefs and the Southern Chiefs Organization to come up with a new plaque text that would incorporate the differing views of the treaty. At the time Parks Canada attempted to develop an oral history about the meaning of the treaty with a number of Indigenous Treaty 1 communities in southern Manitoba. The study was poorly coordinated by the Manitoba Field Unit office of Parks Canada and resulted in little useful information on contemporary Indigenous views of historical treaty making. The report was left incomplete and was never made public. Meanwhile, federal Department of Justice lawyers advised strongly that Parks Canada and the HSMBC not accept the shared use argument. As a result both sides rejected a proposed plaque text that incorporated the two differing perspectives. To this day no revised plaque has been approved, although according to an August 2020 article in the *Winnipeg Free Press*, Treaty 1 First Nations are providing input into a new plaque text.[21]

In 1950, shortly before acquiring Lower Fort Garry, the Board added the fort's role in the fur trade to its national significance, noting

Figure 7. An aerial view of Lower Fort Garry, c. 1940s. Credit: Archives of Manitoba.

over a century of Hudson's Bay Company administrative and supply activities.[22] Four months earlier, Board minutes had noted the fort's location, setting, orientation, and composite elements, commenting that the extant buildings of the site were of particular importance for their assemblage, design, use of materials, and construction technology, as well as their functional and spatial disposition.[23] The federal acquisition of the lower fort and its later development as a major heritage attraction were in large part driven by the growth of tourism in the country, itself the product of expanding time for leisure and recreation. The affordability of the automobile for an increasingly affluent postwar middle class became a major factor in the expansion of the tourism industry and the accessibility of places like Lower Fort Garry. The fort had much to offer as a tourism destination, even if its actual historic role in the fur trade was largely peripheral for much of the nineteenth century. Relatively close to a major urban centre, the fort boasted original and largely intact stone structures from the fur trade era in a setting that was both bucolic and easily accessible. At a time when heritage often focused on the intrinsic value of extant historic structures—a kind of "no building, no history" perspective on significance—the lower fort represented the ideal historic site. In the years before cultural landscapes drew commemorative attention, including a focus on Indigenous spiritual sites and traditional hunting areas, the presence of period architecture—sometimes in its original setting or often represented by relocated period buildings—remained at the heart of most heritage initiatives in Canada.[24] Everything from fur trade forts to stately mansions came to represent the triumph of settler culture and reaffirmed the "no building, no history" theme.

As the postwar tourism industry in western Canada grew alongside the development of nation-building subjects like the fur trade, the significance of the stone fort as the site of the making of Treaty 1, an event increasingly seen by non-Indigenous Canadians as having little historical relevance, was swiftly pushed to the background. Downplaying the significance of the treaty at Lower Fort Garry can be traced to two factors: the growing realization in the 1950s and 1960s that the site presented a tourism opportunity that favoured the perception of fur trade history as colourful and inspiring, not to mention nation building; and the emerging non-Indigenous view that treaties were largely irrelevant in the settler colonial society of the twentieth century. Of course, car culture was central to this shift in the visitor experience. "Automobility," as historian Ben Bradley calls it in his 2017 book, *British Columbia by the Road: Car Culture and the Making of a Modern Landscape,* had much to do not just with simple access to the interior but with changing perspectives on tourism promotion, park development, and historic sites.[25]

With a new and growing source of site visitors and heritage "customers," Lower Fort Garry was primed for development as a major national historic site (or "park" as it was initially called). Historians Michael Payne and C.J. Taylor have written that "a single event such as the signing of a treaty, while almost certainly more significant than [Lower Fort Garry's] limited role as a fur trade site, had limited basis for site programming."[26] Writing in 2003, Payne and Taylor supported the development of Indigenous encampments at fur trade sites but also argued that "heritage agencies will not put the kind of effort into identifying, protecting, and interpreting Aboriginal sites other than those associated with the fur trade that they probably should."[27]

During the 1950s a few fort buildings, at the time under the ownership of the federal government (but prior to the end of the MCC lease), underwent some repairs. Unfortunately, much of this work was heavy-handed and involved poured concrete flooring in the cellar, the replacing of a number of original wood beams and supports and new door and window frames, and the stuccoing of some original limestone walls.[28] Writing in 1956, federal engineer J.E. Wilkins recommended that no attempt be made to restore the fort buildings, including the Big House, commenting that he "cannot see how any attempt to restore it to its original appearance would in any way improve it."[29] Dominion Parks Branch plans in 1956 to create a "fur trade museum" on the main floor of the Saleshop building resulted in the design of the space as a "typical" HBC post of the period. It was only later that research revealed that the Lower Fort Garry trading area was not typical of mid-nineteenth-century posts. Other work included the construction of a paved parking lot outside the fort's north wall, the erection of outdoor directional and interpretive signage, and the resurfacing of the asphalt driveways inside the walls. Despite the fact that no attempt was made to restore the fort buildings to the fur trade era, repair work was carried out over the rest of the 1950s, work that compromised some of the fort's original fabric. However, the lack of funding to carry out comprehensive "improvements" probably ended up saving a good deal of the original materials. Between 1951 and 1965 there was little in the way of attempts to gather historical documentation on the original fort buildings and grounds. No archaeology was carried out at the site prior to 1962, and the historical research that had been pursued was imprecise, quixotic, and often inaccurate.[30]

Yet, interest in developing the site remained high especially among local historians, even if justifications for investment in the property were sometimes eccentric. In 1959 Barbara Johnstone, the curator of the Hudson's Bay Company Museum in Winnipeg (and later the first superintendent of Lower Fort Garry National Historic Site), wrote to Jack Herbert, the director of the National Historic Sites Division (NHSD) in Ottawa, that preserving the lower fort was key to instructing young people about social values and principles. "There is one good selling point to politicians and the public alike," she wrote. "That is missiles come and go, and aircraft, and Dew Lines, treaties and the like are made and broken daily . . . the strength of democratic life lies in the end with individuals of these countries that hold democratic opinions. Now if the young are not receiving lessons about the fur trade, just how long will it take a Communist fifth column to overcome us without the use of missiles?"[31] If Johnstone's justifications for investment in the lower fort might have stretched credibility, a growing public interest in the history of the site would soon result in a comprehensive heritage makeover, a makeover that would ultimately compromise much of the fort's heritage character. Reconstruction would soon masquerade as restoration.

In 1961 the federal and provincial governments entered into an informal agreement for a joint development of the fort and the surrounding properties. The federal government would restore the historic buildings within the fort walls and the government of Manitoba would build a "sympathetic historical development" on provincial land south of the fort. A loosely defined concept, this development was to be a "Red River Colony restoration" and include the relocation to the site of local Winnipeg heritage buildings including Riel House, the construction of other period buildings, and the development of an "Indian Village, Hudson's Bay Trading Post, Red River Ox Cart Rides, Red River Steamer, Early Brewery, [and] York Boat Rides." A few years later the Manitoba government backed out of the proposed scheme, suggesting that the federal government take on these projects. Provincial properties located immediately north and south of the fort were sold to the federal government.[32]

Ottawa considered these plans to be overly costly and the NHSD began its own developments, most notably a proposal to build a museum within the fort walls to house the Hudson's Bay Company Museum Collection. This impressive collection of Indigenous artifacts, artwork, clothing, weaponry, and HBC material culture, what the HBC in 1920 referred to as "historical relics, lore, and souvenirs of the early history of the Company," was created in the early 1920s to mark the 250th anniversary of the founding of the company.[33] Displayed at the Hudson's Bay Company store on Portage Avenue for many years, it was moved to the new museum at Lower Fort Garry in 1964. In 1994 the company gifted the collection to the Manitoba Museum, where it is now on display.[34]

With the departure of the MCC at the end of 1962, the Dominion Parks Branch and the NHSD began an intensive restoration and redevelopment of the site, all centred on the history of the fur trade in the West. As interest in local heritage increased in the 1960s, planning began for the construction at Lower Fort Garry of a fur trade museum containing the "relics" of the past. Later, the fort site would evolve into a sort of pioneer village of the fur trade, an imagined tourism destination of restored and reconstructed buildings, costumed interpreters, and a pan–fur trade interpretation. The path to the modern national historic site such as the lower fort was a long and complex one as resources became available and the development of an "official" or "authorized" heritage was realized. As C.J. Taylor has written, in the 1960s the national historic sites program focused on a number of large-scale projects, driven by ministerial commitments. The reconstruction and restoration of sites like the Fortress of Louisbourg, the Halifax Citadel, and Dawson City quickly became government priorities, as did Lower Fort Garry.[35] At the lower fort, the NHSD built a new museum to house the Hudson's Bay Company Museum Collection, extant stone buildings like the Big House and the Saleshop/Furloft were restored to their mid-nineteenth-century appearance, and other early buildings were reconstructed or moved to the site. Although the eventual development of Lower Fort Garry was impressive in scope, a 1962 plan for the "restoration and reconstruction of the historic buildings at the lower fort" by the Department of Northern Affairs and National Resources called for a much more ambitious plan.

Besides the restoration of the existing buildings both inside the fort walls (Big House, Saleshop/Furloft, Warehouse, South West Bastion, Men's House, Bakehouse, Powder Magazine, and Doctor's Office) and outside (the Engineer's Cottage), the report recommended the reconstruction of a number of original buildings including the barns and stables once associated with the company farm immediately north of the fort, the buildings of the "industrial complex" south of the fort (including the grain barn, storehouse, brewery, distillery, grist mill, sawmill and lathe room, malt barn, lime kiln, miller's house, and the "old wood store"), as well as the reconstruction of the Blacksmith Shop and Farm Manager's Cottage, also located south of the fort.[36] Grand as it was, the plan was ultimately unsustainable and it was soon decided to restore and reconstruct those buildings associated with the 1850s. The original 1953 plan to outfit the Saleshop as a museum for the HBC collection was never realized, and it was not until 1962 that the federal government decided to begin construction of the museum inside the fort walls. The exterior of that museum would replicate the appearance of the historic Retail Store, a wood-frame building within the fort walls that had been built in 1873 and dismantled in 1924. The museum was completed in September of 1965 at a cost of $136,000.[37]

The first large restoration project at the fort concerned the Big House. Built in the 1830s, the house had undergone a fair number of structural and cosmetic changes over the years and looked little like the limestone two-storey, hipped roof building that appeared in the H.L. Hime photo of 1858. Restoration work on the house commenced in the spring of 1966, as did archaeological investigations around the building's perimeter walls. The verandas that had been built in the twentieth century were removed, the structurally unsound north and west walls were demolished, part of the annex was demolished, and all of the more modern interior partitions were removed. As well, the federal government rebuilt the original stone fireplaces and bake ovens, a new basement floor and drainage system were added, and "as found" evidence (floor markings that indicated original walls) was used to completely alter the layout of the first floor with new construction, including plaster walls with period paint colours and wood floors manufactured to look as if they were from the middle of the nineteenth century.[38] The site installed a new veranda to mimic the original seen in the 1858 Hime photograph. In 1968 curators at the NHSD in Ottawa began the furnishing of the house with a handful of original pieces, although most were simply period pieces that were repaired and refinished.[39] (The use of non-site-specific but period-friendly materials would characterize restoration of most of the furnishings of the lower fort. Other pieces were new, manufactured in the style of the original.) In May of 1969 the restored (and partly reconstructed) Big House was officially opened by Jean Chrétien, the minister of Indian Affairs and Northern Development.

The NHSD carried out work on the other stone buildings within the fort walls. At the Saleshop/Furloft they installed a concrete re-taining wall below grade; built a new roof; poured a concrete floor in the basement; repointed the walls with cement mortar; repaired or removed the chimney, fireplace, and interior walls; and installed new joists, flooring, and windowsills and frames. In 1970 the building was furnished as a period saleshop on the main floor; the second floor was furnished as a storage area for merchandise such as tea, tools, and rope; and the third-floor loft was used as a fur storage room.[40] It opened to the public in June of 1971.

Figure 8. The Big House, Lower Fort Garry National Historic Site, 1994. Constructed in the 1830s by the Hudson's Bay Company, the house was restored in the 1960s by Parks Canada. Credit: Parks Canada.

Figure 9. The parlour at the Big House, Lower Fort Garry, n.d. When restored in the 1960s the Big House witnessed many changes to its interior spaces. Credit: Parks Canada.

Comparable actions were taken on the remaining stone buildings inside the fort in the late 1960s. Roofs were replaced, new concrete floors were poured, window and door frames were replaced, and original stonework was repointed with concrete instead of lime mortar. The Men's House, an early 1850s barracks and kitchen for some of the company's servants, was originally built as a rubble-filled timber-framed structure (a French style of construction known as *colombage pierrote*). As in the other restored buildings at the fort, the department installed a new foundation along with a new roof, interior joists, flooring, and supporting beams. Only one half of the lower floor was furnished and opened to the public. Interpretation focused on the daily lives and work of single HBC men at the fort; married servants lived away from the post.[41]

Plans for the large Warehouse building were more ambitious, as the building dated to the earliest construction at the fort in the 1830s. Initial intentions in the early 1970s to restore the building as Manitoba's first penitentiary—a role it served between 1871 and 1877—and then the province's first mental asylum from 1885 to 1886, were shelved in favour of planned exhibits around the theme of building technology at the lower fort.[42] The department then abandoned that plan as well when it was decided in 1976 to interpret the building as a fur trade warehouse in keeping with the theme of the fort's other stone buildings. In keeping with the decision to restore the warehouse to the look of the 1850s, a structural and use history of the building was carried out by Parks Canada historian Greg Thomas in 1977.[43] The intent to use the building to interpret agricultural storage and transhipment was only partially realized due to funding issues. For a time fort operations used the building's second floor for special presentations, and a period restaurant operated by the Lower Fort Garry Volunteer Association occupied the main floor for a few years after 1986. As part of its fur trade "makeover," the government repointed the original walls and replaced the roof along with interior beams and support posts. New sleepers and flooring were installed throughout the building. In the 1980s Parks Canada replaced the foundation at the west end of the building.

With property acquired from the provincial government immediately south of the fort, the NHSD decided to go ahead with restoring the one remaining extant building—the Engineer's Cottage—while reconstructing two other buildings that were once located nearby,

Figure 10. The Ross Cottage at Lower Fort Garry, n.d. Built in the 1840s, the house was partly reconstructed in 1970 as the Engineer's Cottage and has undergone periodic work since then. Credit: Parks Canada.

the Farm Manager's Cottage and the Blacksmith Shop. (No historic reconstruction would be complete without a smithy to provide the predictable, and expected, sounds and smells of pioneer life.) In 1970 the Engineer's Cottage was partly reconstructed (one wall was rebuilt) and the roof and interior floor were replaced. The department removed an 1860s-era annex.[44] In the 1980s, as part of a revamped interpretation program at the fort, Parks Canada renamed the house the "Ross Cottage" to mark the brief time when retired HBC factor Donald Ross and his family lived there in the early 1850s.

Archaeological investigations in the area in 1967 revealed the nearby location of what was once the Farm Manager's Cottage. Rather than reconstructing the building, the department decided to purchase and relocate an extant 1835 Red River frame house located in the district of Kildonan that had once belonged to Scottish settler James Fraser. The Red River frame building was placed adjacent to the original house site at the fort. For several years the relocated house was known as the "Fraser Cottage," but was later renamed the "Farm Manager's Cottage" for the period when the post farm manager, Alexander Lillie, lived with his family in the no longer extant cottage once located on adjacent ground. Since it was moved to the site in 1970, approximately

90 percent of the log timbers of the Fraser house have been replaced, as has much of the interior woodwork.[45]

The first forge at Lower Fort Garry most likely dates from the 1840s. The HBC replaced it with a second and larger blacksmith shop in the late 1850s, but it was destroyed by fire in 1877. Initially, the plan was to reconstruct the second shop based on archaeological excavations and period descriptions, and Parks Canada files in Library and Archives Canada (LAC) contain engineering drawings for this work.[46] However, in 1971 a surviving Red River frame house located only a few kilometres south of the fort, but much smaller than the proposed reconstruction, was purchased by the department and moved to the site; its door was widened and windows were moved in order to replicate a blacksmith shop.[47] No explanation for this change of plan was given in the government files, although the much-reduced cost involved in moving an existing period building must have factored into the decision. In the 1990s much of the original fabric of this relocated building was lost when Parks Canada's Regional Restoration Workshop replaced major elements of the structure with new materials.

A principal heritage resource at Lower Fort Garry, and one that helped mark its distinctiveness in the architecture of the fur trade, are its limestone walls. Begun in the early 1840s, more as a symbol of authority in the local settlement than for protection, construction of the walls at the fort was not completed by the company and the visiting British Sixth Regiment of Foot until 1848. Almost a century and a half later, the restoration of the walls became a major task and was not undertaken until the late 1980s, although some repointing, the installation of an asphalt cap, and landscaping to facilitate drainage had been carried out periodically between the early 1920s and the 1950s. With virtually no work on the walls between then and the 1970s, it was reported that, by 1974, 30 to 40 percent of the stones exhibited serious deterioration.[48] Recommendations for the protection and restoration of the walls stemming from the 1974 report —minor repointing, grade-level water barriers, repair of spalled stones, and improvement of drainage—were very much in keeping with the "minimal intrusion" principles of heritage restoration. Unfortunately, the report's recommendations were not followed, and by the late 1980s the walls had further deteriorated. In 1987 Parks Canada initiated a multi-million-dollar program of restoration that began with a careful dismantling of the east wall (individual stones were numbered, taken down, repaired, replaced, and repointed) but soon degenerated into a simple knock-down of the north wall using a backhoe; most of the stones were discarded and replaced with new limestone. Project delays and available funding were cited as the reasons for the accelerated, if ham-fisted, approach, and what began as a sympathetic restoration program would become the destruction of original fabric followed by new construction, a technique largely prohibited by Parks Canada policy. The agency's Cultural Resource Management Policy, while technically allowing for the reconstruction of resources, does indicate that reconstruction can be considered only if "there are no significant preservable remains that would be threatened by reconstruction; and the action will not compromise the commemorative integrity of the site; and there is sufficient research information to support an accurate reconstruction."[49] Clearly, the approach undertaken by Parks Canada's Regional Restoration Workshop did not fall into this category.

Eventually, professional and fort staff with Parks Canada intervened and the work was halted. With plans developed by a restoration architect, the Restoration Workshop adopted once again the concept of minimal intervention: they installed a concrete cap atop the surviving west and south walls to stop drainage into the rubble core of the walls and implemented a repointing program. This earlier destruction of an original heritage resource was the product of poor planning and the decision to not engage in regular, sustainable, and ongoing maintenance but opting instead for a quick but expensive fix.[50] As many people in government will attest, it is often, and paradoxically, easier to gain access to large capital expenditures than it is to run smaller year-over-year maintenance budgets. It is a funding approach that works well with federal Treasury Board policies but does little to protect heritage resources on an ongoing basis.

The situation with the wall restoration project to some extent echoed much of the work that had gone on at the fort over the previous two decades, although admittedly the "restoration" of the lower fort walls was far more heavy-handed. That being said, building restoration during the 1960s and early 1970s was approached less as a sympathetic and respectful treatment of cultural resources than as a plan to get the fort up and running as a significant tourist site, the largest in western Canada. Although historical and architectural research was carried out on the various surviving buildings at the fort, the plan to develop a major heritage animation program carried the day, and building interiors, for instance, were developed more for tourist satisfaction than for accuracy, though "accuracy" always seemed to remain a vague and indefinable goal. Visitor expectations of what a fur trade fort should look like—Indigenous encampments, usually minimal in size, were integral to this "look"—often influenced such things as room layouts, traffic flow, and accessibility. Cleanliness, order, neatly mowed lawns, and well-maintained pathways were considered critical to visitor enjoyment, avoiding the disorder and dirt of what such places actually looked like during the historic period. Fur trade recreations and reconstructions in these environments become a sort of talisman, a prized object, rather than an idea or a place with meaning. While of course not charged with any magical force, the material culture of the fur trade is effectively employed to symbolize or represent a much larger and more complex phenomenon, and the more exact the symbolism, the easier it is to attract notice and acceptance. The heritage of the fur trade in prairie Canada is for the most part the heritage of things, both genuine and manufactured. Meaning, insight, and even narrative are often sacrificed for the curatorial experience and the placement of objects in expected places—all part of the "visitor experience."

With its extant, restored, and reconstructed buildings, Lower Fort Garry was well suited for the development of a major interpretive program. The site's proximity to Winnipeg and Selkirk gave it a reservoir of visitors (not to mention summer travelling Canadians and Americans), especially at a time when heritage tourism was expanding. Costumed interpreters in restored and reconstructed buildings animated daily life as it was in the mid-nineteenth century, or at least as it was imagined to be by public historians, interpretive specialists, and site managers. "Living history," itself a form of reconstruction, was much in vogue by the early 1970s, following the success of places such as Colonial Williamsburg in Virginia, Louisbourg in Nova Scotia, and Sturbridge Village in New England. At Lower Fort Garry, the limited interpretive efforts of the 1960s were expanded in the 1970s to a full-scale animation program with costumed interpreters role-playing a variety of historical personalities who lived and worked at the fort in the 1850s and 1860s. As part of an intense commemoration and development of historic sites across the country during a period that saw the increased link

Figure 11. Costumed interpreters at Lower Fort Garry National Historic Site, 1994. Once a major component of the fort's interpretive initiatives, cutbacks to the animation program over the years have considerably weakened the quality of presentation at Lower Fort Garry. Credit: Parks Canada.

between heritage and tourism, Lower Fort Garry National Historic Site became a major showpiece in western Canada and approached in scale the vast research and restoration/reconstruction programs carried out at Louisbourg and the Halifax Citadel. The nascent heritage tourism of the 1950s and 1960s that would expand in the 1970s resulted in increased visitation to the fort, making it one of the most heavily visited sites in the West. It very much illustrated what Board historian C.J. Taylor has called "the era of the big project."[51]

In the process of becoming the foremost national historic site in western Canada, Lower Fort Garry was the subject of considerable published and unpublished research carried out by historians, archaeologists, and curators in the employ of Parks Canada. Building histories, landscape histories, interpretive histories, and curatorial and archaeological investigations—the standard fare of public history research—were completed over a period of four decades. These investigations contributed much toward not just the physical look of the site and its interpretation but also toward the construction of a particular heritage perspective, or how at the lower fort the federal government recreated a version of the past in the present.[52] In the 1970s, in keeping with the fort's role as a fur trade tourist site (and downplaying its part in the signing of Treaty 1), a new federal plaque was erected at the site. It reads:

> One of the finest collections of early stone buildings in Western Canada, Lower Fort Garry was built for Governor George Simpson of the Hudson's Bay Company between 1831 and 1848. Schooners linked Norway House to the fort which was a focus for industry and transport in the lower Red River Settlement. Its farm helped supply food for boat brigades and oxen for Red River carts. After 1870 the fort was used as a federal prison and the first training base for the North-West Mounted Police. It housed the Motor Country Club from 1913 to 1962 and was given to Canada by the Hudson's Bay Company in 1951.[53]

Years later, in 2007, these basic topics were front and centre in the development of the site's Statement of Commemorative Intent (SOCI), although the significance of Treaty 1 was added. Its SOCI states:

> 1. Lower Fort Garry is one of the finest collections of early stone buildings in Western Canada; 2. Lower Fort Garry, as a Hudson's Bay Company post, was a focus for industry and transport, as well as a supply and distribution centre for the fur trade of the company's Northern Department; 3. Lower Fort Garry was the place where Treaty Number One was made between the Saulteaux (Ojibwa) and Swampy Cree First Nations people and the Crown; and 4. Lower Fort Garry was used by the federal government for public purposes in the 1870s, notably as the first training base of the North-West Mounted Police.[54]

In defining the commemorative intent of the fort, a number of "character-defining elements" were listed in the statement, many of which speak to the significance of place in the heritage of the lower fort. These include its location and setting in relation to the Red River; the relative locations of the fort and the historic First Nations encampments related to Treaty 1; the spatial distribution of individual structures within the fort walls; the integrity of natural and constructed landscape features related to the fur trade use of the fort; and surviving viewscapes from the fort towards the river and adjacent open spaces, to nearby Métis river lots, as well as views up and down the river.[55] In recent times, however, these last elements have been compromised as considerable modern construction on both sides of the river now obscure many of the older landscape features of the area. The lower fort once included a 202-hectare farm located west of the fort. Much of that area is now occupied by Lower Fort Garry Estates, a modern subdivision.[56] And, of course, Highway 9 now passes through the area where Anishinaabe and Cree groups camped in the late summer of 1871 during negotiations for Treaty 1.

It is important to note that Lower Fort Garry has traditionally been considered by heritage advocates as representative of fur trade life in the West—a pan–fur trade interpretation—despite the fact that the fort played a relatively minor role in the Hudson's Bay Company's trade in Rupert's Land. The post's interpretation as archetypal of life in the fur trade, as nation building, and in effect a memorial to colonialism in a post-colonial age, reveals how socially constructed views of heritage help to construct an official memory, a landscape of memory that defines a collective meaning that is both current and utilitarian. As a national historic site Lower Fort Garry remains, at least in part, a socially constructed place of significance. Visitors learn more about a generic "life in the fur trade" as interpreted by public historians, site managers, and interpreters, and about such activities as candle making, blacksmithing, and the leisure pursuits of the officer class, than they do about the history of this particular place. When interpretation does focus upon the history of the lower fort, it is often exaggerated or misleading. For instance, site interpreters frequently appropriate for the lower fort the more important role of Upper Fort Garry, located in the heart of the Red River Settlement. This includes the upper fort's role as an administrative entrepôt in Rupert's Land, a focus for the social and political life of the settlement, and a link between Indigenous economies, European markets, and a global trade in commodities.

If much research has gone into the representation of material authenticity at sites such as Lower Fort Garry, less attention has been given to how history is portrayed or how visitors engage with the past.

At many historic sites, especially at fur trade sites like the lower fort, the interpretation of Indigenous history has essentially been grafted on to site interpretation and site spectacle, at best a clumsy diminution of the real roles of Indigenous peoples as social, cultural, and political players. Small encampments comprised of one or two (usually canvas) teepees, almost always outside the fort walls, characterize Indigenous life as an appendage to the fur trade, their economies and daily lives represented as part of colonial culture and the fur trade mode of production. Although some encampment interpreters are Indigenous, others are not, and their conversations with visitors often revolve around topics related to material culture such as cradleboards, teepees, and beadwork. This "outside the palisades" interpretation of Indigenous life during the fur trade is characteristic of many of these sites, even if some have moved in recent years to address the one-dimensionality of cross-cultural relations.[57] While Indigenous families might share place with white people, they are physically and symbolically relegated to the sidelines. But if that has been the broad trajectory of management and interpretation at Lower Fort Garry since the 1960s, a 2018 Management Plan for the site suggests that Indigenous perspectives, in particular perspectives regarding Treaty, might be gaining a greater foothold.[58]

A number of ambitious strategies have been proposed for the site, all centred upon expanding the Indigenous role at the fort while foregrounding treaty making in the interpretive program. A goal of collaboration with Indigenous communities and expansion of the presentation of Indigenous culture will attempt to incorporate their knowledge and perspectives into management planning and decision making. Treaty 1 First Nations and Métis peoples will be invited to engage in traditional and cultural activities while sharing their perspectives at Lower Fort Garry. They will be asked to use the site to perform ceremonies, conduct cultural celebrations, and actively share their stories and traditions related to the fort. It is anticipated that these activities will comprise a minimum of 25 percent of interpretive programming, the majority of this Indigenous programming to be created and presented by Indigenous people with a historical connection to the site. Parks Canada has declared that it will collaborate with the Treaty 1 First Nations to establish a land holding at Lower Fort Garry NHS, presumably an important step to recognizing treaty rights and traditional territories.[59] Outreach and education related to the site will

Figure 12. Costumed interpreter at the Indigenous encampment at Lower Fort Garry, 2010. Credit: Parks Canada.

take on greater scope, including the history and legacy of residential schools, treaties, Indigenous rights, and the United Nations Declaration on the Rights of Indigenous Peoples.[60] The establishment of a land base at the site and independent Indigenous programming are small steps forward for Parks Canada and the federal government, a change at least in the way that historic sites deal with Indigenous peoples. Of course, whether these lofty intentions are actually achieved remains to be seen. Interpretive objectives, as with most Parks Canada management plans, remain conspicuously vague with goals such as: "The site's unique and authentic tourism offer has been strengthened."[61] It appeared from a visit to the fort in August of 2020, however, that none of these initiatives had been realized, although because of COVID-19, site interpretation was considerably limited, and visitors were not allowed into any of the fort buildings, including the interpretive centre.

Despite these intended initiatives it is difficult to portray post-colonial histories at places that were built on the assumptions of colonialism. Decades of investment in the architectural and material culture history of the nineteenth-century fur trade might not be easily jettisoned for alternative perspectives. Such a transition will necessitate a nuanced view of the past that might be beyond the competencies of a public organization not known for its sophisticated understanding of history. To date, the representation of Indigenous cultures at fur trade sites like Lower Fort Garry has been largely a failure, in part because of the weakness of the interpretation but for the most part because such representation portrays Indigenous peoples as inhabitants only of the past, as never considered in modern contexts, or as any real challenge to the dominant discourse, "their edges still produced in the shadow of Canada's commemorative ideals."[62]

At Lower Fort Garry the site's once ambitious restoration and reconstruction program, its traditional generic and pan–fur trade interpretation, its focus on material culture, and its overall use of space reveal a great deal about heritage as a cultural process, about the distortions of tourist entertainment, and about how the aesthetics of place are used to create the past in the present. Heritage here is defined through a particular lens, a lens that sees a construction of the past to meet tourism expectations, not the endurance of the past in the present. The use of space and the kinds of curatorial decisions that go into reconstructions and restorations remain largely hidden from the visitor, suggesting that what lies in front of the tourist is "real" rather than the product of research, speculation, and assumption (all affected by fluctuating budgets). As Canadian museum director Barbara Kirshenblatt-Gimblett has pointed out, for heritage programmers to achieve what they consider to be "authenticity" "requires that the interface, the means by which the representation is staged, be muted or concealed."[63]

While the lower fort has continued to maintain its usefulness as a tourist site, visitation numbers have decreased dramatically from decades past. For instance, in 1973 more than 300,000 people visited Lower Fort Garry. By 2006 visitation had plummeted to 35,000, an almost 90 percent drop. New and competing attractions in Winnipeg and throughout southern Manitoba are among the reasons for this decline, although the lack of a change in programming and the drop in popularity of living history were also factors.[64] However, it is at the local level that the fort has less significance as a place of memory and identity, arguably being a state-sponsored monument that stands apart from the community in which it is located. And while the nationalizing tendencies of heritage are often enlisted to sustain the character of the state, they regularly butt up against contested perspectives: the sub-national forms of memory that tie the meaning of place to personal acts of engagement or to local acts of communication and perception that make meaning in and for the present. Local heritage values can often stand apart from, and even challenge, national designations. I recall a conversation years ago with an elderly local historian in the Selkirk area named Frank Walters. Mr. Walters disagreed with the nearby lower fort's federal fur trade commemoration; instead he felt quite strongly that the site was better suited as a place to honour those from the Selkirk area who had died in the First and Second World Wars. For Walters, such a monument would be more personal and more closely tied to the values of the community and its history. The fort as a national historic site, he believed, had little resonance in the community. For Mr. Walters, the fur trade was "a long time ago," whereas the wars remained in recent memory. (That Mr. Walters was himself of the Second World War generation no doubt influenced his opinion.) That is not to say that as a national historic site Lower Fort Garry should commemorate home-grown involvement in world wars, but it does indicate that for many like Frank Walters, heritage is personal and local.

Although we can accept that our understanding of history is open to revision, can we say the same about heritage and our memory of place? At places such as the lower fort, too often interpretation remains stagnant and single voiced. Change comes slowly. Some visitors arrive and depart unmoved in their thinking—the "tourist gaze," as discussed in the Introduction—while others arrive with certain expectations but might challenge the messages they are given. At times reflecting the tourist gaze back to visitors, heritage agencies unwittingly reinforce conventional views of the past and, at some fur trade sites, even a traditional racialized version of history. Such versions of the past become predictable. For instance, the familiar domestic setting at sites such as Lower Fort Garry usually contain the material culture familiar to many visitors: the machine-made furniture fabricated to look rustic and handmade, the mandatory wash basin, and the small straw mattress bed in the corner. When the quizzical visitor asks about the undersized bed, the nineteen-year-old costumed animator will predictably respond with "people were shorter in the old days," to which the visitor will nod approvingly, and think, "Ah yes, that makes sense." Thus, in presenting the past as commodity, heritage places often authenticate what they imagine the visitor wants to see, a constructed and authorized past that is knowable, predictable, and reassuring.

"Founding Father" Narratives and New Voices

Heritage often expresses "founding father" narratives and authorized messages to forge a sense of common identity based on the past. New interpretations can potentially alter this trajectory and bring new stories and new voices to the table. A Manitoba illustration of this can be seen with the national commemoration of Prince of Wales Fort near Churchill. Commenced in 1731 by the Hudson's Bay Company but not completed for four decades, the massive stone fortress was part of a plan to defend company possessions on Hudson Bay from seaborne attack. The fort, located at Eskimo Point on the Churchill west peninsula, was also crucial to HBC trade with the Dene and Inuit peoples of the region. In 1782 the HBC surrendered the fort to a French force and the structure was partly destroyed. The federal government began a partial restoration of the fortress in the 1930s, although it was not completed until 1960.[65]

When designated as a national historic site by the HSMBC in 1920, the fort's importance was based solely on its role in the eighteenth-century rivalry between France and England for control of the resources of western Hudson Bay. In the decades since designation a variety of other themes emerged alongside this early colonial perspective and centred on the Indigenous history of the region, both during the fur trade period as well as for the almost continuous occupation and resource use that occurred for thousands of years in the area prior to the arrival of European traders. New voices appeared to challenge the "founding father" narrative of imperial rivalry, providing alternative views of heritage and place on the Churchill west peninsula. The west peninsula comprises the west bank of the Churchill River across from the modern town of Churchill, Manitoba. It contains a variety of historic sites and from a heritage

Figure 13. Prince of Wales Fort, Churchill National Historic Site, 1995. Constructed in the eighteenth century by the Hudson's Bay Company, the fort was partially destroyed in 1782 by Jean-Francois Galaup, comte de la Perouse. It was restored/reconstructed by the federal government beginning in the 1930s. Credit: Parks Canada.

perspective is generally considered to be the region extending from Eskimo Point in the north to the remains of Fort Churchill National Historic Site (1783 to 1930) in the south.[66]

Following Prince of Wales Fort's designation as a national historic site—the first in western Canada—the federal government obtained ownership from the province of 20.2 hectares of land around the fort in 1922.[67] However, it wasn't until nine years later in 1931 that the Board approved and erected a plaque at the fort. It reads: "Built upon plans drawn by English military engineers to secure control of Hudson Bay for the Hudson's Bay Company and England. Construction in 1733 [*sic*, 1731] and completed in 1771. Surrendered to and partially destroyed by a French naval force under La Perouse in 1782. Its ruins are among the most interesting military remains on the continent."[68] What is interesting about this plaque text is the way that it conflates the interests of the HBC and England, a comment, no doubt, on the role of chartered companies in furthering imperial strategies in the eighteenth century. Of course, England was not alone in creating such companies to promote its commercial interests worldwide.[69]

Figure 14. The Churchill west peninsula, 2010. Prince of Wales Fort is in the foreground. Seahorse Gully is located farther to the south. Credit: Parks Canada.

Prince of Wales Fort would take forty years to complete. Initially the fort was considered finished by 1741. However, the poor workmanship and design of the original construction would necessitate another three decades of rebuilding. In the end it was an impressive (if anachronistic) achievement, a stone structure to rival others of the period and built in an inhospitable environment with a very short construction season. Over 27.9 square metres in size with outer walls twelve metres thick and six metres high, the fort contained four large flankers, a parapet, and embrasures for the forty large cannons that would guard every approach. The interior consisted of the governor's quarters, barracks for the officers and men, storehouses, tradesmen's shops, and a powder magazine, along with sheds and stables. Despite its impressive construction, the fort was severely undermanned and was captured without a shot in 1782 by a French naval force under the command of Jean-Francois Galaup, comte de la Perouse. La Perouse mined the fort walls and reduced the fort to mostly rubble before sailing south to capture York Factory.[70] The HBC returned the next year to build Fort Churchill some six and a half kilometres upriver.

In the minutes of the HSMBC meeting for May of 1933, a motion was carried for the nearby sites Sloop Cove and Cape Merry to "be considered as part of the general historic site associated with the old fort at Churchill."[71] Sloop Cove, located three kilometres south of the fort on the west peninsula, harboured the wooden sailing vessels used by the HBC for whaling expeditions and northern trade with the Inuit of western Hudson Bay. The cove was designated as nationally significant because of the inscriptions left there by the men who lived at Prince of Wales Fort. One of these names, that of trader and explorer Samuel Hearne, is elaborately inscribed on the rocks above the cove. During the eighteenth century there were approximately three metres of water in the cove at high tide. Iron mooring rings, still visible today, were driven into the rocks to secure the sloops. Today the cove is mostly dry due to isostatic (post-glacial) rebound and because of hydro diversions located upriver on the Churchill River. Cape Merry National Historic Site is located on the northern tip of the eastern peninsula on the town side across from the fort. It consists of two gun batteries built by the HBC in 1744 and 1747, located across from the fort to help defend the mouth of the river.

Figure 15. The ruins of Cape Merry Battery, c.1920. The federal government reconstructed one of the two batteries at the site in the late 1950s. Cape Merry is located at the mouth of the Churchill River across from Prince of Wales Fort. Credit: Archives of Manitoba.

Unlike historic places such as Lower Fort Garry, the historic sites of the Churchill area are better able to communicate a more authentic language of place, even if the emphasis on eighteenth-century French–English conflict and the fur trade is only part of the story of that region. By being less contrived, less circumscribed, and more open to new voices, the region (and here I am talking about the whole of the peninsula) suggests the possibility of innovative vistas and new landscapes that might tell a bigger story, an Indigenous story in the case of the Churchill west peninsula. Here, heritage does not try to simply replicate a version of the past; it does not overtly attempt to manufacture authenticity but remains rather a part of it and a part of the larger landscape. It avoids the imagined *reproduction* of the past, opting instead for the *survival* of the past. Of course, the partial restoration of Prince of Wales Fort, rather than its interpretation as a ruin, introduces a degree of artifice, and its impressive presence, like many examples of historical architecture, can focus perceptions of the past in narrow and conventional ways. For the average visitor to the west peninsula, the fort is what draws their attention.

Interest in protecting the ruin that was Prince of Wales Fort began in November of 1929 when the chief engineer of the Department of Railways and Canals in Ottawa recommended that to prevent "further deterioration" of the fort, repairs be carried out to the "front portal [front gate] including digging out of the old guns partially buried" and a house be constructed for a watchman to prevent vandalism at the fort site.[72] Two years later the National Parks Branch under the leadership of J.B. Harkin asked that Railways and Canals go further and carry out "minimal repair" to the ruins of the fort walls. In reply the department provided an estimate of the work required to provide nominal repairs at the fort: a total of $20,000 and twenty men working for four months to partially repair the exterior walls, restore the entranceway, and lift the cannons and place them on concrete slabs.[73] Even with the limited work proposed for Prince of Wales Fort, interest in the project soon grew. One visitor to the site, F.L. Farley, wrote to Harkin in the summer of 1931, commenting, "Within the next ten years this old Fort will become one of the greatest attractions to travellers not only from Canada but from the U.S. who undoubtedly will soon make the trip to the Bay to see its wonders in the same manner as they go to Egypt to see the pyramids."[74]

More extensive work on the fort did not begin until the summer of 1934 as part of a Depression-era federal public works project. Records kept from that time, as well as period photos, show that restoration and reconstruction concentrated upon the exterior walls. In some places the walls had been reduced to rubble; in other locations much of the original construction remained. Interrupted by the Second World War, the project continued in the 1950s with work concentrating upon the interior stone structures. This involved the demolition of the heavily damaged second storeys of most buildings as well as the partial reconstruction of others. Archaeological work continued at and around the fort during the work and after.

It is evident that some aspects of the fort's original workmanship were altered during restoration. For example, concrete was employed extensively as coping on exterior and interior walls and as back-up material where whole sections of walls were rebuilt. Despite these interventions, a 1994 study by the Architectural Division of Parks Canada determined that the 1930s and 1950s work retained most of the original material of the fort in situ.[75] Significantly, the report also concluded

S. W. Bastion Aug. 26, 1935.

Figure 16. Workers restore the Southwest bastion at Prince of Wales Fort in August of 1935. While minimal work on the fort was suggested in 1929, the bulk of the restoration was undertaken in the 1930s, suspended during the war, and completed in the 1950s. Credit: Archives of Manitoba.

that the form and scale of the eighteenth-century fort remained un-impaired, as was its relationship to the surrounding landscape. Despite more recent threats to the stabilization of the fort walls (a section of wall collapsed in 1997), Prince of Wales Fort retains the integrity of place and its significance as part of the cultural landscape of the west peninsula.[76] A comprehensive research program, begun in the 1990s, included archaeological assessments of the rampart and foundation, an analysis of the physical properties of the stones used in construction, and the installation of instruments to monitor the thermal and moisture regime of the walls.

Although the fort continues to maintain its situational integrity, its story is only a small part of the narrative of that region. Emerging alternative views of its history as well as new narratives regarding the multi-millennia history of the west peninsula speak to a much grander heritage. That the HSMBC in 1920 ignored the fact that the Churchill west peninsula contains resources that speak to over 3,000 years of occupation by Indigenous peoples is hardly surprising, given that the cultures of these people were little understood or appreciated at the time. Since that era, however, research has shown that there are in fact few areas in Canada that so clearly display the long continuity of human occupation and resource use as does this relatively small area of the Churchill west peninsula. For hundreds of generations peoples of the Arctic Small Tool Tradition (the Pre-Dorset and Dorset), Thule, and modern Inuit occupied this area where they hunted, fished, and traded. Physical and archaeological evidence of these occupations in the form of tent rings, cache sites, kayak rests, graves, and the remains of summer camps can be found throughout the Seahorse Gully and Button Bay areas, and speak to the great antiquity of the Indigenous presence in the region.[77] The west peninsula also contains the remains of the HBC post of Fort Churchill, which was occupied by the HBC from the late eighteenth century until 1930. As a cultural landscape few regions in the country can rival the Churchill west peninsula, and in the 1990s the Manitoba government considered nominating the area as a UNESCO World Heritage Site. Unfortunately, the nomination never went forward, as it was felt at the time that too many sites from first-world nations were being put forward at the expense of potential sites elsewhere in the world.

That same decade, the introduction of notions of commemorative integrity and commemorative intent into the national historic sites program resulted in a strategy that ultimately restricted a more broadly based interpretation of the ancient history of the west peninsula. While an area plan approach to the Churchill west peninsula was simply a casualty of this Ottawa-based national initiative, the ultimate goal of the policy was to restrict a wider thematic interpretation of many historic sites across the country by relating historical interpretation of place to original HSMBC recommendations, a great number of which, like the commemoration of Prince of Wales Fort, dated to the early decades of the twentieth century. For Parks Canada, according to its commemorative intent policy, the reasons for designation had to be taken directly from Board minutes or from approved plaque texts.[78]

If the 1960s and 1970s witnessed the development of new national historic sites in Manitoba and across the country, a retrenchment occurred after 1980 as fewer sites were acquired. Although Parks Canada's System Plan[79] expanded designations to include emphasis on the history of Indigenous peoples, women, and ethnocultural communities, most development resulted only in the installation of new plaques. The arrival of commemorative intent policy, however, signalled a more conservative era of interpretation, especially in regard to place. In relying almost exclusively upon sometimes very old Board recommendations, the idea of heritage place was narrowed rather than expanded. As discussed in Chapter 1, Parks Canada's National Office grew anxious about the more inclusive cultural narratives that regional public historians were developing around many national historic sites, including a changing focus from "site" to "place" and the broader interpretations that went with it. Commemorative intent effectively limited the discourse to older and more conventional historical narratives. The policies of what historian and heritage manager Frits Pannekoek once called "the cautious intellectual bureaucracy of Parks Canada" meant that at places such as Churchill, historical interpretation remained bound to older colonial themes such as French-English military rivalry.[80]

The chance to broaden the narrative, to bring in changing perspectives and to expand, both temporally and geographically, into new areas of commemoration and protection, especially regarding Indigenous histories (much of the rich archaeological resources of the Churchill area remain without federal protection), was therefore lost, as it was at a number of national historic sites across the country. The 3,000-year cultural history of the Churchill west peninsula (along with its unique natural history) is a place of continuity and meaning, and the history of the region should be treated in its entirety. The focus on the comparatively short history of the fur trade and the imperial rivalry of the eighteenth century is exclusively related to European occupation. Such a practice is not simply Eurocentric but represents only a very small part of the heritage of that place.

Remembering Kihciwaskahikan

At York Factory the history of the old post and its people continues to resonate with a sense of the past in the present, a feeling that its inhabitants had left the place only shortly before you arrived. For almost three centuries the most important fur trade post in western Canada, York remains a space of meaning and a landscape of memory, its significance captured in a sense of place that resonates particularly with the Indigenous people of western Hudson Bay. Yet, the site retains a foot in two worlds: a Muskego Cree world of community and kinship (if at times also one of cross-cultural dissonance) and a Euro-Canadian tradition of commerce and colonialism once woven into the experience of the local and the national. For the Muskego, York, although not a place of origin, is nonetheless a homeland with a legacy of identity that continues to be a space of social and cultural belonging. From the massive and still-standing Depot Building, largely constructed with Indigenous labour in the 1830s and the storehouse for much of Rupert's Land's furs and trade goods, to the silence of the nearby cemetery where tilting and deteriorated wooden crosses mark the graves of those once associated with the old post—names like Beardy, Spence, Saunders, and Wastasecoot—York embodies a sense of place that brings value, memory, and meaning to the landscape.

The commemorated heritage of Prince of Wales Fort and related sites—at least at the federal level—is linked to the significance of place, although the full scope of this heritage is restricted by the limited interpretations of an official past. Though interpretation is influenced by the choices made in determining heritage place, there are also the limitations of temporal interpretation, or the imposition of a particular historical significance on a chronology or time period that best fits a socially constructed understanding of what is heritage and what is not. The history of York Factory (known in Muskego Cree as "Kihciwaskahikan"—the "Place of the Great House"), a nationally commemorated fur trade site in northern Manitoba, is a case in point. Built in the late seventeenth century near the mouth of the Hayes River on Hudson Bay, the post persisted for almost three centuries, closing in 1957. For much of the nineteenth century, York was the Hudson's Bay Company's major entrepôt and trans-shipment centre in the Northwest when most trade goods and pelts in the West made their way through this bayside factory. It is that time period, along with the earlier period of French-English conflict, that provides the focus for much of the site's commemoration and interpretation. Today the Statement of Commemorative Intent for York Factory, first developed by Parks Canada in the late 1990s and modified in 2017, reads: "York Factory is commemorated for its critical role in the French-English struggle on Hudson Bay for control of the fur trade, as an important Hudson's Bay Company trading post and entrepôt for over two and one half centuries, and for its role in the expansion of the fur trade into the interior of Western Canada."[81]

For the Indigenous peoples of the western Hudson Bay region, almost three centuries of contact and commercial exchange not only

Figure 17. Young Cree men freighting on the Hayes River for the Hudson's Bay Company, c. 1890. Credit: Archives of Manitoba.

influenced traditional modes of production but also affected social and political development, domestic relations, and seasonal movement. The Muskego Cree had a centuries-old relationship with York Factory as traders, consumers, provisioners, and labourers. Although their involvement in domestic production persisted well into the twentieth century, fur trade mercantilism helped create a system of credit and debt that increasingly brought the Muskego peoples of Hudson Bay into a global capitalist system. Locally produced goods were replaced by European commodities, accompanied by a decline in the resource base of the district, the commercialization of social relationships, and significant demographic alterations that resulted in increased poverty and depopulation, and ultimately marginalization. As elsewhere, the introduction and articulation of European capital paved the way for the replacement of Indigenous production—the domestic economy—particularly as wage labour and the production of commodities such as fur and country provisions for Euro-Canadian traders was established by the HBC in their efforts to accumulate capital.

Over its long history York helped integrate Indigenous economies into an international structure of commodity production and trade, and introduced Muskego and Métis peoples into a global economy that

Figure 18. Interior of the store at York Factory, 1910. Credit: Archives of Manitoba.

was based upon a colonial exploitation of resources. Just as unsustainable commodity trade and food hunting on the prairies brought plains peoples into a wider economic and colonial affiliation, creating asymmetric power relations among traders and establishing what historian George Colpitts has called "the bioregional history of the West," so too did the peoples of the Subarctic and their environments become part of a transnational capitalist structure.[82]

But it was York's precipitous decline after 1870 that greatly impacted the Muskego Cree of the region and helped to set the trajectory of the economy of the Subarctic for decades to come. The deterioration of the resource base of the region and the resulting, and significant, demographic alterations were manifested in increased poverty and depopulation, and ultimately in the marginalization of the Indigenous peoples of western Hudson Bay.[83] The decline of York Factory during the last decades of the nineteenth century and the early years of the twentieth was more or less replicated at fur trade posts throughout much of Canada's Subarctic. Declining prices, the growing scarcity of game and fur-bearing animals, and the development of resource industries in the South all contributed to the impoverishment of a great many Subarctic Indigenous groups.[84] Scarcity was, of course, not uniform across the Subarctic in the late nineteenth and early twentieth

Figure 19. The Reverend Richard Faries and his wife Catherine (right) with lo-cal people at York Factory after signing the Treaty 5 adhesion in August of 1910. Credit: Archives of Manitoba.

centuries, but reduced access to resources was a common feature of that territory and that time period.

York Factory is one of the oldest commemorated sites in western Canada, being designated as nationally significant in 1936, although the site was still operated by the HBC until 1957. In May of 1936 the HSMBC recorded, "That in the opinion of the Board the struggle for Hudson Bay is an event of national importance in the history of Canada and that it should be commemorated by the erection of a memorial at York Factory."[85] A plaque text was approved by the HSMBC in 1938 but for unknown reasons did not get ministerial approval until 1954 and was not erected at the site until three years later in July of 1957. It read: "Established by the Hudson's Bay Company in 1682 as Port Nelson. During the contest for Hudson Bay between France and Great Britain its possession changed hands six times. It was finally restored to Britain by the Treaty of Utrecht in 1713."[86]

When, after almost three centuries of continuous operation, the Hudson's Bay Company closed York in the summer of 1957, local Indigenous people left for inland communities at Shamattawa and Fox Lake. Both settlements had started as wintering encampments and were established as permanent communities decades prior to the closing of York in 1957, although they were not recognized as separate

Figure 20. Muskego Cree family camping near York Factory, c. 1915. Credit: Archives of Manitoba.

bands by the federal government until 1947.[87] The main contingent of York people were resettled by the Department of Indian Affairs at the newly created community of York Landing on Split Lake, 250 kilometres inland from the bay. Today York Landing remains the home of the York Factory First Nation, though many Elders return yearly to the old Hayes River site to rekindle memories from their childhood. Younger Muskego accompany the Elders on these trips, curious about their heritage as a coastal people. From these excursions and reunions we see that even today, the history of the people of that community and that region continues to speak to the historical centrality of Indigenous people as kin, as labourers, and as consumers at the places that were colonized.

Initially hoping to lease the site to Northern Affairs and Natural Resources, an overture rejected by the federal government, the HBC in 1959 leased the 105-hectare site to a former HBC post manager, Harold Bland. Bland, a long-time company employee, had managed York between 1934 and 1954. Planning to run the site as a hunting

Figure 21. Gravesite at York Factory, 2002. Credit: Robert Coutts.

lodge, Bland agreed to protect the surviving resources at York, including the 2,787-square-metre Depot Building, a massive warehouse constructed between 1832 and 1838.[88] Other historic resources at the site included the small library building, the ruins of an early nineteenth-century stone powder magazine, a cemetery (its use might have dated to the late eighteenth century), and thousands of artifacts left at the site and stored in the Depot Building. Other than these above-ground resources, it was York's landscape that provided evidence of a once bustling place.[89] Drains, palisade lines, building depressions, and the remains of piers and summer camps spoke to the importance of this place in the nineteenth and early twentieth centuries. Archaeological resources—many excavated in the post-1978 period—were abundant.

By 1959 the federal government (at the urging of the HSMBC) began to show interest in York as a historic site. At the invitation of the HBC, a site survey was completed that year, as were structural drawings of the Depot. That same year T.C. Fenton, the supervising engineer for the National Historic Sites Division, recommended that the government acquire York Factory and "take reasonable steps to re-tard [the Depot's] deterioration and prolong its life as long as possible." "Replacement cost if it were lost," he adds, "would be very consider-able."[90] From no interest in acquiring the site in 1957 to contemplating acquisition and the cost of reconstruction just two years later was a large step for the department in terms of preserving heritage resources in the Subarctic. Lobbying by outside agencies such as the Hudson's Bay Record Society (HBRS), the Manitoba Historical Society, and even the Minnesota Historical Society urged the federal government to acquire York, with Willis Richford, the director of the HBRS, suggesting that the site be kept in repair by "private enterprise," as "Canada's record has not been too good in preserving her historical relics, which is much better than building replicas."[91]

Over roughly the next decade, with other heritage places such as Lower Fort Garry taking up considerable funding, little was done to-wards acquiring York Factory, the federal government no doubt wary of the costs of preserving such a remote historic site.[92] Not surprisingly, York's isolation worked against its protection and preservation. Northern Affairs Minister Walter Dinsdale, in a 1961 letter to Churchill Member of Parliament Robert Simpson, wrote that "the Factory has a good history, but its state of isolation is a very grim factor." York, he argued, presented "practically insurmountable drawbacks of terrain and inac-cessibility, and the affect [sic] they would have on supply, labour, and tourist flow make it a poor risk for the foreseeable future."[93] Despite his reticence, the minister did note that the earlier survey of the site was a "historical record against the day when York might again come alive."[94]

In 1967, as the federal government busied itself with other fur trade projects in Manitoba, the provincial government proposed the idea of dismantling the Depot Building at York Factory and moving it to The Pas. The provincial minister of Tourism and Recreation, Sterling Lyon, in a letter to Arthur Laing, the federal minister of Indian Affairs and Northern Development, proposed, "In light of the vandalism and fire risk for the depot bldg., I would like to propose for your consideration a project whereby York Factory would be dismantled and transported to The Pas where it would be re-assembled and converted into a museum showing the development of the fur trade in Canada." Lyon added that, "while this may appear a formidable task, I am informed that the frame of the [Depot] building is prefabricated and held together with hooks which would provide for fairly easy dismantling and reassembling."[95] According to Lyon, the building components would then be moved in winter to The Pas by tractor train. Where Lyon and his advisors got the notion that the Depot Building at York was "prefabricated and held together with hooks" remains a mystery. Although some hooks were used in the building, in fact, the depot represented early nineteenth-century balloon construction, painstakingly erected with studs rather than joinery, wooden knees to tie and reinforce roof trusses and beams, a shallow wooden foundation to allow for shifting permafrost and easy replacement, and interior wooden wedges that were used to raise and lower support posts as dictated by the movement of the permafrost.[96] Interior walls were comprised of planking that had been painstakingly beaded. Although a preliminary costing for the move came in at $275,000 (no doubt an optimistic figure, even in 1967), the federal department outright rejected the plan. Peter Bennett, the assistant director of the NHSD, remarked that he "was completely opposed to moving the building from its present site."[97] However, Lyon's scheme had two welcomed consequences. First, in reacting to the plan, the HSMBC recommended that the federal government acquire the site from the HBC ("we entered negotiations with the Hudson's Bay Company . . . to acquire York Factory precisely in order to forestall the proposal by the Government of Manitoba"); and, second, it helped spur the Board into developing a policy stating that historic buildings like the Depot cannot be moved from their in situ location.[98] This policy and its various iterations would guide the NHSD for years. Perhaps more importantly, it reinforced the importance of place in defining and evaluating heritage value at a time when the relocation of historic buildings was somewhat commonplace throughout the country.

After months of negotiation with the HBC, transfer of York Factory to the federal government occurred in 1968. At a ceremony held at Lower Fort Garry in July of that year, Jean Chrétien, then the minister of Indian Affairs and Northern Development, officially announced the acquisition of York, stating that Canadians can visit the site and "renew their understanding of bygone days." Continued Chrétien, "I am told that although York Factory changed hands many times . . . it ended up in the hands of the English. Is there some hidden significance in today's ceremony? Not really, for today we are all Canadians and we own things jointly and together. A more constructive arrangement I think."[99]

Figure 22. Aerial view of York Factory National Historic Site, 2017. Credit: Gordon Goldsborough.

The transfer of York Factory heralded the beginning of decades of research and stabilization work by Parks Canada. Land use and structural histories, a social history, a five-year archaeological program that ran between 1978 and 1983 (as well as later archaeological salvage programs), stabilization studies, restoration work, management planning, research into riverbank erosion, and a controversial plan to replace the rotting main floor of the Depot Building all helped to protect and interpret this significant northern resource. Periodic archaeological digs continue at the site, and in the 1990s a large, modern Parks Canada residence replaced the rudimentary accommodations (a small cabin and trailer) that had once occupied the site. Unfortunately, this modern building compromises the integrity of place at the site, its location too close to the historic resources. The nearby Silver Goose Lodge, once operated by the York Factory First Nation on property adjacent to the historic site, has now closed down. Because of the site's continuing isolation, visitation remains low, averaging fewer than 300 people per year.[100] In recent years tours to York from Winnipeg have been organized.

▲ ▲ ▲

At places such as York Factory, Prince of Wales Fort, and Lower Fort Garry, it is still often the "business" of heritage that supports the formation of cultural identities that are authoritative, that often replace memory with history, and that fashion a present disconnected from the past. But if history can generate overarching narratives, it is often place that can bring out diverse meanings, landscapes of memory that challenge these dominant discourses. Where, for instance, Lower Fort Garry is an attraction and an authorized and at times contrived portrayal of the past, York Factory, despite some interventions, remains a true "place," with layers of memory and meaning that have resonated over centuries. I make these comments not as a neutral observer but as someone who worked in the historic sites program for many years. And I write as someone who believes that what we say about the past is shaped by the present at the same time that it informs that present. To look at new places, or old places with new perspectives, we see that "heritage work" is not always "authorized" or the exclusive terrain of the professional. Neither does it have to be the inevitable product of a dominant discourse.

At the same time, at places such as York Factory heritage interpretation is hamstrung by a bureaucratic focus on a narrow period of significance. But significance for whom? For Euro-Canadians, an emphasis upon an early period of imperial rivalry or York's emergence as a commercial hub of the fur trade defines the site as nationally significant, at least in the eyes of the HSMBC. It is framed as a positive, confident, and nation-building story. Yet, there is another story, the account of how Indigenous economies were drawn into international commodity production, a transnational economy based upon the exploitation of resources. And then there is the story of decline, a story that for modern heritage agencies has little resonance on the commemorative map but for Indigenous peoples becomes critical to their economic and cultural survival, to their history of adaptability, their history of marginalization, their history of being sidelined. Yet, these are stories not seen to be worth commemorating. For many people in northern Manitoba, "outside the palisades" describes more than just trade relations; it is the heritage legacy of the fur trade.

Arguably, it is this story, a story that continues to resonate throughout northern Manitoba and in fact through much of the Subarctic, that should be an important component of the interpretive focus, as it helps to tell the history of colonialism and the consequences for those who are colonized. That it is not part of the official heritage of the site or a part of the dominant discourse raises issues around who in fact speaks for the past. Whose voice dictates the preferred narratives of history, in the case of York Factory a commemorative emphasis on the period of European growth and influence prior to 1870, and for the Churchill west peninsula the prominence of European occupation over Indigenous histories? Is commemoration simply or mostly about Whig stories of "progress" and "advancement" and how these terms have come to be defined? And can we publicly remember and recognize something other than what Cecilia Morgan calls "the sweeping stories of national progress and uplift ... that have little room for the histories of marginalized groups"?[101]

With contemporary heritage sites that "celebrate" the fur trade in prairie Canada, it is cultural processes and contemporary views that provide the overarching interpretations that form the authorized heritage discourse. Idealized views of a colonial past and the emphasis on early European commerce and settlement frequently overshadow the ancient histories of heritage place, the impact of an asymmetrical commodity trade, or the significant time periods of Indigenous life that continue to resonate in the present day.

CHAPTER 3

"We Came. We Toiled. God Blessed": Settler Colonialism and Constructing Authenticity

Heritage distils the past into icons of identity, bonding us with precursors and progenitors, with our own earlier selves, and with our promised successors.

David Lowenthal, "Identity, Heritage, and History"

"Firsts" have played a critical role in the shaping and reshaping of heritage, place, and memory. As discussed in the previous chapter, the commemoration of the fur trade has often laid claim to such distinctions—the first post inland from Hudson Bay, the first post west of the Rockies, the first white man to explore such and such a river. American historian Jean O'Brien has argued that nineteenth-century white settlers in New England used local histories and their claim to modernity through "firsts" to marginalize Indigenous peoples and promote the myth, one that even today remains a part of American perception, of Indian extinction.[1]

It is with settler colonialism where such claims have been used to express authenticity, to sustain claims to place, and, in the West, to authorize the prairie narrative. With the remaking of the prairie landscape we see the influence of "founding father" narratives, the "firsts" of arrival and settlement and their importance to the formation of the group dynamics that would eventually lead to the recognition within specific groups of what Frances Swyripa has called "shared pioneering credentials."[2] At the local level the renaming of place, the construction of churches, the creation of new forms of land tenure, and the erection of shrines and historical markers all showed, Swyripa says, how settler colonialism imposed "order and meaning on the prairie landscape at the most basic and human level."[3] Remaking the "commons" was the aspiration; commemorating it was the reward. The quotation in this chapter title reflects that perspective—"We Came. We Toiled. God Blessed." This text appears on a plaque celebrating the centennial of Mennonite immigration to Manitoba erected at the Manitoba Legislative Building in 1974.

Eventually, at a more macro level the internal narratives of the settlement frontier would become part of the wider heritage movement, the new prairie ethnoscapes being recognized as critical to nation building and cultural advancement. In the 1980s the Historic Sites and Monuments Board of Canada commissioned a major report on prairie settlement patterns, treating these landscapes as a phenomenon that could be represented tangibly through their structural and spatial aspects. With the goal of establishing new national historic sites, candidate landscapes were required to contain an acceptable level of extant historical resources, the significance of those resources to be ultimately determined by the Board. The Board limited the study to agricultural settlement and included rural occupancy of either individual farm settlements or nucleated communities. The Métis river-lot patterns of the Red River Settlement and the South Saskatchewan Valley were not considered in the study. According to the report, "river lot farming . . . was minimal and had little impact, other than as an adjunct of the fur trade, on the economy of the region."[4] In fact, river-lot farming was more than minimal, was not simply an "adjunct" to the fur trade, and did have considerable impact upon the economy of the region at the time. "Individual farm settlements or nucleated communities" generally referred to Anglo-European and Anglo-Canadian farming, the latter to the establishment of ethnocultural and ethnoreligious settlements on the prairies in the late nineteenth century. The 1984 study and the subsequent heritage nominations it generated were critical steps in the official recognition and commemoration of settler colonialism, defining authenticity, supporting claims to place, and entitling the prairie narrative.

The interpretation of historic place in the rural West came to assign an attachment to the soil to private property, to capitalist labour markets, to the cult of individualism, and to the perception of an empty land in the territories occupied by Indigenous cultures and fur trade mercantilism. It is a story that derives from what Irene Spry called "the tragedy of the loss of the commons," or the transition in western Canada from common property resources, to open-access resources, to private property.[5] More importantly, it tracks the commemoration and celebration of this tradition, how that commemoration was created and how it evolved over time; how settler colonialism became an "authentic" past worthy of designation, preservation, and the creation of its own heritage mythology.

Patterns of popular history making have been reflected in certain cultural communities, including the processes by which they have come to shape an oftentimes pervasive view of a settler past. With settler colonialism, place becomes significant through the development over time of traditions, myths, and cultural narratives. Landscapes become ethnoscapes where local and national memories are located in pioneer histories and group founding stories, monuments and shrines, the preservation of architecture, or by speculative reconstructions.

A variety of sites illustrate the designation of settlement heritage and the "construction of authenticity" in western Canada. By focusing on a handful of historic places that commemorate the pioneering tradition, I illustrate the goals and limitations of the commemorative ritual and I consider this tradition more broadly. These places include the River Road Heritage Parkway that commemorates early Anglo-Métis settlement in Red River, and the distinctive European cultural ethnoscapes of such places as Neubergthal Street Village National Historic Site and the Doukhobor settlement at Veregin in Saskatchewan, a recently designated national historic site. I also focus on Manitoba's Mennonite Heritage Village, an outdoor "museum" of early Anabaptist settlement in Manitoba, as well as upon the commemoration of Motherwell Homestead NHS, an example of late nineteenth-century Anglo-Ontarian settlement in southern Saskatchewan. Beyond describing the origins, commemorations, and sense of place for each, I look at each within the broader heritage designation of settlement patterns across the prairies.

In reviewing national and provincial commemorative documentation, local community histories, and texts relating to ethnocultural settlement, we can consider how these writings portray land and settlement, how memory is cultivated and celebrated, how community cohesion is achieved (or at least attempted), and how the sense of progress, especially as it relates to place and site, is reified. Arguably, these commemorations are broadly representative of settlement heritage on the prairies. They typify a particular theme in Canadian history through the reshaping of the landscape, the official recognition of "founding father" narratives, and the spatial dynamics of ethnoscapes. Each, in its own way, represents attachment to place and soil as well as the entirety of the settlement experience.

Although the heritage of ethnocultural settlement had long been recognized at the local or community level through markers and memorials or by local histories, they were underrepresented nationally, especially the impact of ethnoreligious settlement in the West. In attempting to broaden commemoration across the country, Parks Canada's System Plan, developed in the late 1990s and published in 2000, placed greater emphasis upon the designation of ethnocultural communities, along with the commemoration of women and Indigenous peoples.[6] It represented a major step for the HSMBC, a group that had traditionally concentrated upon such themes as military history, the fur trade, and early Anglo settlement.

Canadians are involved in history, especially family and community history. When talking about "heritage," it is often the local and regional that tend to capture their awareness. In the chapter "Places and Pasts," the authors of the 2015 book *Canadians and Their Pasts* discuss the significance of local heritage, citing the poet and critic Eli Mandel, who described "the overpowering feeling of nostalgia associated with the place we know as the *first* place, the *first* vision of things, the *first* clarity of things." They go on to note "our sense of the past is also established by relations with others and accumulate as we work together in a process described as the 'production of space,' in which our perceptions and the dimensions of the world around us are shaped by human activities."[7] As such, public history agencies that commemorate place, just like museums, have an obligation to contextualize the regional within a broader story. According to historian Gerald Friesen, there is "a very real public interest in what institutions such as museums and [historic] sites do and say, and to recognize that for many people exhibits and plaques are more believable—and interesting—than academic monographs. This means that what heritage agencies do in the area of commemorating ethno-cultural history matters."[8] To this I would add the essential commemoration of place, and the acknowledgement of the memories evoked by the views, values, and appreciation of the landscape.

"A Thoroughfare for an Extended Village"

The topic of setter colonialism in western Canada most often suggests themes related to European, Anglo-Ontarian, and ethnoreligious settlement on the prairies. The settlers are usually described as "pioneers" in popular treatments, their toil narratives, square lot surveys, or characteristic communal land patterns most often used to illustrate the impact of immigrants upon the physical landscape. Yet, the creation of ethnoscapes in any significant form really begins decades prior to the 1879 National Policy with the early nineteenth-century establishment of river-lot agriculture in the Red River valley and the later Métis settlements along the South Saskatchewan River. Although Métis life in these settlements tended to focus upon hunting, fishing, freighting, and trade, agriculture also played a substantial role in the foundation of a new form of cultural landscape in the West: the narrow river lots patterned after the seigneurial system of New France.[9] Situated north of Winnipeg is the modern-day historic site known as "River Road Provincial Park." There, we can still see the vestiges (although fast disappearing due to modern exurban expansion) of the old river-lot system of the Red River valley. First surveyed by Peter Fidler of the Hudson's Bay Company in 1813 for the Selkirk Settlers, river lots became the principal landholding order in Red River. Their expansion beyond the Red River valley ended in 1869 with the sale of Rupert's Land to Canada and the establishment of the square lot survey.

River Road Provincial Park (named the "River Road Heritage Parkway" until 1997) commemorates the early settlement of the lower region of the Red River Settlement, a western Canadian colony that dates to the first decades of the nineteenth century. First known as "The Rapids" settlement and later as "St. Andrew's Parish," it was established in the late 1820s on the Red River by English-speaking Métis, many of whom had been declared surplus by the HBC, and by retired Scottish fur traders and their Métis families. Here, they farmed their narrow river lots, hunted and fished, worked seasonally on the York boat brigades, and engaged in trade with the company and with local Cree and Ojibwa people.

River Road is located approximately twenty kilometres north of Winnipeg in the modern-day municipality of St. Andrew's. It is a local byway with a long history. Curving along the west bank of the Red

Figure 23. Ojibwa bark lodges on the banks of the Red River near the Middle Settlement. Photographed by H.L. Hime, 1858. Credit: Archives of Manitoba.

River, the road first appeared on settlement maps in 1836 and linked the narrow lots that angled back from the river's edge. Originally known as the "Inner Road," it partly connected the sprawling parishes that originated at the forks of the Red and Assiniboine rivers. Eventually, this inner road was replaced by the "King's Road" located almost two kilometres to the west. For the people of old St. Andrew's Parish, River Road was, for much of the nineteenth century, as Jean Friesen and Gerald Friesen describe it, a "thoroughfare for an extended village, a kind of back street for a parish that had no proper main street because it possessed too little commerce to require anything so grand."[10]

Some distance along this now popular country drive, at a sweeping bend in the Red River, modern travellers get their first glimpse of St. Andrew's Church, its familiar steeple rising prominently above the low horizon of the shallow river valley. As the oldest extant church in Western Canada (it was constructed in 1849), St. Andrew's-on-the Red, as it has become known, stands today as a pastoral reminder of a time when church and community were among the integral constituents of everyday life.

The history and significance of place, to some extent at least, is still visible along River Road. But the region has lost much of its earlier

Figure 24. St. Andrew's Church, n.d. Construction of the church began in 1844 and was completed in 1849. The oldest extant church in western Canada, it was declared of "national architectural and historical importance" in 1974. Credit: Robert Coutts.

heritage because of the development of the area as a prosperous commuter community not far beyond Winnipeg's outer suburbs. Heritage memory is carried less by place than by standardized forms of interpretive signage. Only vestiges of the parish's once thriving river-lot geography remain, and they are increasingly receding with the erection of each new substantial house, two- or three-car garage, and manicured lawn. However, at one time St. Andrew's and River Road, like all of nineteenth-century Red River, were riparian settlements. This developmental pattern was the result of a variety of factors that effectively served to restrict habitation to the long narrow lots that bordered the Red and Assiniboine rivers. These rivers and their tributaries facilitated transportation, and their banks provided the timber necessary for both fuel and shelter. Only near the river's edge was the land considered viable for cultivation, the rivers and creeks providing the main source for the settlement's water as well as fish to supplement the local diet.

The geographic pattern throughout the colony was hybrid in nature. Its topographical layout was based on the Quebec river-lot model, although actual land use mimicked the infield and outfield system found in Scotland and brought to Red River by the Selkirk Settlers. The settler's home, assorted outbuildings, and small kitchen garden were located near the river's edge. Behind the farmstead was situated the infield, or the small fenced and cultivated "parks" where the farmer grew his cereal and garden crops. Beyond the infield, and occupying the rest of the two-mile (about 3.2 kilometres) lot, stretched the larger outfield. Some settlers used the outfield for occasional cropping but most grazed livestock in their unfenced areas. As well, each landowner possessed what became known as the "hay privilege" on the two miles of land extending beyond their river lot. Beyond the hay privilege, Red River colonists possessed equal rights to the wild hay and timber of what was called "the commons." Of course, the extent of cultivated acreage, as well as the number of livestock, varied from landowner to landowner. Those Métis who occupied the bulk of their time on the HBC York boats or on the buffalo hunts had less time to cultivate and seed beyond a few hectares and relied primarily upon smaller kitchen gardens. Others depended less on wage labour and hunting and often cultivated a greater acreage or kept livestock such as cattle, oxen, and horses.

The Red River Settlement in general, and St. Andrew's in particular, presents a sense of identity established not simply by the uniqueness of land and place but by the practices and traditions of an adaptive economic strategy. For local settlers the peculiarities of climate, geography, and technology, and the lack of commercial markets, forced local families to exploit the resources of the rivers and plains—an expedient, if not profitable, tactic for life in a restrictive economy.

With the Red River Resistance of 1869–70, the passing of the Manitoba Act, and the subsequent alienation of Métis lands in the new province, life changed in old Red River. The transition to a new political order after 1870, along with the influx of Ontarian settlers, altered the character of the community. Some people departed the River Road area to seek new economic opportunities elsewhere or left as the result of dispossession. Those who remained found their influence challenged by a federal policy that promoted mass immigration to the province and to the North-West Territories. Colonization beyond the borders of the old parishes such as St. Andrew's and the development of Winnipeg as a distribution and supply centre consigned St. Andrew's to the periphery of the new large-scale agricultural economy of western Canada. Despite the survival of some impressive limestone architecture, the River Road district settled into the slow life of a rural backwater,

Figure 25. Unidentified family with their two-storey Red River frame home, St. Andrew's Parish, c. 1890. Credit: Thomas Sinclair Collection. Courtesy of the Sinclair family.

its meagre land base unable to compete with the large-scale agriculture of the "New West."

But as interest in the history of the area increased with the development of tourism in the twentieth century, River Road and the surrounding area began to enjoy new popularity as a heritage destination. A 1977 report to the provincial government noted that River Road was one of the most significant historical districts in western Canada. "No other identifiable area," the report concluded, "possesses the wide variety of historical structures and sites that represent all aspects of early settlement life from fur trade to religion, education, and farming in such close proximity to one another and along a road and river that are in themselves historical."[11] That both the river and the road are "in themselves historical" is interesting; they are effectively labelled "heritage" by their mere existence, though, of course, both witnessed the evolution of local economies and local ways of life.

Across the country the increasing demand for heritage conservation and the provision of outdoor recreational opportunities resulted in the

1972 announcement by Prime Minister Pierre Elliott Trudeau of the Byways and Special Places Program, which focused on recreational opportunities for heritage river corridors. A year later it was enhanced by the federal-provincial Agreement for Recreation and Conservation, known simply as the "ARC program."[12] According to the Concept Plan, ARC developed the concept of "federal-provincial cooperation in the planning, development, operation, and management of areas containing important historic resources."[13] The agreement was a milestone in the development of historic resources across the country, partnering federal and provincial heritage and financial assets with a greater emphasis on heritage tourism.

In Manitoba, a number of sites along the Red River were considered suitable for a federal-provincial partnership under the Manitoba ARC Authority Incorporated (the partnership's full name). The ARC program was the first to consider rehabilitation of the Red River as a natural and cultural corridor, following a century of neglect and of urban and exurban development away from the rivers. The overall plan set aside $13 million on a number of sites from St. Norbert and the La Salle River in the south to Netley Marsh on Lake Winnipeg in the north. They were to be anchored by a federal development at the forks of the Red and Assiniboine rivers. The Forks site, once a centuries-old meeting place for prairie Indigenous nations, the centre of the Red River Settlement, and the location of Upper Fort Garry, had become an increasingly disused railway yard and an empty and derelict space alienated from the city core. Though beyond the scope of this study, the story of the development of The Forks—first the creation of green space by Parks Canada and later the commercial and recreational initiatives that emerged from private-public development—did go a long way in rejuvenating Winnipeg's history as a river-oriented settlement. As historian Claire Campbell writes, The Forks "was a massive project of urban reclamation, to reinvigorate a derelict industrial core into an economically self-sustaining complex of farmers' markets and cafes, performance spaces and public sculpture, and a riverside park."[14]

The Manitoba ARC agreement was concluded in October of 1978 with River Road selected as a key heritage development in the Red River Corridor plan.[15] With the details of the River Road design yet to be worked out, planners did identify the overall challenge for the project to be that of "controlling and acquiring the adjoining landscape for required visual and planning improvement"; this was planning jargon for creating a landscape environment and place that reduced the impact of surrounding modern development.[16] As we will see, the original lofty goal would not be achieved in the years to come.

The 1982 River Road Parkway Concept Plan identified the settlement of River Road (and St. Andrew's Parish) as "a major development in the initial settlement of the Canadian West and the role of the Hudson's Bay Company in that settlement."[17] Four themes were identified for interpretation at various nodes along the road: river-lot agriculture; English Métis society; social class; and the transition between 1860 and 1890 of political, economic, and social institutions in the region.[18] This last theme represented a major narrative for the whole of Red River and for the Indigenous peoples who lived within its boundaries. Surviving resources and interpretive signage could adequately relate the story of the last three themes; as for river-lot agriculture, a century of changing land patterns had effectively diminished the historic role of place in the old parish. Although descriptive narratives could provide visitors to the area with some idea of traditional land holdings, no provision was made by the ARC Authority to acquire and preserve a river lot in the area. And while that particular land-use pattern was still visible at the time of planning (1982), today the increase in suburban sprawl along River Road has all but obliterated on-the-ground traces of the agricultural pattern that characterized the earliest European and Métis settlement in the West. The decision to not protect the heritage of place but to focus instead upon the development of scenic vistas and recreational nodes, and the acquisition and restoration of the built heritage of the area, represented an opportunity missed.[19]

The final plan for the parkway proposed the development of six natural, recreational, and heritage nodes, many of the latter represented by nineteenth-century examples of stone architecture. These included Twin Oaks; Kennedy House, the stone house built in 1866 by William Kennedy, the Métis former HBC employee and Arctic explorer; and Scott House, a more modest structure that was partly dismantled in the 1980s because of structural issues and is now interpreted as a "ruin fragment." According to the 1982 River Road Parkway Concept Plan, "selective destruction of the building is recommended with the leaving of a ruin fragment," a technique used with various heritage buildings

Figure 26. Kennedy House, River Road, 2015. Credit: Gordon Goldsborough.

throughout Europe. Initial plans for Scott House included a vegetable garden and enclosures for pigs, horses, and hens—all animals that had once been a part of farming in the area. However, the addition of livestock at the property never occurred.[20]

One of the largest restoration developments along the road was St. Andrew's Rectory, a national historic site like the nearby church. Constructed in 1854, and for many years a private museum, the rectory was declared of national historic significance in 1962 and was purchased by the federal government in the 1970s. The site's later heritage interpretation focused on stone architecture and the role in the settlement of the Church Missionary Society, a London-based Anglican evangelical order founded in 1799 as the Society for Missions to Africa and the East.[21]

Funding for work on the rectory fell to Parks Canada. The "restoration" of St. Andrew's Rectory NHS was a major undertaking and was completed in the early 1980s. Much like the walls at Lower Fort Garry, however, the work on the rectory more closely resembled reconstruction than restoration, as much new material was used for both the exterior and the interior. At nearby St. Andrew's Church, structural

Figure 27. Work on St. Andrew's Rectory, 1980. Much new stone was used to rebuild the rectory while the interior was largely gutted. Credit: Parks Canada.

and cosmetic repairs to the historic building began in the 1930s and continued intermittently until the 1980s.[22] Although no monies were made available under the Canada-Manitoba ARC Agreement for work on the church, the building was later restored under the National Historic Sites Cost-Sharing Program with structural work completed in the spring of 1995.[23]

As elsewhere along River Road, funding went largely towards the restoration and maintenance of built heritage, a built heritage that did not represent the historic life of the community and its origins as an agricultural community.[24] Overall site development failed to incorporate the commemoration of the historically unique land-holding system of the region. Other than what is related on some interpretive panels, the visitor learns little of the remaking of the riverine landscape and the importance of the land in the formation of community culture. What would eventually become the transformation of the commons through large-scale prairie agriculture and the later recognition, even celebration, of that transformation would not form part of the commemoration of the historical culture of Red River. The Métis loss of land to speculators and incoming Ontarian settlement after 1870

Figure 28. The reconstructed St. Andrew's Rectory, n.d. The original rectory was constructed in 1854 and declared a national historic site in 1962. Credit: Parks Canada.

would instead be underscored by the commemorative erasure of that heritage and language of place. A preoccupation with the preservation of a non-representative built heritage would ultimately skew the historical understanding of life along River Road in the nineteenth century, suggesting that the typical Indigenous freighter and hunter of the region lived in the grandeur of limestone halls.

After nine public meetings between 1980 and 1981, the development of the River Road Heritage Parkway was undertaken by five jurisdictional interests including Parks Canada, Manitoba Highways, Manitoba Historic Resources Branch, Manitoba Parks Branch, and the Rural Municipality of St. Andrew's, which included the Selkirk and District Planning Board.[25] The proposed project plan laid out in detail the kinds of management systems that would be required in developing, managing, and operating the parkway. After reviewing a number of options, the report recommended that the provincial Historic Resources Branch take on the role of "formal lead agency" with Manitoba Highways to continue to maintain the actual road maintenance and the Selkirk and District Planning Board to take the leadership in any future planning endeavours.[26]

However, the recommended management regime did not occur. When the ARC Authority was eventually disbanded an informal management approach was adopted and a number of provincial and federal departments maintained control over components of the parkway. Over time the lack of centralized management led to funding issues, particularly the lack of financial support for ongoing maintenance. For example, the interpretive nodes and scenic pull-offs were poorly maintained and the bicycle pathway between the road and the river was soon overgrown. Although the interpretive signage contained accurate, interesting, and well-written material, the physical condition of the signage deteriorated over time, despite the parkway's being designated a provincial heritage park in 1997. In the early 2000s the road was paved and in 2007 the provincial government replaced the interpretive signage at the different parkway nodes. While providing an overview of the history of the road, the community, and local river lots, the new signage also developed "A Family Journey," which followed the journey of the fictitious Thomas family as it made its way north to Lower Fort Garry.[27] In 2013 Manitoba Parks and Natural Areas Branch assembled a new Draft Management Plan for River Road. This thin, eleven-page document adds little in terms of strategy for the parkway. Other than to clarify the parkway's management under the current Parks and Protected Spaces Branch, the document simply repeats the original ARC goals "to preserve several sites containing 19th century homes, promote public awareness and appreciation of these sites and provide recreational opportunities along the Red River."[28]

In small part the significance of place can still be glimpsed along River Road. It remains rural to some degree. However, where the meaning of some historic places has been sacrificed to tourist comforts and an invented past, the heritage of River Road is being lost as the result of neglect and from the gentrification of riverside properties. Only remnants of the area's river-lot geography and cultural landscape remain, though they continue to disappear with the building of each new upscale house. Like so many heritage plans, River Road represents an opportunity lost. In the Introduction to a 1973 plan for prospective zoning for the road, there is a discussion of the importance of the visual landscape and how it should be considered as a natural resource "prone to depletion and destruction, highly sensitive and difficult to renew."[29] It suggests that for the proposed parkway, "The visual field

Figure 29. Scott House, River Road, 2016. Because of the current condition of this "ruin fragment" and the obvious lack of maintenance, the property has been closed to the public. Credit: Eric De Schepper.

experienced in the act of viewing [River Road] is the manifestation of all the landscape resources, including plant communities, topographic variety, harmonious land uses . . . and unique features incorporating cultural, historic, and natural systems."[30] The proposed parkway, the document recommends, should maintain "a high degree of visual continuity throughout its length."[31] Since those forty-seven-year-old proposals, much has been lost in one of Manitoba's oldest communities. Once little more than a muddy cart track, River Road is a vanishing reminder of a Métis heritage of hunting, fishing, freighting, and trade, and the overland trail that helped integrate these activities within the community.

"Clean and Well Kept Grounds"

Much of the late nineteenth-century non-Indigenous occupation of western Canada centred on ethnoreligious settlement, especially immigrant settlement from central and eastern Europe. In terms of commemoration, the founding narratives of groups such as Mennonites, Ukrainians, and Doukhobors, among others, moved beyond national mythologies to a greater emphasis on regional contexts, the celebration of the immigrant settler generation, and the possession, meaning, and importance of the land itself. For the descendants of ethnoreligious settlers, the national narratives around political and cultural ascendancy that defined Anglo-Canadian and Anglo-European settlement were largely supplanted by the specifics of the settlement experience and by cultural and religious persistence. Frances Swyripa has argued that by the 1970s, "as nostalgia for the past and its artefacts gathered momentum, the material heritage of the [ethnoreligious] settlement era—defining the land, recalling its human dramas—acquired unprecedented symbolic value."[32] She adds, however, that the settler generations regarded pioneering as temporary, so little of their original vernacular architecture, other than churches, cemeteries, and a handful of houses and farm buildings, remained.[33] What did endure was the land itself and often the cultural landscapes that marked the signposts of possession. Despite the desire to link history with space, much of the modern heritage movement attempts to establish a memory of place without the actuality of place or at least the originality of place. Creating contrived and often romanticized reproductions of the built environment, from churches to barns, from one-room schoolhouses to early log cabins in pastoral village settings with all their fabricated material culture, has long been a part of Canada's commemorative tradition.

The origin of the open-air museum, as it has been called, can be traced to Skansen, an open-air museum in Sweden that opened in 1891. With relocated farm buildings, the site included interpreters in traditional costumes, live animals, folk music, domestic settings, and demonstrations of crafts and conventional occupations such as blacksmithing, carpentry, and other activities. Skansen, which remains one of Sweden's leading tourist destinations, thus set the pattern for such heritage reconstructions in other countries, including in North America, where many people were impressed by such romanticized replications of a pastoral past.

One of the earliest such imitations in Canada was Black Creek Pioneer Village, located in the North York area of Toronto and opened in 1960. It interprets an 1860s Anglo-Ontario farming community and includes both relocated and reproduced "pioneer" structures. Upper Canada Village opened in 1961 near Morrisburg, Ontario, along the St. Lawrence Seaway, and includes forty reproduced and relocated heritage buildings including mills, stores, and trades buildings.[34] Upper Canada Village also interprets life in an 1860s Anglo-Ontario farming community. A more recent, and western, example of a reconstructed/ restored heritage site is the Ukrainian Cultural Heritage Village near

Edmonton. Founded in 1971 (and designated a provincial historic site in 1975), it is described as an "open-air museum" and brings together a number of surviving buildings from the region to interpret Ukrainian settlement in central Alberta in the early decades of the twentieth century. In describing open-air museums such as the Ukrainian Cultural Heritage Village, historian Karen Gabert writes: "Museum curators are able to win over the most sceptical of visitors at open air sites, in part because they stay invisible. Traditional museum exhibits bear the clear marks of their creators; open-air exhibits can erase or at least ignore all such evidence and encourage the fantasy of having happened upon an in situ historic wonderland."[35] While Gabert's point is an interesting one—open-air museums do encourage the fantasy of revisiting the past—most visitors, I believe, are well aware of the quixotic if not questionable integrity of their surroundings. When I was a child our family visited Frontier Town, a sort of Hollywood-style Western town in upstate New York. I was well aware, even as an eight-year-old, and as fun as that site was, that we had not happened upon some "in situ historic wonderland" (even if I did not know what "in situ" meant).

Another example, and closer to home, is Mennonite Heritage Village Museum established in 1967 near Steinbach, Manitoba. The open-air museum interprets the story of Mennonite culture from its origins in the sixteenth century but focuses primarily upon the story of ethnoreligious settlement on the eastern prairies of Manitoba in the late nineteenth and early twentieth centuries. As the outdoor museum has developed over the years, it has become a major tourist attraction and has attracted thousands of visitors each year since it opened. According to a 1975 report prepared for the Manitoba Department of Tourism, Recreation, and Cultural Affairs entitled "A Survey of the Mennonite Heritage Village Museum," which was based upon a 1974 study of the site's more than 30,000 visitors, "at the museum, the Manitoba Mennonite Historical Society has constructed a village characteristic of Mennonite communities in Manitoba in the 1870s and 1880s." The report went on to conclude that "the Museum has two major objectives: to protray pioneer life in Manitoba and Western Canada, and to preserve the Mennonite heritage."[36]

The creation of the village was the brainchild of the Manitoba Mennonite Historical Society, which was formed in 1958, although concern for the preservation of Mennonite heritage in the Altona area dates back to as early as the 1930s.[37] In a province that moved quickly to commemorate a pioneer past—the Manitoba Historical Society was founded in 1879 as the Historical and Scientific Society of Manitoba, just nine years after the province joined Confederation—much is revealed about staking claim not only to the land but to "founding father" narratives. That the first Mennonites were looking to preserve their settler past just half a century after arriving in the new province in 1874 further underscores the colonizer preoccupation with entitlement and the swiftness characteristic of the colonialist project.

The idea of a museum based on artifacts collected by John Reimer, a teacher in the Steinbach region, was proposed early on. The Mennonite Historical Society, however, had bigger plans, and eventually a sixteen-hectare site was purchased just north of Steinbach in 1965, where a building to house the artifacts was completed by 1967.[38] Other buildings would soon follow that would "provide a graphic representation of life in southern Manitoba from 1874 to approximately 1930 for the purpose of preserving for present and future generations, the contributions made by Mennonite settlers . . . an important part of Canadian heritage."[39] The first historic building moved to the site was the Waldheim House, constructed in 1876 south of Morden. A log structure, Waldheim House was originally built with a thatched roof and an attached barn. Other buildings moved to the site and restored include a Semlin, or sod, house; a housebarn originally constructed in 1892 in the West Reserve near Winkler; an outdoor oven; a livery, which is now a restaurant; the Chortitz Old Colony Church, built in 1881 also near Winkler and moved to the village site in 1967; a school; an 1892 granary; a blacksmith shop; a general store; and the Hochfeld House, constructed in 1877 and moved to the village in 1986. The centrepiece of the village is the large operating windmill, a reconstruction of the first mill built near Steinbach in 1877 and augmented by parts from a period mill in Germany. A number of memorials, gardens, an orchard, a visitor centre, and of course a gift shop also form part of the site. Funding for much of the village development changed over the years. While admissions revenue has remained substantial, the site has also relied upon grants from the city of Steinbach, the Rural Municipality of Hanover, and the federal and provincial governments. Annual operating and special initiative grants to Mennonite Heritage Village have consistently remained among the highest given by the province to heritage initiatives. Special community fundraising campaigns have also traditionally accompanied specific building projects such as the construction of the windmill and the Village Centre. In the 1980s, to help solidify museum funding on a more long-term basis, the provincial Historic Resources Branch encouraged the museum board to formulate a long-term plan that looked at attendance and market analysis, a review of programs, facility requirements, and a financial review. Until that time the museum board had often come to governments for funding assistance after a capital project had already been developed.[40]

The Mennonite Heritage Village website, like the promotional material for so many heritage developments, uses the phrase "Travel Through Time" as its overarching theme, urging visitors to "explore our rich history and be inspired."[41] In the language of heritage and place, virtually all history is considered rich, as a usable past meant to inspire us in the present. The site advertises a "broad range of activities and demonstrations, from wagon rides to bread baking . . . in this bustling village that offers a fresh experience with each visit."[42] In his recent work, *Time Travel: Tourism and the Rise of the Living History Museum in Mid-Twentieth-Century Canada*, Alan Gordon contends that the creation of the Mennonite Heritage Village was more than an expression of multiculturalism: it represented a shift in the mainstream Mennonite community toward a greater engagement with the rest of Canada. The village focus upon material culture, he argues, echoes museum (and outdoor museum) approaches elsewhere, and with the pioneer stories recasts memories of the Mennonite experience as part of a larger strategy of integration and the reformulation of Mennonite identity.[43]

Such sites are often referred to as "museums," and like the original intent of the Mennonite Historical Society, the village near Steinbach remains a museum, albeit a large and outdoor one. Like Black Creek Pioneer Village or the Ukrainian Cultural Heritage Village, these types of developments continue to be popular with visitors who prefer their history neatly packaged and easily accessible. At such sites history is always promoted as *rich* and *inspiring* where the past (or a version of it) is to be *experienced*. As David Lowenthal has suggested, such descriptions of the past can transcend nostalgia as we search for what he labels "a fancifully imagined or surrogate yesteryear."[44]

Figure 30. Reconstructed windmill at Mennonite Heritage Village, n.d. Credit: Mennonite Heritage Village Incorporated.

The appeal of places like Mennonite Heritage Village is the presentation of *origins*, even if these depictions are idealized and formulaic. It is perhaps obvious to characterize settler sites in general as the struggle against obstacles—obstacles such as climate, rudimentary technology, and the overall challenge of the land. But while the idea of struggle ("Look how they had to grow their own food to survive," or "Look at how simple the technology was") helps to define the spaces of settler history, there is at the same time a contrived simplicity, even naïveté, about it that provides visitors with a kind of comfort in the past and the sense that they (through their ancestors) have worked hard and deserve their present reality and position of ascendency in overcoming the harshness of the environment around them. The typical layout of the outdoor village museum can often convey conflicting messages, the simplicity and convenience of the artificial site in fact portraying comfort and security rather than the struggle and adversity the visitor typically associates with settler culture. While perhaps not the explicit intentions of those who create such artifice, it is messages of community and intimacy that might inadvertently supplant those of hardship and adversity.

These values can lie at the core of how a person might experience the past; by portraying the past in the present, we often channel present values. When visitors to Mennonite Heritage Village were asked for their opinions on the site, the expected comments of "enjoyable," "authentic," and "educational" were logged. Only somewhat less frequent were compliments regarding the "clean and well kept grounds."[45] Such *prima facie* values help to organize a past that is comforting, even if the present and the future are not. The golden age that the time traveller enters bears no resemblance to anything real; the escapist nostalgia of the "in-situ historic wonderland" that historian Karen Gabert describes might in fact represent all that is missing in the modern world.[46]

"This Is a Place that Will Be Lived In"

In a 2015 article published in the *Pembina Valley Online*, Margruite Krahn, the chairperson of the Neubergthal Heritage Foundation fundraising committee, discussed the plans of a Mennonite family to live in a housebarn recently moved to Neubergthal Street Village National Historic Site. "We are not the Steinbach Museum [Mennonite Heritage Village]," she wrote, "this is a place that will be lived in."[47] In writing about the historic Mennonite village located near Altona, Manitoba, in what was originally the West Reserve, Krahn touched on the dissimilarities between the living history museum and a heritage place where the cultural landscape is both real and evolving. In authenticating early European settlement on the prairies—in portraying the physical and emotional ties to land and place and how such places are comprehended and recognized—it is at communities like Neubergthal where we see the way that a particular type of settler colonialism imposed a distinct order and world view upon the landscape at the human level.

At such localities as Neubergthal it is the land that best exemplifies the persistence of the past in the present. It is not through the nostalgia of performance that the past is made sense of, or at those places that Lowenthal called "the past as a foreign country with a healthy tourist trade."[48] In a 1990 article entitled "Heritage: The Manitoba Experience," historian Jean Friesen comments upon the growth of heritage-related activities in the province such as the ethnocultural festivals and celebrations that take place at sites like Mennonite Heritage Village. These "bland, populist, neutral version[s] of the past," she argues, have become part of "pioneer ideology," an acceptable past for non-Mennonite visitors that would be seen as "immodest, worldly and undesirable" by Old Colony Mennonites.[49]

The community of Neubergthal is located in south-central Manitoba and has a small population of less than 200 people. When Mennonites began arriving in the province after 1874, they settled first in an area known as the "East Reserve," a block of eight townships located southeast of Winnipeg. Because the land was considered of poor quality, many people soon left for the seventeen townships that made up the West Reserve situated just west of the Red River. Here, the new settlers found a treeless prairie rich in black and clay loam soils. They were one of the earliest groups to farm on the prairies, and their success encouraged the Canadian government to expand its immigration strategies to attract European settlers to the West. As a result of this developing agriculture, supply centres were quickly established in the region. To survive the harshness of the prairie winter in a land once thought completely inhospitable, the Mennonites recreated a form of settlement that had developed over centuries in their homelands in northern Europe and the steppes of Russia. This settlement pattern

became known as the "street village," a shared experience on the land
and a unique perspective on the landscape and the settlers' place in it.[50]

Founded in 1876 by a group of related families, Neubergthal would
be one of over 100 street villages in southern Manitoba established
between 1875 and 1900. The street village is characterized by a single
main road lined by housebarns (a distinctive architectural feature of
early Mennonite communities and reminiscent of structures found
in Holland, Germany, and parts of Poland) and surrounded by narrow fields. Tree plantings along this road protected the village from
the winter winds. Originally the land was owned cooperatively and
villagers shared much of the work. Later, in 1909, the collectivization
of land ownership ended, though farm work often continued to be
collaborative. Life in Neubergthal revolved around a close cooperation
among residents. Villagers assisted their neighbours with harvesting
and threshing, butchering and building. Leisure time was usually spent
collectively, and the church was the central institution of village life as it
defined values and behaviour, how residents made their living, and how
the people governed themselves. The village school was another centre
that helped to transmit cultural and religious values.[51]

Neubergthal, one of approximately seventeen remaining street
villages in Manitoba, was recognized to be of national significance by
the HSMBC in February of 1989. The selection of the village derived
from the 1984 Parks Canada study of prairie settlement patterns,
recommending that "the agricultural settlement of the Canadian prairies
is a theme of national significance."[52] Although the Board advocated
commemorative concentration on the era of the wheat boom (identified
as the period between 1900 and the beginning of the Second World
War), it also noted the need to identify the ethnic diversity of the region.
In recognizing Neubergthal and the street village land-use pattern as
described in the 1984 report, the Board in 1989 stated: "Mennonite
Street Villages are prairie settlement forms of both national historic
and architectural significance and they should be commemorated at
New Bergthal,[53] Manitoba, which not only possessed a considerable
amount of resource integrity but an apparently unique 'sense of place.'"[54]

It is important to note that the entire landscape of Neubergthal has
been declared a national historic site. The particular layout of the street
village from the main road, the rows of planted cottonwood trees, the
original narrow ten-acre (four-hectare) strips of farmland of which

Figure 31. Neubergthal, Manitoba, 2009. The village, founded in 1876, was declared a national historic site in 1989 as an example of the distinctive form of group settlement known as the Mennonite street village. Remnants of the original narrow lots that fronted the main road can still be seen. Credit: Parks Canada.

vestiges can still be seen, fence lines, and gardens are all considered to be what Parks Canada calls "Level 1 resources," or heritage resources directly related to the overall reason for national significance. Joining these aspects of the cultural landscape is the vernacular architecture of the housebarns that sheltered families and farm animals under one roof, some original houses and outbuildings, and public buildings. The Statement of Commemorative Intent for Neubergthal echoes the 1989 commemoration almost word for word. Discussions between the federal government and the community of Neubergthal regarding the development of a cost-sharing agreement began in 1994 and the Commemorative Integrity Statement (CIS) for the historic site was developed collaboratively. The CIS, developed by Parks Canada in the 1990s, was designed to narrow interpretation to the original intent of the Board in its initial designation of a site, no matter how old that designation.

Figure 32. Neubergthal Commons housebarn, 2019. Credit: Used with permission.

Neubergthal continues to project a strong sense of place today. Although the communal system of farming has long been replaced by individual cultivation, the central village street remains the prominent orientation, as do the long narrow yards, the traditionally placed gardens, fence lines, and rows of trees.[55] The local community takes a strong interest in the preservation of its cultural heritage. Incorporated in 1997, the Neubergthal Heritage Foundation works in partnership with Parks Canada to "preserve aspects of this heritage and find ways to share this heritage."[56] An important component of that mission is to restore and maintain buildings that were originally built and moved to Neubergthal during the time of settlement, especially the housebarns that were so idiomatic of early Mennonite architecture in Manitoba. New structures are integrated as much as possible into the overall historic character of the landscape. The "language of place" remains strong in Neubergthal; one can savour it as genuine and real. People live there. The village is a historic place that is not frozen in time, and neither does it attempt to represent itself as an open-air museum. However, in a larger sense the narrative of the Neubergthal community, like so many early settler cultures across the West, especially ethnoreligious settlements, celebrates the tradition of attachment to soil and place, the "shared pioneering credentials" that have helped establish the archetypal commemorative traditions and mythologies around survival and prosperity.

Spirit Wrestlers

Another ethnoreligious group that has shared the commemorative traditions of those claiming pioneering credentials is the Doukhobors, whose early twentieth-century settlement in Saskatchewan is now the national historic site at Veregin known locally as "National Doukhobor Heritage Village" or by the federal government by the more clumsily worded "Doukhobors at Veregin National Historic Site of Canada."[57] Founded in 1904, the village of Veregin, near the present town of Yorkton in southeastern Saskatchewan, was the administrative and distribution centre for Doukhobor settlement in the region after their arrival from Russia two years earlier in 1902. Largely abandoned by the 1940s, Veregin was reborn in the 1980s as a heritage village intended to commemorate early Doukhobor history in the region. Over the years the three remaining buildings in the village (the large, impressive prayer home, a machine shop, and grain elevator) were restored, while seven period buildings from the surrounding area were moved to the original site. A modern museum/reception centre is also part of the village setting.

In 1982 Saskatchewan declared the Veregin Prayer Home a provincial heritage site. A superbly crafted building with elaborate metalwork and a two-storey wraparound balcony, the Veregin Prayer Home reflects long-standing Doukhobor architectural traditions. Unlike other Doukhobor villages in Manitoba and Saskatchewan where the local prayer home was part of a central street village concept similar to Neubergthal, at Veregin the large home was located at the head of the village, signifying its prominent role in the community and its function as the residence for community leader Peter Verigin.[58]

The Doukhobor movement originated in the seventeenth century in southern Russia in what is now Ukraine. A breakaway sect from the Russian Orthodox Church, the movement came to be known by the Russian term *Dukho-borets*, which translates as "Spirit Wrestler" and describes those who wrestle against the spirit of God and the established Church. The name was intended pejoratively, but the sect adopted the name for themselves, defining it instead as those who "wrestle with the spirit of truth."[59]

Late in the nineteenth century, Clifford Sifton, the federal minister of the Department of the Interior, negotiated an agreement with the

Figure 33. The restored Prayer Home at Veregin, Saskatchewan National Historic Site, 2017. Credit: National Doukhobor Heritage Village.

emigrating Doukhobors, an agreement that some authors have since argued was left ambiguous in relation to the terms of the Dominion Lands Act of 1872, and which would lead to future disagreements between the Canadian government and these Russian-speaking "sons of the soil." In essence, the conflict revolved around the belief by the Doukhobors in the collective ownership of property and the contrasting federal policy of populating the West with independent, owner-occupant farmers.[60] Eventually, Sifton negotiated four reserves with the Doukhobors: three just north of Yorkton and one farther west near Prince Albert. Veregin is located in the South Colony, located close to Yorkton and comprising fifteen townships, or 540 square miles (1,399 square kilometres).[61] The Doukhobors sought to establish communities based upon collectivism and pacifism, and the layout of their villages, with a central street, a distinctive prayer home, communal residences, and a community-owned infrastructure including farmland, farm buildings, and elevators, reflected this assimilationist approach to settlement.

Although the federal government had approved block settlement and communal farming for the Doukhobors, under the terms of the 1872 Dominion Lands Act, each settler was expected to register individually for a land grant at the end of the three-year "proving up" period.[62] While the so-called Independent Doukhobors did register individually, Sifton was able to negotiate an agreement with most of the settlement where individual grants were registered under the names of Peter Verigin and a number of community Elders. Sifton's agreement was later reversed by Frank Oliver, his successor at the Department of the Interior.[63] While Oliver's hard line resulted in the growth of the Independents, the Community Doukhobors or the "Sons of Freedom," as they were called, had their homestead entries cancelled. Moreover, their refusal for religious reasons to swear an oath of allegiance to the Crown resulted in growing tensions, and many Doukhobors protested the punitive application of federal policy. In the end many of the Community Doukhobors left Saskatchewan for new colonies in British Columbia. Their lands were sold to incoming non-Doukhobor settlers.

While Peter Verigin remained in exile in Russia until 1902, the early layout of Doukhobor villages followed his views regarding community property, most reflecting what was called the "*strassendorf* plan," with houses facing each other across a broad central avenue. Stables and barns were located behind the living quarters, including housebarns similar in style and layout to early Mennonite housebarns. Prayer homes and other public buildings in most Doukhobor villages were part of the central avenue, but at Veregin, as mentioned above, the large Prayer Home (and residence of Peter Verigin) occupied a central location at the head of the village. The Veregin home hosted communal gatherings, weddings, funerals, and spiritual assemblies.

The National Doukhobor Heritage Village was submitted for consideration as a national historic site to the Historic Sites and Monuments Board of Canada in 2003 and was designated in 2006 as the Doukhobors at Veregin National Historic Site of Canada. According to the Board, Veregin is of national historic significance because "the original Veregin settlement, including the surviving buildings, was the administrative, distribution and spiritual centre for the region during the first period of Doukhobor settlement in Canada; and the spectacular prayer home reflects the settlement's importance to the Doukhobors as a religious and cultural centre, as well as the authority and the vision of the leader of the Doukhobors, Peter V. Verigin."[64] Among the character-defining elements of the site, the Board noted "the location and interrelation of the original surviving buildings . . . the flat site with central open area . . . the volumes of the original and relocated buildings . . . and internal disposition of spaces."[65]

As with Neubergthal, Veregin projects a strong sense of place and, like Neubergthal, the communal system of farming has long been replaced by individual cultivation. However, unlike the Mennonite community in southern Manitoba, Veregin has lost much of its original spatial orientation and architecture. In some ways Veregin as a historic place is a hybrid of Neubergthal and Mennonite Heritage Village; it has relocated buildings and it functions as a site for visitors to learn about Doukhobor culture and history. At the same time the site retains much of its authenticity and remains an active location for traditional Doukhobor religious and cultural activities on the prairies, including prayer services, congregational singing, and the commemoration of the 1895 Burning of Arms, a pacifist protest in Czarist Russia that led to their expulsion from that country. If the historic language of place is diminished at modern-day Veregin, the village is not frozen in time and does not present as an open-air museum. As an early twentieth-century ethnoreligious settlement on the prairies, Veregin marks an attachment to place and the distinctiveness of a religious group whose immigration, settlement, and particular land management were a part of the religiously motivated movements that made up much of early European settlement in the West.

Proving Up

If ethnoreligious communities on the prairies brought their distinctive settlement patterns to the landscape, it was the broader patterns of Canadian, European, and American settlement that helped to define the common look of land-use patterns across the West in the last decades of the nineteenth century and the early years of the twentieth. The "Hamlet Clause" of the Dominion Lands Act of 1872 outlined the organization of the landscape particular to certain groups, but it was the square lot township survey, also a product of the Dominion Lands Act, that would come to largely define space and place in the West. It was the grid pattern of townships and sections that transformed the plains from the grasslands of the commons to a work of the hand, heart, and mind—what historian Richard Allen once called a "region of the mind"—that would come to reflect the colonial ideologies and obsessions of those who created it.[66] Prairie historians and literary critics have more or less continued to pursue this region of the mind motif and have defined the West in more than a physical or geographical sense, as socially constituted space shaped by individual and collective perspectives that shift dynamically over time.[67] Yet, as Simon Schama and others have argued, all landscapes are to some degree cultural and more than the sum of their geography, even those we might classify as less than arcadian in their presentation. They are a work of the mind and the product of the memories and meanings of those who inhabit them or simply view them.[68] The prairies, like the parklands and the northern boreal forests, are all socially constituted space in the West with different histories, different meanings, and different memories.

To entice settlers to this challenging region, the federal government undertook an ambitious program of advertising and recruitment. The rise in grain prices by the turn of the century, the improvements in agricultural technology including irrigation, the development of new strains of cereal crops, the expansion in the number of rail lines, and the relaxation by the federal government of its pre-emption restrictions all allowed for large-scale cultivation by the first decade of the twentieth century and a massive influx of new immigrants by the First World War. The earlier decades of "proving up," where immigrants were required to stay on the land for a specified period and demonstrate "improvements," had given way to larger and established agricultural operations. From these factors emerged the settlement patterns that would define much of the prairies. The survey grid determined the spatial configuration of fields, roads, and irrigation ditches, while also influencing farmstead placement to allow easier access to roads and road allowances.[69] Barns and other outbuildings associated with the farmstead, along with gardens and yards, were orientated according to topography, drainage, and prevailing winds.[70]

Searching to find a historic and cultural landscape to represent prairie farming during the era of the wheat boom, the HSMBC chose Motherwell, a surviving farmstead and house in southeastern Saskatchewan near the community of Abernethy. Yet, it was not the survival of the farm and its buildings or its layout or representation of Ontarian settlement on the prairies that led to Motherwell's federal designation in 1966. Rather, it was the career of W.R. Motherwell, a former Liberal minister of the Department of Agriculture that led to his designation as a person of national significance by the Liberal government of Lester Pearson. Later, the designation of significance was expanded to include his house. The Motherwell site was acquired by Parks Canada in 1968 and after restoration was opened to the public in 1983.[71] As Agriculture minister between 1921 and 1930, Motherwell helped develop what came to be known as "scientific agriculture" on the prairies. The Statement of Commemorative Intent for the site reflects the expanded commemoration and notes its architectural significance, the career of W.R. Motherwell, and the site as an example of a well-to-do homestead of the settlement period in the West.[72] According to the site's character-defining elements as defined by Parks Canada, the Motherwell Homestead exhibits elements of the scientific approach to agriculture, including the use of shelterbelts to protect against wind and soil erosion, the siting of the farmstead near a rail line and the communities of Abernethy and Indian Head, and the division of the landscape into functional quadrants defined by domestic occupations, farmyard operation, garden, and water supply.[73] Later, when the Board expanded the designation, they added the homestead as an example of the settlement period as well as its buildings (primarily the fieldstone house and the large barn) as being of architectural interest. The current federal plaque at the site reads: "In the early 1880s, William R. Motherwell arrived here as part of a large wave of homesteaders from Central Canada, capitalizing on the federal government's offer of free land grants to settle the West. Over the next twenty-five years, he expanded his original quarter section and built an impressive barn and fieldstone house that recalled the architectural styles of his childhood. Motherwell divided his model farmstead into four quadrants, all ringed with shelterbelts of trees, illustrating an Ontario settler's approach to farmstead design and scientific agriculture on the Canadian Prairies."[74]

Motherwell Homestead National Historic Site consists of nine historic buildings built between 1897 and 1918 on just over 3.2 hectares of property.[75] Established by W.R. Motherwell, a former Ontarian, in 1882, the site was named Lanark Place after Motherwell's birthplace near Perth, Ontario, in Lanark County. In 1901 Motherwell co-founded the territorial Grain Growers Association in Saskatchewan, later serving in the newly formed Saskatchewan Legislature between 1905

Figure 34. Built in 1882 of fieldstone construction, the restored Motherwell Home is known as Lanark Place. Its Italianate style mimics similar era farmhouses in Ontario, where W.R. Motherwell was from. Credit: Parks Canada.

and 1918, most of those years as provincial minister of Agriculture. In 1921 he was elected to Parliament as a Liberal and served as the federal minister of Agriculture between 1921 and 1930. The two most prominent surviving buildings on the property are the impressive two-storey stone house and the large, L-shaped wood and stone barn. As second-generation farm buildings, the house and barn were variants of the common Ontarian building types transplanted to the prairies.[76] However, the larger use of space at the site also reflects the configuration of an eastern Ontario farmstead from the period, including the landscaping, building styles and locations, agricultural techniques, and overall physical organization.[77]

When Lanark Place was at its peak in the first decade of the twentieth century, the Motherwell farm consisted of six quarter sections, totalling almost 405 hectares. By the time of Motherwell's death in 1943, the farm had been reduced to just over 121 hectares, as a number of quarter sections had been given to Motherwell's various children. Unable to keep the farm operating, the family sold the property in 1965, and a year later 3.4 hectares were donated to the Province of

Figure 35. Motherwell National Historic Site, Abernethy, Saskatchewan, n.d. Credit: Parks Canada.

Figure 36. Restored 1907 barn at Motherwell National Historic Site, n.d. Credit: Parks Canada.

Saskatchewan. The W.R. Motherwell property was given federal designation in 1966 and title was transferred to Parks Canada.[78]

Throughout the long process of restoration, Parks Canada relied upon a number of historical, architectural, and archaeological studies carried out by the agency over several years.[79] These studies looked at broader settlement and land use in the Abernethy region, the architectural history of the various buildings associated with the Motherwell homestead, and the study of the landscape architecture of Lanark Place, specifically the distinct quadrants of the local landscape and their characteristics.

It was W.R. Motherwell himself who designed the layout of the farmstead. He had shelterbelts planted for protection from the winds and to trap drifting snow, a dugout was created for water collection from the snow stopped by the trees, and ornamental hedges and flowerbeds were installed. His intent, like other well-off farmers in the region, was to mimic an eastern Ontario farmstead. To this end, Lanark Place was laid out in quadrants. Each had its own purpose and was separated by a treeline, which provided both beauty and shelter. These included the water dugout quadrant, a garden quadrant for fruits and vegetables, the barn quadrant that denoted mixed farming operations that were at the centre of the homestead, and the house quadrant containing the imposing Italianate-style stone house built in 1897, a flower garden, ornamental trees, and even a tennis court. Each of the quadrants was surrounded by shelterbelts, the rows of trees that became ubiquitous across much of the prairies.[80] The quadrant system utilized ornamental fencing in addition to the shelterbelts and separated the living area from the work areas. The ornamental gardens, laid out in geometric fashion, and the other decorative aspects of various quadrants were intended to reflect the formality of Victorian society. The larger open fields for crops and grains surrounded the four-quadrant farmstead.[81] The year 1912, the height of agricultural operations at Lanark Place, was chosen by Parks Canada as the date for restoration.

Today, Motherwell National Historic Site offers the usual assortment of tours, school programs, day camps, and special events. Like in many historic sites across the country, activities such as music festivals, although not linked with the heritage of the site, are used to entice visitors. In the era of falling attendance at historic sites, such events, for Parks Canada at least, have become a mainstay of visitor programming.

The agency's periodic management plans lay out a vision for each national historic site across the country. But where such plans were once detailed and thorough, current plans are for the most part short and vague. At sites like Motherwell and Lower Fort Garry, "living history" approaches are now largely underfunded. That they are frequently ill-conceived or overly mannered in their technique is often the result of a lack of perspective by those who write management plans for ministerial approval. Motherwell's most recent (2011) management plan remains imprecise and almost deliberately obscure. For instance, the rather flowery site vision reads:

> This is the first emotive vision for the site, painting a picture of the desired future for Motherwell Homestead as a place of living history, linking the past to modern Canadian life. The quiet sounds of the prairie—rustling grasses and a burst of bird song, provide the backdrop for the sounds of work on an early 20th century farm—stomping hooves, clinking harnesses and powerful snorts as the team draws the plough, releasing the scents of freshly turned soil. Under watchful eyes, sown seeds sprout and grow, nourished by the powerful forces of sun and rain. As the autumn sun shines, join our friends and neighbours working the fields. All hands are working hard to store the grain and gardens' bounties for the long winter ahead—binding, stooking, threshing, storing, pickling. In a quiet moment, ponder what far-off families in foreign countries will be nurtured by the grains from these fields. Motherwell Homestead is a place to discover life as it was. Well cared for, bright buildings draw you into the homestead. Pride of ownership is evident in every facet of the site. Through the sensory experience of food, travel the path from field to fork. Hop on a wagon and tour the grounds, explore the nooks and crannies in the huge barn and magnificent stone house, get your hands dirty with the farm equipment, animals and gardens. Live history from the ground up.[82]

Unfortunately, with equivocal objectives such as "active site management will continue to improve the state of the site" or "visitors of all ages will have fun," much of the thin twenty-eight-page management plan provides little information on how such worthwhile goals will actually be achieved.[83] Of course, the dramatic cuts to programming at Motherwell NHS in the spring of 2012, part of the Harper government's slashing of the Parks Canada budget across the country, have severely restricted the scope of interpretation and the development of new projects at the site.

As with many historic sites, limitations to the scope of the original land base have restricted interpretation. At Motherwell, for instance, though the site boasts the presence of farm animals and some animation about period agricultural practices, the limited size of the site and the interpretive stress on the romance of early farming make it difficult for visitors to appreciate the significance of place, the scope of the new agricultural economy, the historic impact of the township survey, and, most importantly, the impact of colonization and the displacement of Indigenous peoples. (For example, little is said about Treaty 4 and the lands occupied by the Cree, Saulteaux, and Assiniboine in southern Saskatchewan where Motherwell NHS is located or the role of Catherine Motherwell as principal of the nearby and notorious File Hills Residential School between 1901 and 1908.) These are the critical factors that came to characterize the enormous change in both the landscape and the cultural life of the prairie West in the latter decades of the nineteenth century.

▲ ▲ ▲

This chapter on the commemoration of settler colonialism builds upon the previous investigation of the geography of fur trade commemoration by continuing the study of heritage, place, and memory within the colonialist narrative. Regional and national commemorations of Euro-Canadian settlement history in the West in the second half of the nineteenth century and the early decades of the twentieth reveal the contours of the national paradigm of progress and nation building throughout that period and how quickly history became heritage. Interpretation of historic place in the rural West came to assign the development of private property, capitalist labour markets, and individualism (and the collectivism of ethnoreligious settlements) a prominent status in the territories once occupied by Indigenous cultures and fur trade mercantilism. By examining the spaces of settler culture, we are in effect examining landscapes of sovereignty and how these places enter our national psyche through the establishment of popular history making. It is these pervasive chronicles that turn challenging historical, cultural, political, and economic differences into a celebratory narrative that, as anthropologist Eva Mackey has written, employs "a mythological celebration of difference to create a unified (although hybrid) narrative of national progress."[84] She adds, moreover, that in settler culture "representations of Aboriginal people are appropriated to help the settler nation find and articulate a 'natural' link to the land—to help settlers become Indigenous."[85] On the other hand, the commemoration of settler colonialism can be viewed as almost predatory, endeavouring to rationalize its existence, indeed its superiority, by erasing or expunging the memories of early Indigenous cultures through characterizing them as inferior and transitory. Or, worse, settler occupation stories can portray Indigenous history as one of savagery and their cultural downfall as inevitable. As the American historian Laurel Thatcher Ulrich has written, these histories have often "transformed the violence of colonial conquest into a frontier pastoral."[86]

The selection of historic sites described in this chapter provides snapshots of settlement heritage in western Canada. Unlike most analyses of settlement patterns in the West, I quite deliberately begin with the interpretation of River Road in Manitoba as an example of the undervalued impact of Métis agricultural and land-use practices and the incorporation of the economies of the settlement's Indigenous peoples into global markets. From there the chapter moves to the commemorative myths and symbols of the distinctive European ethnoreligious landscapes at places such as Neubergthal and Veregin. In examining the heritage interpretation of Motherwell Homestead National Historic Site, the chapter takes into account the broader patterns of Canadian, European, and American settlement that facilitated the widespread township land-use pattern across the West during the boom years of the settler-colonial period. These places, along with their national and regional texts, reveal how land is understood and valued, how real and imagined histories of community are celebrated, and how memory is cherished, burnished, and invented. They reveal, as well, how landscapes were reshaped as colonial topographies and how "founding father" narratives came to define the land as legacy and the patriotic backdrops of cultural communities.

CHAPTER 4

Contested Space: Commemorating Indigenous Places of Resistance

Places have many memories and the question of which memories are promoted and which cease to be memories at all is a political question. Places become sites of contestation over which memories to evoke.

Tim Cresswell, *Place: An Introduction*

Place and Resistance

In Canada, concepts of heritage and historic place continue to evolve, especially for Indigenous peoples, who, since the 1970s, have mounted a growing resistance to outsider and often racialized views of their history and their cultural places of significance. By the 1990s, administrative strategies from government such as Parks Canada's Cultural Resource Management Policy facilitated the incorporation of Indigenous places of significance into traditional interpretive models, although the process remained slow, largely ill-defined, and very often set within the context of a settler colonialist perspective. More often than not, Indigenous themes were simply grafted on to the interpretation of existing historic sites, especially at fur trade forts that had for decades told stories only of the expansion of mercantile colonialism. As a growing Indigenous influence helped to establish new priorities and new narratives, we began to see in western Canada an increasing emphasis upon the heritage and significance of Indigenous space. Yet, as Cole Harris has argued, histories and commemorations involving Indigenous populations as a whole rarely approach the topic from the perspective of space or what he calls a "spatialized" understanding of how a people are defined and how a landscape is reimagined.[1] If not attached in some subordinate way to colonialist histories, these commemorations continue to portray Indigenous places as essentially pre-contact spaces and landscapes, putting less weight upon post-contact sites of occupation and, most importantly, the contested spaces and sites of resistance that inherently challenge the commemorative traditions of the settler discourse. Eventually, through new priorities and the emergence of new narratives from Indigenous and non-Indigenous writers, activists, and public and academic historians in western Canada, we have begun to see greater emphasis on the heritage of Indigenous space.

But discussing Indigenous space in the West leads to issues around economies both regional and beyond, as well as political (and economic) relations with the state. As well, perceptions of family, kinship, culture, and social life help to define space, particularly in regard to the origins of the Métis in the West. Historian Heather Devine explores such contexts in her study of ethnogenesis and the concept of kinship within a larger socio-cultural understanding beyond the simple classifications of blood and race. Using a method known as "prosopography," or the application of genealogical reconstruction and the knowledge of naming practices found in primary documents such as parish records, census data, Indian Affairs documentation, and Métis scrip, Devine is able to reconstruct kinship patterns and socio-political alliances to track migration patterns and the adoption of First Nation, Métis, or European-Canadian self-identification within particular families. Using the types of sources mentioned above (and others), Devine studied the Canadien Dejarlais family and its descendants over four centuries. Her work makes the point that Indigenous people defined themselves less as a racial category than a community (or communities) related by affiliations acquired through kinship and the commonality of social and economic patterns reflected in such things as settlement or mobility, as well as Christian practices. As in Red River, where class and patterns of subsistence helped to define Métisness, the families of the Athabasca region, as Devine demonstrates, viewed themselves in much the same way.[2] Key to such a definition are space and place and the history of a kinship-based or economic Indigenous presence that would be contested with the intrusion of settler culture.

In Manitoba and Saskatchewan, resistance to national narratives and designations has helped to redefine the character of those places that have long been associated with Canadian colonialism. Although such sites as the Battle of Seven Oaks and Upper Fort Garry in Manitoba are often associated with fur trade and settlement history, they can stand apart as meaningful spaces of Indigenous resistance to colonial hegemony. Similarly, and perhaps more evidently, the commemorated 1885 battle sites of Saskatchewan establish a similar counternarrative, an oppositional memory that disputes the authority of a state-sponsored heritage. This chapter will trace how the local, regional, and national heritage of these places has evolved since original designation, sketching out the way contemporary Indigenous perspectives have challenged the authority of commemorations as well as their interpretations over time. We can also better understand the link between an evolving historiography and the commemorative paradigm regarding the heritage of Indigenous place in the West as we gain a new perspective on Indigenous peoples as historical, cultural, and political players in the struggle for contested space. Such contested places represent the interrogation of memory, raising questions about which memories are invoked and which are forgotten—in essence, commemoration as a political act.[3] Agendas are politicized in order to serve the interests of individuals, of racial or religious communities, of colonizers, and of the state.

It is perhaps at battlefields, or at contested spaces in general, where the values of heritage, place, and memory most visibly and distinctively come together. Here we find defined places and physical landscapes, although many have been lost to urbanization or are no longer contextualized within a broader historical setting. Yet, those that survive more or less intact and are commemorated for their historical significance can demonstrate the evolution of specific interpretations in familiar places. These spaces and monuments may tell stories of conflicts that are often univocal and occasionally multi-voiced; they can potentially relate historical events that are transformative or invoke some great passion and reflection. Changing interpretations over time can also indicate shifting cultural values and the way the past informs the present. Designated as "official heritage," however, they demand a certain level of attention and help to provide a usable past. How that "usable past" is defined and by whom remains a subject of debate, as do the issues surrounding contested space within post-colonial theory.

Looking more broadly, contested space and the changing perspectives around the interpretation of battlefields as places of memory are discussed by American historian Thomas Brown in his book *Civil War Canon*. Brown suggests that in the U.S Confederate canons of memory have traditionally assisted white southerners in negotiating shifting political, social, and economic positions. These canons of memory, he argues, have adapted to address the challenges of modernity since the end of the Civil War, as some people (and here we might include the southern romantics) use these places to renew a faded myth, while the children of the civil rights era look for what he calls "a useable Confederate past."[4] As I write this, however, America is in the process of removing the approximately 700 monuments to the confederacy throughout the South and elsewhere, essentially memorials to the glorification of a slave past. By far, the greatest number of these public statues and monuments were erected not during Reconstruction (1865 to 1877) but between 1900 and 1920, arguably the peak of segregation, Jim Crow, and Klu Klux Klan activity in the South. Interestingly, a small spike of monument building occurred in the early 1960s, around the passing of the Civil Rights Act in 1964.[5] The removal of these monuments has occasionally been accompanied by white supremacist violence as in Charlottesville, Virginia, in August of 2017. There are few state-sponsored memorials to slavery that exist in a land where arguably the "lost cause" narrative of the Confederacy continues to override the consideration of secession as treason and slavery as criminal.

Seven Oaks and Contested Space

It is fitting, I think, to begin an analysis of the commemoration of Indigenous places of resistance in Manitoba with the Battle of Seven Oaks, as it is commonly known in English, or La bataille de la Grenouillère, as it is called in French. Seven Oaks has enjoyed an honoured, if controversial, place in the historiography of western Canada, and is generally recognized as a seminal event in the colonization history of the West. For Métis peoples, Seven Oaks has traditionally represented the emergence of strong nationalist sentiments, with the events of June 1816 at Red River occasionally characterized as the "birth" of the Métis Nation, although that interpretation is often overstated.[6] On the other hand, an older and conventional Anglo historiography once represented the battle as the violent struggle of European settlers against the "forces of barbarism," a civilization-versus-savagery model that telescoped colonial relations in the era of European expansion and consolidation. The historiography of a more recent era, however, has tended to be less inflamed, usually choosing to view the battle in tragic terms as either the resistance of a marginalized people against economic domination or more frequently as the inevitable outcome of a commercial war in the West among rival fur trading concerns.[7] Despite this changing historiography, the Battle of Seven Oaks continues to represent a significant example of the colonialism/resistance paradigm in European-Indigenous relations. The first commemoration of the battle was by the Historical and Scientific Society of Manitoba when they erected an obelisk monument in a small park alongside Main Street in Winnipeg in 1891.[8] Later, in 1920, the monument site was declared to be of national historic significance by the Historic Sites and Monuments Board of Canada. A federal plaque, dating from 1951, is affixed to the monument.

Paradoxically perhaps, Seven Oaks represents a unique perspective on memory and place in that the exact site of the battlefield, located in what is now the City of Winnipeg, has been lost to the rapid suburban expansion of what became the district of West Kildonan in the North End of the city. Originally part of the municipality of Kildonan, the area was split into eastern and western halves in 1914 and assumed its present configuration in 1921. The approximate site of the battle is marked on Peter Fidler's 1817 rough map of the Red River Settlement in the area known as la Grenouillère, or Frog Plain, a river-edge prairie slough now part of old suburban Winnipeg. However, the present-day site of the Battle of Seven Oaks monument on the east side of Main Street near Rupertsland Avenue in north Winnipeg is only an approximation of the historic place. Fidler's 1817 map shows the battle site to have been on lots 8 and 9 "a little to the N.W. of the Road from Fort Douglas to Frog Plain." A grove of oak trees is depicted just north on lots 10 and 11.[9] The Aaron Arrowsmith 1819 map of the Red River Settlement also locates the battle site on lots 8 and 9, although this map is based largely upon Fidler's earlier map with some topographical details added.

Lack of precise historical knowledge of the location of the battle-field might be due in part to the changing nature of historical writing on the event. Various texts on the battle, as historian Lyle Dick has argued, "chart a trajectory from the raw pluralistic origins of prairie historiography in the early nineteenth-century controversies over Seven Oaks to the polished hierarchical structures of twentieth-century historical writing."[10] After citing the 1818 Coltman Report on the battle, Dick, in his examination of the narratives that surround "story" and "discourse" in the historical writing about the conflict, surveys the version of events found in the works of Charles Bell (an amateur historian) and George Bryce (a cleric and academic), before examining later interpretations when conflicting perspectives were "rewritten, overwritten, or erased by its rival."[11] Here the accounts of Seven Oaks by twentieth-century historians such as Chester Martin, George Stanley, and William L. Morton are cited in the ascendency of the "massacre" narrative. Ultimately it was the changing narrative on Seven Oaks and the perspective of the savage Métis "Other" that would emerge in western Canadian writing, a perspective that would help justify the earlier dispossession of Métis lands. It was arguably the pluralism of many of the early accounts of the battle—writing that incorporated a multi-voiced approach—that did not concentrate upon the significance of place or at least did not view as critical the designation of the exact location of the conflict. That importance did not come until later with the erection of the 1891 monument and the hegemony of the massacre narrative that would elevate the significance of Seven Oaks in the campaign against an Indigenous past. By that time, however, place had been lost, although the erection of the monument signalled the creation of a new image for Anglo-Canadian settler society on the prairies.

Considerable background goes into telling the story of the events of the 19th of June, 1816. By the early years of the nineteenth century, the forks of the Red and Assiniboine rivers had begun to play an important role in the extensive provisioning network of the North West Company, a role that was central to the development of a Métis economy in the West. With the establishment of Fort Gibraltar at the forks in 1810, the North West Company enjoyed a significant advantage over their rivals in the control of the pemmican trade of the Red River and Assiniboine River valleys. Keenly aware of this, the Hudson's Bay Company (HBC) determined that a presence at the forks was required. The ambitious settlement scheme of Thomas Douglas, the Fifth Earl of Selkirk, a major shareholder in the HBC, would help combat Nor'Wester influence in the lower Red River district, disrupt the Canadians' critical supply line to the interior, provide a home for retiring HBC servants, and potentially become the supplier of agricultural foodstuffs to the fur trade. Although the first party of Selkirk's Scottish settlers who arrived at the forks in 1812 met no opposition from the Métis inhabitants of the district, the story of the first years of the settlement was marked by increasing friction with the North West Company and its Métis employees, leading ultimately to the pemmican embargo of 1814, the burning of the Selkirk Settlers' crops and homes in the summer of 1815, the sacking of Brandon House by the North West Company, and the destruction of Fort Gibraltar by Colin Robertson of the HBC in 1816. The stage was now set for the events at Seven Oaks; the intense competition for furs and the gathering storm over commercial and geographical control of the Red River district would lead to the conflict between a fur trade empire under challenge and its lightly regarded opponent.

In June of 1816 a large party of Métis freighters under the leadership of Cuthbert Grant, a North West Company clerk and trader, was in the process of moving a supply of pemmican from the upper Assiniboine to Nor'Wester canoe brigades on Lake Winnipeg. Hoping to avoid the forks, which was now controlled by the HBC, Grant's party left the Assiniboine in the vicinity of what is now Omand's Creek and moved overland, coming within a few miles of Fort Douglas, the colony fort located approximately one and a half kilometres north of the river junction. They were spotted by the inhabitants of the post, and a small group of settlers under the command of the colony governor, Robert Semple, moved out to meet Grant's party, intercepting them some distance northwest of Fort Douglas, near la Grenouillère. A verbal confrontation between the hostile parties led to a general exchange of gunfire (Anglo-Canadian historiography generally accused the Métis of firing the first shot, although the 1818 Coltman Report concluded that it was in fact one of Semple's men who opened fire) and resulted in the death of twenty-one settlers, including Governor Semple, and one Métis man. Grant then seized Fort Douglas while the surviving colonists embarked for York Factory. Later, Lord Selkirk and a contingent of hired De Meuron soldiers recaptured Fort Douglas, and colony settlers, who had been encamped near Lake Winnipeg, were persuaded to return to the settlement. The merger of the two competing fur trade companies four years later in 1821 put an end to the open hostilities between the Métis and the HBC-sponsored colony along the Red River. Ultimately, Red River would be transformed into a largely Indigenous settlement and would remain so until the arrival of the Canadians and other immigrants after 1870.

As Manitoba and the West increasingly came under the control of Anglo-Canadian immigrants, their version of the events at Seven Oaks—the massacre narrative—became the dominant one. Métis perspectives, as well as the official record of the battle as represented by the Coltman Report of 1818, were lost to the ascendency of settler colonialism, the racialization of the Métis, and, to a lesser extent, the official commemoration of a prevailing and authorized heritage. Only in recent times have rival perspectives challenged the socially and politically invoked memories that are embedded in place as competing viewpoints challenge the accepted historiography and defy traditional tourism commodities.[12]

Public commemoration of the Battle of Seven Oaks began with the erection in 1891 of a monument near the battle site by the Historical and Scientific Society of Manitoba. On land donated by the Inkster family, and with funds from the Countess of Selkirk (the daughter-in-law of Thomas Douglas, the Fifth Earl of Selkirk), the almost three-metre-high (nine feet) monument was unveiled on 19 June 1891, the seventy-fifth anniversary of the battle. It was a solemn ceremony with a number of dignitaries, including Lieutenant-Governor John Schultz, historians George Bryce and Charles Bell, the Rev. Samuel Matheson (later the Anglican archbishop of Rupert's Land), and John MacBeth, the president of the Manitoba Historical Society and a direct descendent of an original Selkirk Settler. Among the crowd were other representatives of the old Scots-Irish families of Red River. Some of the speeches from that ceremony were reproduced in the Historical Society's *Transactions,* a series of lectures published intermittently between 1879 and 1980. The account of the Seven Oaks ceremony is contained in the 1891 series written by Charles Bell and George Bryce.[13] In reading the speeches from that day, one is struck first (and not surprisingly) by their serious tone but as well by the absence of bellicosity in the remarks. The word "massacre" was never uttered—that interpretation would come later with revisionist Anglo historiography—and, instead, a tone of sadness and tragedy seemed to mark the day. If Rev. Canon Matheson described the memorial as "the scene of a battle bitter in its cruel intent," the lieutenant-governor noted the "differences of opinion as to the causes which led to the

Figure 37. The 1891 monument to the battle of Seven Oaks, surrounded by more contemporary interpretive signage related to the battle and its aftermath, 2019. Located on the east side of Main Street in north Winnipeg, the monument represents the oldest historical commemoration in western Canada. Credit: Robert Coutts.

combat and loss of life these stones record," while President John MacBeth described Seven Oaks as "an unfortunate conflict" and a "lamentable affair." Under the title "Seven Oaks," the inscription on the monument reads simply: "Erected in 1891 by the Manitoba Historical Society through the generosity of the Countess of Selkirk on the site of Seven Oaks, where fell Governor Robert Semple and twenty officers and men, June 19, 1816." No mention is made of the one Métis person killed in the incident.

In 1920 the Seven Oaks monument came to the attention of the Historic Sites and Monuments Board of Canada, which had been formed only one year earlier. Unable to pay the taxes on the monument site, the Lord Selkirk Association of Rupert's Land, the organization that owned and maintained the monument, approached Prime Minister Arthur Meighen to find a suitable owner for the site. Meighen passed along the request to the HSMBC. According to the minutes of the Board, in January of 1920 it agreed to assume ownership of the monument and the land.[14] Further, it was agreed that the site was of national historic significance and should "receive attention in the way of preservation."[15] The land was eventually transferred to the Crown three years later in 1923.

Unlike HSMBC recommendations from more recent decades, no reason was given for the Board's decision to declare the Battle of Seven Oaks a national historic site, and no background paper (now referred to by Parks Canada as an "Agenda Paper") was prepared. At the time the minutes simply noted the decision of the members of the Board and no discussion was recorded. No plaque text was presented prior to designation, as the Board simply highlighted the original 1891 inscription engraved on the monument.[16] Notably, the battle was declared a national historic "site," not a national historic "event," even though the exact location of the battle was unknown. The site became simply the monument and small plot of land adjacent to Main Street and, like a lot of monuments, only indistinctly connected to the larger concept of historic place. In 1951 the Board attached its own bronze plaque to the monument, although, according to the minutes, it chose to retain the original inscription.[17] In 1956 the Board abandoned plans to install a plaque bearing the names of those killed in the battle when the marker did not include the one Métis member of Grant's party who died on the battlefield.[18] In 1977 the Board installed a revised plaque (although the 1951 date remains). The current text reads:

> Here at the Frog Plain, on June 19, 1816, Robert Semple, Governor of the Red River Settlement, and about 26 men confronted a North West Company brigade from the Assiniboine River, led by the young Métis clerk, Cuthbert Grant. The Métis saw the settlement as a threat to their way of life; Semple, brave but obstinate, was prepared to insist on his authority as Governor. Tempers flared, a shot was fired, and Semple and twenty of his men were cut down. Regardless of what Grant's plan had originally been, he was now committed to action, and went on to capture Fort Douglas, headquarters of the Settlement.

Although this current plaque text does not use the word "massacre," and it is the Métis who are "confronted," it does couch the battle in very passive terms with phrases such as "tempers flared" and "a shot was fired."The roughly 600 characters of a standard federal plaque text rarely allow for interpretive subtleties. More importantly, however, one sentence—"The Metis saw the settlement as a threat to their way of life"—suggests the continuation of a settler-colonialist perspective. The 2009 Statement of Commemorative Intent, the Parks Canada policy that lays out the reasons for national significance, expands on the sentence but continues the colonialist narrative by indicating that Seven Oaks "represents the conflict between two different ways of life, that of the Métis and the Red River Settlers."[19] What was in essence a commercial and territorial conflict is reduced instead to a cultural one. Neither the plaque nor the Statement of Commemorative Intent mentions the Pemmican Proclamation,[20] an act of hostility and a direct attack on Métis livelihoods, leaving the reader to infer that Indigenous people were unable to cope with changing circumstances without reverting to ferocity, or what historian William L. Morton called the "wild blood of the brules."[21] What were these "two different ways of life" described in the federal document and why is there an assumption that a bloody conflict was the inevitable result? With the history of early colonies such as Red River, we deal with the interpretation of intercultural spaces of contact, the borderlands or contact zones, that often remain perceptions of an idealized past and, in the case of Seven Oaks, a racialized history that not so subtly underscores the theme of the "Native savage." Such spaces of contact are often used to maintain the hegemony of the colonialist narrative and the inevitable triumph, after much hardship and adversity, of the "superior way of life" of the colonizer.[22]

If official government interpretations of Seven Oaks did not engage with the massacre narrative, at least not overtly, such was not the case with the mid-twentieth-century works of historians such as Marcel Giraud and Morton. With a selective and biased use of sources, both helped to establish a historical perspective on the battle as a manifestation of Métis savagery, creating a historical discourse that fostered and celebrated the ascendency of Anglo prairie culture.[23] And it was that academic interpretation that strongly influenced more contemporary attitudes in the years to come. More recently, there is Lyle Dick's thorough and nuanced account of the historiography surrounding Seven Oaks and the construction of a historical tradition; however, this is not the place to examine that scholarly literature in detail.[24] Suffice to say,

Figure 38. A modern depiction of the Battle of Seven Oaks. Commissioned by Parks Canada in the 1980s, this painting, much like the C.W. Jefferys 1945 drawing of the battle, erroneously depicts mounted Métis charging Robert Semple's men, who are on foot. In fact, the Métis had dismounted shortly after the first shots were fired. Credit: Parks Canada.

though, in more recent times scholarly treatment of the battle has been far more balanced and the massacre narrative has all but disappeared, at least in the serious histories; less so in some popular sources, however.[25]

How has Seven Oaks as contested space been interpreted in non-scholarly treatments, most particularly in the commemorative media? The ceremony that marked the opening of the 1891 monument, as well as the installation of government plaques and the development of the federal Statement of Commemorative Intent, were generally civil endeavours, although the language, at least in the 1891 ceremony, remained distinctly colonialist in its tone. More recently, on the bicentennial of the battle in June of 2016, a number of interpretive panels were erected adjacent to the Main Street monument, the result of funds provided by the federal and provincial governments as well as cultural and community organizations.[26] The panels provide the historical background leading up to Seven Oaks, as well as an account of the battle and its legacy in the history of the West. The interpretation begins with a portrayal of the establishment of the colony and a short history of the Métis peoples of the region. Signage then provides a description of the Pemmican War, and in a panel entitled "A Storm is Gathering . . ." the story is told of the immediate events leading up to the battle. A description of the battle itself is told in a text imaginatively labelled "Red Sky in the Evening," and a postscript panel is simply called "Legacy." An additional panel entitled "Finding the Past in the Present" tells the story of how the grade four class at Governor Semple School in north Winnipeg studied the battle in 2011 and their reunion five years later to reminisce about the experience. Throughout the various public texts, the interpretation focuses on the economic and territorial stresses that led to the conflict at Seven Oaks and avoids the traditional cultural stereotypes that see the Métis actions as the result of "the conflict between two different ways of life." It is a subtle, yet very significant, change of language, removing the clash-of-cultures narrative and the implied inferiority of Indigenous populations. Seven Oaks did not create a sense of nationhood for the Métis but was instead an expression of that identity. As with most cultures, the freedom to practise commerce is critical to nationhood, but it was with the Battle of Seven Oaks that the Métis moved further toward commercial independence and to establishing a sense of place in the West.

With Seven Oaks we see how contemporary Indigenous viewpoints have challenged the authority of commemoration. An evolving historiography and the recognition of Indigenous resistance in the West can lead to an enhanced understanding of Indigenous peoples as historical, cultural, political, and, most importantly, contemporary players in the struggle for contested space.

Place and Replace: Seven Oaks to Upper Fort Garry

"Place" can mean simply geographical mapping and territoriality, but of course it has a much wider significance. Emma LaRocque, in tracing Métis ideas of place, describes the concepts of "attachment, rootedness, groundedness, materiality, familiality, home, homelands."[27] Similarly, identity, meaning, and the power of memory, especially those memories associated with space and place, provide the reality for expression and experience. When we recall events associated with place, the landscape becomes a centre of meaning, not an abstract physical location but a geography charged with personal significance that shapes the meaning of community, identity, and social and cultural belonging. If the Battle of Seven Oaks has come to signify historical and cultural claims to place, it is the image of the buffalo hunter and the paddling voyageur, the dispossessed of the Red River Settlement, and later the "Road Allowance People," that illustrates how the story of contested space has remained a persistent theme in the history of Indigenous peoples in Manitoba.

For early Manitoba Anglo historiography Seven Oaks became a sort of founding storyline, a heroic mythology and master narrative in the colonialist project. In this scenario Indigenous people were presented, according to Lyle Dick, as "lawless, violent, unstable, and irresponsible."[28] To underscore this outlook, the trajectory of Indigenous insurgence was continued to the Red River Resistance of 1869–70 and onward to 1885. Writing in 1885, the historian George Bryce wrote that, "having tasted blood in the death of Governor Semple, they [the Métis] were turbulent ever after . . . and preserved their warlike tastes. . . . It need not that I should recite to you the doings in the rebellion of 1869–70, it was simply the outbreak of the 'Seven-oaks' and 'Sayer' affairs again."[29]

While Bryce, Morton, and others drew such straight-line connections, did public commemoration follow the same path? As with the Seven Oaks battlefield, Upper Fort Garry and its role in the Red River Resistance of 1869–70 can stand apart as a meaningful space of Indigenous resistance to colonial hegemony. The events of that critical period in the province's history, like Seven Oaks before it, embody a landscape of memory and meaning, a racialized place charged with social, political, and cultural importance. Yet, has the heritage commemoration of the upper fort evolved since its original designation as a national historic site, and can we trace the way contemporary perspectives might have challenged the authority of commemoration and interpretation over time?

Upper Fort Garry, the massive stone fort built by the HBC in the late 1830s and enlarged in the 1850s, was the centre of a sprawling community of diverse peoples living on river lots that fronted the Red, Assiniboine, and Seine rivers. The fort was a critical supply and transport hub in the western fur trade, and for much of the eighteenth and nineteenth centuries, Upper Fort Garry and its predecessor forts at the forks linked the economy of the region to a system of trade throughout western North America.

Surrounding the upper fort was the Red River Settlement. For much of its existence, at least until the influx of settlers from the Canadas after mid-century, the colony was a Métis settlement. A small population of Scottish descendants of the Selkirk Settlers, a handful of retired Orkney servants of the HBC, some French-Canadian settlers, and First Nations peoples were dwarfed by a much larger population of French- and English-speaking Métis who inhabited the settlement's various parishes. Reliant upon a mixed economy of agriculture, hunting, trading, provisioning, and seasonal wage labour with the HBC, the Métis of Red River adapted to the realities of a self-sufficient life in an isolated colony.

Throughout much of the nineteenth century, Upper Fort Garry at the forks remained the centre of Indigenous Red River, the focus for commerce and trade, administrative activities, civil government, and judicial proceedings. From Upper Fort Garry grew the roots of a new Indigenous commerce, a challenge to the HBC monopoly in the old settlement and, later, the development of Winnipeg and a burgeoning economy of supply, manufacture, and transport. Canadian annexationists began to arrive in the settlement in the late 1850s, and HBC rule in the Northwest came increasingly under attack by Canada and Great Britain. Indigenous influence in Red River also came under siege. As negotiations to transfer the region to Canadian authority commenced in the 1860s, the Métis inhabitants of the West became alarmed that their land and cultural rights, including the protection of language, faith, and education, would not be respected.

As with previous threats to land and commercial liberties, many of Red River's Indigenous population rose up in opposition to colonial influence. Louis Riel soon emerged as the leader of Métis resistance in Red River. In the vacuum that was civil government in Red River, Riel seized Upper Fort Garry in early November of 1869, consolidating his authority in the settlement. His decision to seize the upper fort reinforced Indigenous claims to space, especially the racialized and contested space of the fur trade in which the Métis had played a subordinate role. In December of 1869 Riel declared a provisional government and drafted a list of rights, and in January 1870 met at Upper Fort Garry with Donald Smith, the HBC official and special

commissioner from the Canadian government, in front of a crowd of
1,000 mainly Métis local settlers. Riel's decision to work with a representative assembly ensured that peace and relative unity would prevail
in Red River. When he permitted the execution of an unruly Canadian
prisoner, Thomas Scott, in March 1870, he introduced a flashpoint in
Ontario politics, although that debate did not immediately disrupt
affairs in Red River. The English-speaking Métis of the settlement
joined their French-speaking counterparts in the Legislative Assembly
of Assiniboia and voted unanimously to accept the Manitoba Act and
to enter Confederation as the first new province. Later that summer
Riel was forced to flee the settlement ahead of the arrival of Colonel
Garnet Wolseley's troops that had been sent west from the Canadas.
While the Provisional Government had won concessions and a new
province was created, the Métis were soon subjected to the "Reign of
Terror," as incoming troops and Canadian colonizers used violence
to show their displeasure with Métis status in the new province.[30]
The history of Winnipeg in the early 1870s demonstrates how these
early Canadian immigrants and their armed force effectively limited
Indigenous rights to place and cultural worth in the old settlement and
drove many from Manitoba to seek new lands to the west. As contested
space, decisive moments in the history of western North America took
place on the ground at the forks and within this fort, a site about the
size of several city blocks and containing only a dozen or so buildings
and a few hundred residents.

Upper Fort Garry was an early commemoration of the HSMBC; its
national designation in 1924 made it part of "Forts Rouge, Garry, and
Gibraltar National Historic Site of Canada." Like other commemorations at the time, no specific reason was given for the designation,
and the plaque still affixed to the surviving stone gate of the fort in
downtown Winnipeg reads rather cryptically: "Near this site stood the
following forts: Fort Rouge, under La Verendrye, 1738; Fort Gibraltar,
of the North West Company, 1810, became Fort Garry of the Hudson's
Bay Company, 1822; replaced by Upper Fort Garry, of stone, begun
1835, extended in 1850's when this gateway was erected, demolished
1882."[31] Although the specific designation pertaining to Upper Fort
Garry is early, the forks of the Red and Assiniboine rivers, where the
upper fort was located, was not declared a national historic site until
1974 and focuses on a thematic history that dates back thousands of

Figure 39. Interior of Upper Fort Garry, c. 1880. Credit: Archives of Manitoba.

years.[32] The HSMBC plaque reads: "Strategically located at the junction of two major rivers which form part of a vast continental network, this spot has witnessed many of the key events of Western Canadian history. This was a traditional native stopping place and for this reason La Vérendrye erected Fort Rouge near here in 1738. It has been a centre for trade and exploration, a focus for the first permanent European settlement in the Canadian West, cradle of the province of Manitoba, nucleus of the city of Winnipeg, a hub of rail and road transport, and the gateway for the settlement of the prairies." The boundaries of the site are somewhat vague. However, the commemoration does recognize a larger sense of place and the development of pre-contact trading networks, the expansion of the post-contact fur trade, and the early development of Winnipeg as a hub for rail transport. Despite the breadth of the historic themes developed for The Forks, the land now designated by Parks Canada as The Forks National Historic Site, and indeed the wider commercial and recreational area known in Winnipeg as simply "The Forks," does not include the St. Boniface side of the Red River where the significance of heritage place is as much a part of the historic river junction as the west side of the river.

The roughly 6,000 years of history commemorated at The Forks makes the site the most temporally extensive, still inhabited, historic location in the country, with Upper Fort Garry representing only a limited element of its heritage. The Forks as a multi-millennia "meeting place" has remained the site's overarching theme since its development in the late 1980s, even if that claim has been at least partly exaggerated as part of the long-term marketing campaign by both Parks Canada and The Forks North Portage Partnership.[33] As Claire Elizabeth Campbell has argued, ironically it has been The Forks's historical identity as a meeting place that has effectively encouraged extensive modern developments of an ahistorical character. "By characterizing the Forks as a meeting place," she writes, "whether six thousand years ago, two hundred years ago, or last Saturday, we can insert present-day activity into a genealogy of use."[34] Outside of the modest Parks Canada–controlled green space, The Forks today is dominated by commercial, retail, recreational, and cultural developments (the nearby Canadian Museum for Human Rights being the largest). Once an almost forgotten railway yard, The Forks is now largely a commercial attraction (and occasional gathering place) with only oblique or vague marketing connections to the history of that site.

For nearby Upper Fort Garry, which was demolished in 1883, the only remaining vestige of the original structure was the post's north gate, a stone archway hidden among the buildings of the city's down-town core and adjacent to a gas station. In the early 1980s the gate was augmented by a reconstructed north wall and accompanied by outdoor interpretive signage that focused on the layout of the HBC fortification in the nineteenth century. Little coverage was given to the larger role of the stone fort or to the daily lives of its Métis and Scottish inhabitants. In 2004 much of the original land where Upper Fort Garry once stood was declared by the City of Winnipeg as surplus property. The newly formed Friends of Upper Fort Garry submitted a proposal to develop the site as a historic park and, with money raised from private and public donors, assumed title to the property in 2009.[35] Archaeological work at the site was followed by such physical developments as the use of stone to outline the location of original buildings, the creation of pathways, the planting of trees, and the building of a Heritage Wall that mimics the location of the fort's original west wall. (In the case of Upper Fort Garry, the sense of place is realized more with landscape elements than with attempts to speculatively reconstruct the buildings of the original fort.) Website materials provide information for the

Figure 40. Entranceway, interpretive signage, and original stone gate at Upper Fort Garry Heritage Provincial Park in downtown Winnipeg, 2020. Credit: Robert Coutts.

public and for school groups, and QR (Quick Response) codes at the site provide material on buildings, events, and personalities. In 2010 the site was designated a provincial park and was opened to the public in the summer of 2015. Planned developments included the construction of a National Métis Museum and interpretive centre adjacent to the site.[36] However, more recent plans have the Métis National Heritage Centre located at the heritage Bank of Montreal building located on the southeast corner of Portage and Main streets.

As part of the development of Upper Fort Garry Provincial Park, a historical overview was developed along with a number of themes related to the history and significance of the site. Early on it was decided to focus a good deal of the interpretation upon the Indigenous history of the fort and more specifically its role as the "birthplace of

Manitoba," referring generally to the events of 1869–70. Under the thematic title "Upper Fort Garry and the Red River Resistance: The Birth of Manitoba and Winnipeg and the Growth of Canada," much of the interpretation emphasized the fort's role in the entry of Manitoba into Confederation.[37] While other topics such as the history of the fur trade and the role of the Selkirk Settlers were given coverage, it was the struggle for Métis rights in the West that gave the upper fort its real commemorative significance as an Indigenous sense of place that emerged from conflict, attachment, and nationhood.[38]

Decentring the Commemorative Narrative:
The 1885 Resistance in Saskatchewan

Sociologist John Urry's phrase the "tourist gaze" describes the set of expectations and perspectives that visitors often have when they participate in heritage tourism and the search for an "authentic" experience.[39] This "gaze," or a similar set of expectations, can influence how people interact with historic places, especially when these spaces are presented as tourism commodities to be consumed. While heritage can be approached in many different ways and for many different reasons, it is, as Urry suggests, the socially and politically embedded memories that form a part of place that are frequently the source of disagreement.[40] In western Canada the historically contested sites of the 1885 Northwest Resistance reveal a social and political heritage embedded with a variety of memories and meanings. Within a manifest destiny perspective, these places have traditionally represented the expression of the Canadian and colonial narrative: the expansion of dominion policy. For Indigenous people, however, these places represent loss and opposition to this narrative, yet at the same time symbolizing the survival of culture and identity. Curator and historian Matthew McRae has argued that while in the early twentieth century there were no Indigenous monuments to 1885 other than at Batoche (although a number of monuments had been erected to Canada's soldiers who fought in the campaign), the Indigenous memory of 1885 survived in the oral traditions of the Métis and First Nations people throughout the West. "And when English Canada tried to impose its own narrative in the heartlands of these memory communities," McRae writes, "conflicts arose."[41] For decades, commemoration and designation created tensions as Indigenous communities were portrayed as outside, and opposed to, a single and unchallenged national story.

Like nationalism itself, federal designation customarily searches for a heritage that is centralist, unambiguous, and "useful." However, as both literal and commemorative battlefields, contested heritage places such as the 1885 sites signify landscapes of memory that have pluralized the past, or have at least decentred that past from the single-voiced messages of authorized commemoration. The ongoing renegotiation of the past in the present reveals that certain places carry additional layers of meaning and thus more potential for dissonance, conflict, and resistance to a sanctioned discourse.[42] "Dissonance," for Saskatchewan sites such as Batoche, Fort Battleford, Duck Lake, Fish Creek, and others, refers to their roles as places of tourism consumption—the tourist gaze—as well as their political roles as Indigenous sites of resistance.

Traditional commemorations of the 1885 resistance sites, not unlike Seven Oaks and Upper Fort Garry, tend to put emphasis upon history as a chronicle of winners and losers. Historian Walter Hildebrandt has called these "sacred sites" where, ideologically, the past is interpreted as the conquerors see it.[43] Fort Battleford, commemorated as a North West Mounted Police post that helped further Canadian expansionism in the West, is also the place where eight First Nations participants (five Cree and three Stoney) in the 1885 uprising were hanged; their story of resistance, along with their mass gravesite, is not a part of designation and forms little of the site interpretation. In more recent times, and much like the federal interpretation of the Battle of Seven Oaks, interpretive perspectives have been, on the face of it at least, more moderate. However, like Seven Oaks, site interpretation at places such as Battleford is increasingly noteworthy for its passivity. On the site's website, for instance, visitors are encouraged to "discover the perfect storm of events which led to a confrontation between members of local Cree First Nations and the scarlet serge-clad officers of the North West Mounted Police," and where in1885 "things take a tragic turn."[44] "Perfect storm" and "tragic turn" are anodyne phrases with little meaning, serving to disempower and disassemble history as being without cause and effect, essentially rootless and inert. Conflict is minimized, and, as authorized heritage, it is safe history where some may learn but none (except Indigenous visitors) will be offended.

Figure 41. Commanding Officer's Residence, built in 1876, at Fort Battleford National Historic Site. Credit: Parks Canada.

Fort Battleford, located along the North Saskatchewan River near its confluence with the Battle River in the west-central part of the province, was designated as nationally significant in 1923, although the site remained a community-based museum until its transfer to the federal government as a national historic park in 1951.[45] The original HSMBC plaque, erected at the site in 1924, reads: "Sacked by the Rebel Cree Indians under Poundmaker. Here on 26 May, 1885 after the battle of Batoche and the capture of Riel, Poundmaker and his band surrendered to General Middleton."[46]

Despite the terse language (and misinterpretations) of this original plaque, it, like other commemorations of the Northwest Resistance, came under early criticism, particularly by the journalist W.A. Kennedy, who criticized the "looseness of the language" and the exaggeration of Poundmaker's influence over his followers.[47] In 1951, when Fort Battleford was gifted to the federal government, a new, more fulsome plaque was installed at the site. It read: "Here, in July 1876,

Superintendent James Walker established a post of the North West Mounted Police in the heart of Cree country. "The Fort" grew to a strength of 200. During the uprising of 1885 it gave refuge to more than 400 people and was the base for operations at Cut Knife Hill and Fort Pitt, leading to the surrender of Chief Poundmaker and the search for Big Bear. With the extension of settlement and mechanization of the force it ceased to be the barracks in 1924. Notably, the 1951 plaque played down the "siege" of Fort Battleford by hostile Cree (though in reality it was a desperate search for food by the starving members of Poundmaker's band). Nonetheless, that interpretation remained prominent in many of the site's early publications and is mentioned in the 1997 Statement of Commemorative Intent for Fort Battleford, although the word "siege" is placed in quotation marks.[48] However, no siege occurred, as the fort was never attacked or surrounded and its surrender was never demanded. In fact, Chief Poundmaker went to Battleford to ask for supplies promised to his starving people and to reassure the North West Mounted Police that he had no plans to join Riel. In 2010, after pressure from local Cree First Nations, Parks Canada agreed to cease using the word "siege" in its interpretive description of the events that took place at Battleford in the spring of 1885.[49]

Former Parks Canada historian Alan McCullough has argued that the interpretation of Fort Battleford, like other 1885 sites, has gone through three iterations within the federal system. Early commemoration, he claims, viewed these places as part of "Canada's westward drive to become a transcontinental nation." The second, which appeared in the 1950s, attempted, he suggests, to moderate the colonialist nature of the original commemorations by allowing for the recognition of some Indigenous resistance. The third, McCullough writes, began in the 1970s and, while not abandoning the theme of Canadian expansion, did place greater emphasis upon the societies displaced by this expansion.[50]

Arguably, a fourth iteration exists, the product of changing Parks Canada policy towards historic sites in the 1990s, and specifically the introduction of the Cultural Resource Management Policy (CRM). As part of this policy direction, Parks Canada developed the Commemorative Integrity Statement (CIS) to guide interpretation. At Fort Battleford National Historic Site the Statement of Commemorative Intent, developed in 1997, returns to a largely colonialist interpretation. It reads: "Fort Battleford National Historic

Site of Canada commemorates the role of the North-West Mounted Police at the fort from 1876 to 1885 in extending the Canadian government's interests in the west. The role of the fort during the North-West Rebellion/Resistance of 1885, included its role in the 'siege' of Battleford, as a base for the military operations at Cut Knife Hill, Fort Pitt, and the search for mistahi-maskwa (Big Bear). It was also the site of the surrender of pîhtokahânapiwiýin (Poundmaker) to General Middleton's forces on 26 May 1885."[51] Here, the focus of interpretation remains on the extension of government interests and the fort as a base for military operations. The missed opportunity to broaden the interpretation to describe the negative impact upon local Cree and Métis people, the reactions of starving Indigenous populations, Poundmaker's band in particular, and the role of the fort as a conqueror's bastion against local and regional interests ignores the different voices of history and how they can be revealed in contested space. Instead, as a historic place Battleford continues to speak to the conservatism of public commemoration and interpretation, an interpretation that is centralist and unambiguous, and the reification of traditional narratives.

Perhaps no historic place in western Canada illustrates the themes of contested physical and commemorative space more than Batoche, the site of the penultimate battle in the Northwest Resistance and the subject of much interpretive debate over the decades. Batoche today is a major national historic site in the West, the site of the largest battle of the 1885 campaign, and, more importantly, is viewed as a homeland, or origin community, for Métis peoples, both in the past and today. Each year, "Back to Batoche Days" celebrates the gathering of Métis families in the region who have ties to the site and its origins. Since the late 1970s considerable federal investment has gone into the research, protection, and restoration of the site, including the battlefield, the restored church and rectory, the cemetery and site of the east village, and the remains of the 1885 earthworks—known as a "zareba"—that protected the camp of the Canadian forces under General Middleton during the four-day battle. A large, modern interpretive centre was constructed in the mid-1980s and contains exhibits and a multi-media show. Site tours are also offered to visitors.

The sense of place at Batoche is a critical part of its heritage significance. The landscape is rolling parkland, with fescue grasslands and brush-filled areas in a shallow river valley. The more elevated parts of the site provide a beautiful overview of the South Saskatchewan River. Trembling aspen is the dominant tree species, with some balsam, poplar, birch, and dogwood (red willow) growing near the river. The old river-lot system of land tenure is still visible on the land, as are remnants of the Carlton Trail that once connected early freighting settlements on the prairies between Red River and Fort Edmonton.

While virtually every 1885 site has over time undergone certain changes in its commemoration and interpretation, it is Batoche that has experienced the greatest attention over the decades and, for the reasons stated above, remains the focus of the 1885 Resistance story in the West, not the least for its role as the "headquarters of the rebels."[52] Batoche was commemorated by the HSMBC in 1923, and when a plaque was unveiled at the site two years later on land donated by the Church, controversy erupted when the Roman Catholic Vicar-General of Prince Albert called the Batoche plaque a "gross insult to the men who fought under Riel."[53] Moreover, a delegation from Quebec boycotted the ceremony. Like other commemorative plaques from the period, the text was short, although it predictably reinforced a colonialist and military theme. The text of this first plaque read: "NORTH WEST REBELLION. BATOCHE HEADQUARTERS OF THE REBELS. Its capture by General Middleton after four days of fighting, 9th, 10th, 11th and 12th May 1885, ended the rebellion. The Midland Regiment, the 10th Royal Grenadiers, 90th Regiment, Winnipeg Battery, 'A' Battery, Boulton's Mounted Infantry, and French's Scouts took part in the battle."[54] Despite local protests over the absence of any reference to Riel, Dumont, and the Métis and First Nations defenders, or the fact that the plaque was only in English, the Board refused to change the wording, and, although defaced a few years later, the plaque remained in place for another fourteen years.[55] In the 1930s, as scholarly attention turned to the events of 1885, the historian George Stanley characterized the "rebellions" of 1870 and 1885 as opposition to attempts by Ottawa to control the West. Historical writing of the time also saw the battles, including Batoche, as the conflict between primitive and civilized peoples. As McCullough argues, Stanley's view remained the most widely accepted interpretation in English-language historiography until the 1960s[56] and, while not characteristic of later public history research, it has arguably continued at various historic sites, albeit in a more low-key form, until the present day.

Although the original Batoche plaque was removed in 1939, its bilingual replacement, with at least a mention of Riel, was not erected until 1947. It read: "Batoche. Here, on the 15th of May, 1885, after four days of fighting, the Metis under Louis Riel surrendered to General Middleton commanding the Canadian troops."[57] With regional pressure to acquire Batoche as a national historic park, the National Parks Branch began acquiring assets at the site in the 1950s. The remnants of Middleton's zareba was designated a national historic site in 1950 and the land acquired a few years later. The Batoche Rectory was added in 1955 and the church, known as St. Antoine de Padoue, in 1970.[58]

Not long after, Parks Canada acquired the site of the former east village and the main battlefield (including the remains of Métis rifle pits), the park now totalling approximately 1,093 hectares. With the creation of a Parks Canada office in Winnipeg in 1976 and the hiring of a variety of professionals such as historians, archaeologists, planners, and curators, an extensive program of research was undertaken on the site, on Métis society and history, and on the events of 1885. Plans were soon underway for the development of Batoche as a major national historic site. As part of these advances, the Board developed a new plaque text that signalled an altered direction for the site. It read: "Batoche. In 1872 Xavier Letendre *dit* Batoche founded a village at this site where Metis freighters crossed the South Saskatchewan River. About 50 families had claimed the river lots in the area by 1884. Widespread anxiety regarding land claims and a changing economy provoked a resistance against the Canadian government. Here, 300 Métis and Indians led by Louis Riel and Gabriel Dumont fought a force of 800 men commanded by Major-General Middleton between May 9 and 12, 1885. The resistance failed but the battle did not mean the end of the community of Batoche."[59] This text reflected the changing views of the significance of the site, the evolving interpretation of both the battle and the community, and the sense of place that emerged from a 1972 management plan. The new interpretation, according to the plan, was to focus on "the life style of the Métis in the 1880s," allowing visitors to "think of the story and the action [the battle] from the Métis point of view."[60] The plan effectively advocated for a new voice—the Métis voice—and a view of the story and the place as contested space. As site development moved towards an opening to mark the centennial of the battle in 1985, a subsequent management plan reinforced this direction, focusing on two equivalent

Figure 42. Saint-Antoine de Padoue Church and Rectory at Batoche, c. 1897. Based largely upon the research of Parks Canada historian Diane Payment, the history of the Métis community in the years after 1885 has been an important part of interpretation at this national historic site. Credit: Provincial Archives of Saskatchewan.

Figure 43. Mass grave of nine Métis killed during the 1885 Resistance at Batoche. Credit: Parks Canada.

Figure 44. A reconstructed rifle pit at Batoche National Historic Site, n.d. Credit: Parks Canada.

themes: the Battle of Batoche and the history of Métis settlement in the community. Coupled with this new direction, and based largely upon the work of historian Diane Payment, the history of the community and the region in the post-1885 era was also included in the interpretive storyline at the site.[61] When opened in 1985, Batoche quickly became a major tourist venue, with Parks Canada spending considerable funds on interpretive infrastructure. More importantly, messaging at the site moved away from the traditional and singular focus on the battle, or at least the Canadian view of the battle, to a more inclusive social and cultural history that looked at community and resistance from a variety of perspectives and voices. Visitors were encouraged not only to understand the totality of the site but to understand it as a heritage place and a contested space of ideas and perceptions. Arguably, Batoche NHS had now become the pre-eminent heritage site in the country to challenge, at least implicitly, the colonial viewpoint that for so long had been the accepted narrative.

But if much had changed at Batoche (and at other sites), such local or regional initiatives would not go unchallenged by Parks Canada's National Office in Ottawa. Concerned that they were losing control of the message and the authority of a national narrative to evolving regional perspectives, Parks mandarins initiated the development of Commemorative Intent policy in 1990 that helped to signal a new and conservative era of interpretation, especially in regard to place. Generally opposed to the wider social and cultural narratives that public historians were bringing to many historic sites across the country—including a changing focus from "site" to "place" and the wider meanings that went with it—the new policy effectively restricted interpretations to older (and sometimes much older) historical commemorations. It was a conventional approach, to say the least, and one that used bureaucratic idioms to contest changing interpretations of the past. As Gordon Bennett, at the time the chief of Policy and Strategic Planning for National Historic Sites and one of the architects of commemorative integrity and commemorative intent policies, wrote: "In an era when change is often promoted for its own sake, or when shared values are dismissed as an encumbrance, an anchoring on fundamentals can be powerful indeed, a liberating engine for positive change." The phrases "shared values" and "anchoring on fundamentals" as used here are certainly loaded ones, in essence barely coded language for the ascendancy of a national and colonialist narrative. In such a perspective change is "promoted for its own sake." Added Bennett by way of justification for the new policy: "What does not get measured does not get managed," as if heritage value is little more than quantification.[62]

Other Parks Canada managers were more direct. In a published speech entitled "Commemoration: A Moving Target?" given at a 1994 conference marking the seventy-fifth anniversary of the HSMBC, then Director General of National Historic Sites Christina Cameron described the "insidious influence" of "what we now call political correctness."[63] Singling out a number of sites for having strayed from their original commemorative intent, Cameron then focused on Batoche, where she criticized the emerging public history research and interpretation of Métis persistence in the face of hostile settler colonialism and the military defeat of 1885. However, such a critique sees heritage as removed from place, or more particularly from the layers of local memory and meaning associated with that place. Within the centralist framework of commemorative intent, values are hardly "shared" but are instead handed down from on high. Aspirational goals become more important than scholarly research, and national narratives must be "useful" in order to justify the current hegemony of interests. In the case of Batoche, labelling a much overdue alternative interpretation as simply "political correctness" revealed a truly conventional and colonialist national public narrative. To answer the question in Cameron's title, commemoration should always be a "moving target."

Despite Ottawa's disapproval of the changing interpretation at Batoche, the Statement of Commemorative Intent developed for the site in 1997 by the Prairie and Northern Regional Office of Parks Canada listed a number of factors supporting the commemoration. These included Batoche as the site of the armed conflict between the Métis and the Canadian government, the Métis community of Batoche, and the significance of river-lot use patterns at the site.[64] Supporting messages elaborate upon these main themes, although the battle of May 1885 remains the cornerstone of the commemorative intent.[65] Historic place plays a significant role in the statement and focuses upon the site's symbolic and associative values, including the general setting of the site on the South Saskatchewan River; the surviving buildings, rifle pits, and the Canadian defensive earthworks; the vestiges of the Carlton Trail; "Mission Ridge," which was the site of the final charge of the North West Field Force; and perhaps most importantly the distinctive form of land use that is the river-lot system, which was so integral to community life in the region.[66] This last landscape feature was the subject of a separate 1989 Board commemoration, which stated that the Métis river-lot pattern was a nationally significant part of historical land use on the prairies.[67] By being commemorated at Batoche it symbolizes a geography charged with historical significance and speaks to the cultural and terrestrial significance of the place and the layers of memory and meaning we attribute to it. Batoche today readily reveals the survival of culture, heritage, and identity through place.

Of course, a number of other national historic sites, such as Duck Lake, Tourand's Coulee (formerly Fish Creek), Frog Lake, Fort Carlton, Cut Knife Hill, Loon Lake, and Frenchman's Butte, all factor into the 1885 story, including the role of prairie First Nations under Big Bear, Poundmaker, and several other Indigenous leaders. Each of these sites is marked with a cairn and plaque and is situated on federally owned properties of varying size. Although designated early by the Board, their interpretation has changed over the years, much like Fort Battleford and Batoche. But, unlike these latter sites, they do not possess the same level of development and interpretation, although each represents critical components of heritage place. (The site of the Battle of Cut Knife Hill, located on the Poundmaker Reserve in western Saskatchewan, does host a nearby small interpretive centre run by the First Nation.)[68] For instance, the Duck Lake site, the location of the first battle of the 1885 Resistance, is located on a twelve-hectare space near the town of Duck Lake in Saskatchewan and within the Beardy's and Okemasis Cree Nation Reserve.[69] Tourand's Coulee, twenty-seven kilometres south of Batoche, was the site of the victory of a small force of Métis and First Nations fighters under Gabriel Dumont over 850 troops of the North West Field Force. Heritage place includes the thirty-six-hectare battle site as well as seventeen hectares that comprised Middleton's encampment. The site was commemorated in 1923, but the Board mistakenly considered the encampment land as the battle site; it was not until 1971 that the actual site of the conflict was identified and acquired by the federal government.[70]

Two things become evident when studying the public history of the 1885 sites in the West. One, the impact of these historic places, of these landscapes of memory, still remains as heritage spaces, especially at sites such as Batoche. Two, perceptions of these places and their meaning have changed, though often cautiously and not without struggle. If anything can be gleaned from these sites, it is that how they are understood has changed substantially over the decades. The colonial narrative has been dropped or at least contained. This is not surprising, given the changes in the scholarly record, with published accounts moving away from the early racialized perspectives of Indigenous peoples and their resistance to government invasion. Yet, the passive approach still characterizes much of the interpretation as heritage agencies attempt to strike what they might see as a balanced interpretation, the result perhaps of the illiberalism of central policy makers towards regional goals.

Much of this methodology has come about through the use of the "many voices" technique. With this technique, rather than replacing the authorized heritage voice at historic sites with what was considered to be an equally narrow and single-minded approach, multiple perspectives are enlisted in public interpretation to provide visitors with, as historian Frieda Klippenstein describes it, a "collage of vivid stories and images rather than one authoritative description and explanation of an event."[71] Theoretically, the many voices methodology recognizes the authenticity of various perspectives on an historical event without having to synthesize them, or to judge which is most accurate.[72] Yet, either consciously or subconsciously, most historic sites communicate through site programming, place management, material culture, or antiquarian collections that heritage is a cultural discourse with an authorized view of the past.

Chris Andersen's 2014 article "More than the Sum of Our Rebellions: Métis Histories beyond Batoche" makes a strong argument in regard to the Indigenous presence at sites like Batoche. Indeed, Andersen's views regarding Indigenous perspectives at historic sites go beyond this Saskatchewan site to a variety of historic places across the prairies, including a site such as Lower Fort Garry. Andersen argues that simply increasing the Indigenous presence at historic sites in fact "short changes the complexity, resistance, adaptation, and resilience of Indigenous nations and their communities in the years (sometimes centuries) following the historical locales they emphasize." For him, simply enlarging the Indigenous presence is only "mummifying Métis community in the strands of Canadian commemorative fabric."[73] Like Andersen, I do not necessarily advocate for simply increasing the Indigenous presence or Indigenous perspectives at current sites, for that attempts only to interpret post-colonial history at colonial sites, in some respects portraying Indigenous peoples as existing only in the past. And while I agree with Andersen's points regarding an Indigenous presence at historic sites, I do not concur with his opinion about the work of ethnohistorian Laura Peers, who has studied Indigenous interpretations at a variety of historic sites in Canada and the U.S.[74] Though Peers argues that the inclusion of Indigenous voices in national historic site contexts poses fundamental challenges to the central messages communicated about the past, I do not think that she believes that an increased presence will necessarily counter what Andersen calls the "hegemonic stereotypes about Indigenous authenticity,"[75] as she has also commented on the difficulties of interpreting post-colonial history at colonial sites. This is perhaps most evident at historic fur trade sites. If, on the one hand, places such as Batoche are viewed as sites of contestation, then on the other hand, fur trade sites tend to interpret an Indigenous presence as a representation of cooperation and partnership in a mercantile endeavour that was anything but equal and cooperative.

▲ ▲ ▲

An examination of heritage commemoration and contested space can challenge the traditional racialized discourse of the colonialist narrative, revealing the dissonant nature of heritage. Here, "dissonance" refers to the conflicts and disharmonies between perceptions of the past and contemporary awareness and use. It is created by interpretation where discernible messages about place and past are often in conflict. As geographers Gregory Ashworth and John Tunbridge have argued: "All heritage is someone's heritage and therefore logically not someone else's: the original meaning of an inheritance [from which the word 'heritage' derives] implies the existence of disinheritance and by extension any creation of heritage from the past disinherits someone completely or partially, actively or potentially."[76] For Indigenous people in particular, it is the "disinheritance" of place and the oftentimes biased and damaging discourse of commemoration that lie at the root of contested heritage.

Influencing this discourse can effectively alter contemporary power relations as modern issues around land, space, sovereignty, and economic rights become entwined with perceptions of the past. Intangible and tangible Indigenous heritage—places in particular—are bound together with identity claims and, according to Australian archaeologist Laurajane Smith, remain important "theatres of memory."[77] It is here where heritage is made real, made meaningful, and given expression. On the prairies, the Battle of Seven Oaks and Upper Fort Garry historic sites, along with the Fort Battleford and Batoche sites, are each theatres of memory where contested space and commemoration have impacted the ways we think of heritage and place. By moving away from traditional settler colonial viewpoints, or the conservative and authorized perceptions of hegemonic bias, we might begin to see in Manitoba and Saskatchewan the emergence of a post-colonialist heritage and a new inheritance.

CHAPTER 5

Heritage Place: The Function of Modernity, Gender, and Sexuality

Heritage is a distinctly modern concern in the sense in which the question of what is "old" and what is "new" belongs to a peculiarly modern sensibility.

Rodney Harrison, *Heritage: Critical Approaches*

In this chapter I want to broaden the conversation to examine how modernity, as well as themes such as gender and sexuality, have changed the dynamics of what we commemorate and why. In viewing heritage as the persistence of the past in the present rather than its creation in the present, we can more easily grasp the changing versions of what constitutes the important themes of heritage. Subjects such as gender and sexuality impact the way we view the past, how we assemble and disassemble particular narratives, and how such themes can change the way we think about not only what was important in the past but how these realities have shaped modern sensibilities.

Modernity and Heritage

The term "modernity" can have complex meanings. In the humanities and social sciences, it can describe a particular historical period within the chronology of pre-modern, modern, late modern, and postmodern. It can refer as well to a social and cultural view of the world that focuses on the transformation from the pre-modern to the modern world, a transformation that occurred post-Enlightenment, according to some scholars, and for others much later, in the mid- to late nineteenth century. Generally, these changes occurred in the areas of art, architecture, history, technology, science, intellectual theory, and capitalism. Modernity has been associated with personal subjectivity, scientific rationalization, a decline in formal religious perspectives, the emergence of nation-states and bureaucracy, urbanization, the decline of small-scale agriculture, and the move toward globalized market economies.[1] Michel Foucault adds to this list by including the questioning of tradition, the growth of capitalism and global market economies, individual freedom and democracy, and the growth of secularism.[2] Late modernity might also include the globalization of technology, advances in electronic media, and an increased time for leisure, although postmodernity might suggest a realignment of free time in the face of a diminished time for leisure.

In studies of heritage and place, modernity can have particular relevance. Arguably, modernity created heritage or at least facilitated an emerging preservationist movement. It has created pasts that are part of the present. An essentially recent conception, "heritage" responds to vulnerability and risk, and in a late modernist world has adapted a taxonomic structure relating to systems of collection, organization, classification, and prioritization, first developed in contemporary sciences, to deal with that vulnerability. Modern heritage became about materiality, and these physical reminders of an oftentimes romanticized past helped to underpin the new directions in many areas of culture and society. While public space was always present in the past, modernity has helped to create the idea of a more comprehensive public sphere, or at least has facilitated its emergence and growth. In this expression of modernity those physical resources and places perceived as part of the past and believed vulnerable and threatened came to be increasingly valued as a public affair.

Cultural historian Rodney Harrison has suggested that heritage in the twentieth century became increasingly bureaucratized and removed from everyday life.[3] With the consolidation of the modern nation-state came the creation of state intervention, generating lists of heritage places from local significance to international consequence. The growth of governments and bureaucracies—another signpost of modernity— saw the origin of protection charters and the drafting of legislation to safeguard threatened spaces, places, and monuments. Moving ahead, the year 1972 is often associated with the creation (or at least consolidation) of modernist heritage, as that was the year of the creation of the World Heritage Convention and the more widespread view, in the

West at least, that heritage places were important, and governments were increasingly given *the* role in protecting the past.

Finding Her Place

If the modernist era ushered in a growing worldwide emphasis upon the protection of heritage spaces, in Canada the focus of protection and interpretation remained largely traditional in scope. Great men, or at least the places inhabited and belonging to great men (or their battles or their politics), received the greatest attention by heritage agencies, including those in Canada. Women played only a small part in the creation of official heritage, and even then it was only a handful of individuals who were recognized. Gender in the larger sense, little studied in the academy, was not considered significant for heritage commemoration or interpretation unless it was to see women of the past as servants, helpmates, mothers, and occasionally the domesticized matrons of upper-class domiciles. (Catherine Motherwell, who once lived at Lanark Place at Motherwell, is one example of the latter.) And even in these roles their actual lives were little more than backdrops for the larger stories that were taking place around them—for example, W.R. Motherwell as national politician and scientific agriculturalist. For historic site-animation programs, they were there in much the way a chorus provides support for the lead actors in a play. They helped to fill the room, similar to English feminist writer Virginia Woolf's 1929 misquoted line describing the plight of female writers: "For most of history, Anonymous was a woman."[4]

In an afterword entitled "Proceeding from Here" in the American text *Restoring Women's History through Historic Preservation*, historian Heather Huyck writes: "Historic places tell us who we are as a people and where we have come from. Omitting any significant portion of our history distorts all of it. Historic places, because they contain so much past evidence and are so powerful in conveying the past to the public, provide great opportunities for sharing women's history by simply asking the right questions about landscapes, structures, and artefacts and by seeing the women's history already there."[5] Huyck's prescription, however, is only part of the issue in the attempt to integrate women's history into public history. In Canada, initiatives to recognize women's history in the public sphere have largely underachieved because these strategies have been pursued within an existing and limited commemoration of historic places. Yes, individual women have been commemorated both nationally and provincially, and that is to be commended. Nationally, a 1991 Parks Canada System Plan was the first to identify the com- memoration of women's history as a priority, and a series of subsequent national workshops with mostly feminist scholars deliberated over how this goal was to be accomplished.[6] Yet, as Parks Canada historian Dianne Dodd has demonstrated, as of 2008 (admittedly some time ago), of the 1,942 commemorations made by the Historic Sites and Monuments Board of Canada since 1919, only 6 percent concerned women or institutions associated with women.[7]

Despite these dismal figures, Alan McCullough has claimed that Parks Canada has been able to "refocus" historic sites through its centralized administrative system to "recognize women's history and heritage." The delay in this recognition, he argues, can be attributed to the constraints on public commemoration where, he maintains, "academic history and public memory are not in agreement [and] Parks Canada must search for common ground before proceeding to commemorate."[8] Of course, to assume a disharmony between academic history and public memory is problematic, but, regardless, the presumed lack of "common ground" does little to excuse the agency from taking a leadership role. Dianne Dodd, however, strikes a more optimistic tone, contending, "Through most of HSMBC/Parks Canada history, Canadian women have had difficulty in accessing the needed material [presumably financial] and human resources to acquire, develop, and interpret sites, and to gain site designations once they have developed them. Before 1990, there were only nine women's history sites and most of those belonged to religious communities. However, since the late 1990s when Parks Canada made women's history a program priority, the number of sites, albeit not administered by Parks Canada, has increased substantially as the agency acquired sites that women's groups or local organizations had earlier developed."[9]

Whether the increase in national historic sites (most not owned or administered by Parks Canada) devoted to women's history indicates substantial growth might be a matter for debate, especially as women's history has been a program priority for a good number of years.[10] For example, more recent designations by the Board pertaining to places of women's history have been only indirectly related to gender. Although organizations and buildings associated with particular individuals or

women's groups were included, so too were sites where the designation of women's history had little to do with gender or feminist pasts.
Butchart Gardens in British Columbia is perhaps one of those. An
elaborate garden setting located on the Saanich Peninsula north of
Victoria, Butchart Gardens was designated as a national historic site
in 2004 because it represents "an exceptional creative achievement in
Canadian gardening history."[11] According to the designation, the distinct gardens of this historic place evoke a range of aesthetic experiences
centred on the early twentieth-century beautification movement. The
relationship of this historic place to women's history, however, is because
its founder and designer, Jennie Butchart, was female.

Establishing historic places truly related to women's history has
been more than a program failure. The good intentions embodied in a
number of federal commemorative initiatives were largely derailed by
budget considerations, not by misguided objectives. The issue of deal-
ing with gender history at historic places in western Canada has many
facets, but its application brings significant concern. Since national
and provincial discussions began to increase the number of such commemorations, significant budget cuts to heritage initiatives in the late
1990s and into the 2000s, both federally and provincially, have severely
curtailed the protection of historic spaces and restricted the creation of
new sites, sites that might be devoted to exploring the political, social,
and cultural features of women's history.[12] Where the period between
1970 and 1990 witnessed the establishment of a large number of historic places across the West (and across Canada), since that time few
sites have been created and the vast majority of commemorations by
provincial and federal heritage boards—including the commemoration
of women and women's history—have resulted only in plaques.

The consequence, other than to erect commemorative plaques, has
been to attempt to incorporate women's history into existing interpretive programming at historic sites in provinces such as Manitoba and
Saskatchewan, similar to the Butchart Gardens example cited above.
To label this approach as "problematic" is perhaps an understatement.
At one level, the incorporation of women's history into fur trade sites,
into settler colonial sites, into resistance sites, and into house museums
is a workable option, as women's lives were critical to how such places
functioned. At another level, it too often reduces women's history to
the roles played by domestic servants, farmers' wives, and the genteel

matrons of fur trade posts who tell visitors of their latest needlepoint project.[13] In many instances these interpretations are conservative and static. Of course, women had important functions in all these historical scenarios, although more often than not they are little explored beyond the superficial and are always secondary to what the men were doing.

Women's inclusion within the traditional structures of heritage interpretation mirrors their inclusion in traditional historical writing by second-wave feminists, or what historian Joan Sangster calls "compensatory writing."[14] Where in heritage representation men are most often portrayed as individuals, women are typically portrayed as a type, sometimes because of a lack of historical record pertaining to individual women but most often because their gender is not the focus of the story. In her book *Imperial Plots: Women, Land, and the Spadework of British Colonialism on the Canadian Prairies,* historian Sarah Carter focuses on those British women who participated as farmers in the colonialist project on the prairies, their roles often central to establishing a new agricultural economy. Just as significantly, Carter names many of these women, not just providing individual identities but effectively placing women "at the centre of the story," including their involvement in restricting Indigenous entitlements on the land. Here the idea of place plays a critical part, as a glance at prairie township surveys from the late nineteenth and early twentieth centuries demonstrates, according to Carter, "how the land was not neutral, how ideas about proper gender roles were embedded in the landscape."[15] With the goal of establishing British women farmers on the prairies fading after the First World War due to the persistence of a "curiously strong prejudice," as Carter calls it, "this narrow range of opportunities was worlds away from the vision Georgina Binnie-Clark [an early twentieth-century farmer, author, and advocate for women farmers on the prairies] had of British women colonists raising grain on their valuable imperial plots that would help to make the prairies British by displacing Indigenous people and eradicating the need to bring in 'foreign settlers.'"[16] Carter's study of women's role in agricultural settlement on the prairies, like Sylvia Van Kirk's and Adele Perry's histories of women in the fur trade, demonstrates how gender, like place, has been an overlooked focus in the colonial project and a misunderstood part of the authorized heritage discourse. The masculinization of heritage has long characterized the way we portray the past, with gender playing a less than significant role.

▲ ▲ ▲

The characterization of historical female occupations, as some authors have argued, is historically part of the influence of modernity and a masculine gendering that is based upon views regarding the inferiority of women, along with non-white races and the working class; their roles are defined as pre-modern and localized in the world of nature. At heritage places women are often associated with the organic and natural rhythms of pre-industrial societies, considered as historical players within the household and valued for their reproductive capacities.[17] The impact of modernism in the world of heritage has meant that women's roles at industrial sites, in politics, and in places of commerce and public service are little explored at historic places in Canada.

Parks Canada's Statement of Commemorative Intent (SOCI) relates directly to the heritage issues around the commemoration of gender and place.[18] As part of its strategy to deal with cultural resources, in the 1990s the agency brought in the concept of the SOCI to focus national historic site interpretation on the original reasons given by the HSMBC for commemoration. After much discussion with Parks Canada historians (both regionally and in Ottawa), as well as with managers, archaeologists, and site interpretive personnel, short statements were drawn up for each site that in many cases were simply reworded versions of what the Board had found to be noteworthy when they first commemorated a specific place. While this refocus did not entirely preclude integrating topics such as women's history into site programming, it did restrict their scope, especially when those commemorations were created decades earlier, some as early as the 1920s. With no new national historic sites (or at least no new federally or provincially operated sites with interpretive programming), the interpretation of women as domestics or helpmates has tended to remain the primary focus for gender history in a public setting in prairie Canada. That such a result occurred is not entirely surprising, as heritage, unlike history, is resistant to change and is often managed at official levels by bureaucracies that function within conservative and conventional views of the world. Regardless, the good intentions and calls for more women's history and gender-based heritage of the 1991 Parks Canada System Plan went largely unheeded in the face of later budget reductions.

The absence of women's history from heritage place—by "absence" here I mean its relegation to the background, or to the "scenery" of such places—has so long been a fixture of historic sites that for many people it passes without notice. Architectural historian Gail Lee Dubrow, in describing her family visits to historic places when she was a child, observed that "the historic places we toured so closely fit our shared belief that men were the agents of historical change and the absence of women's history totally escaped notice."[19] Traditionally, it has been at the house museum, once ubiquitous throughout North America but rapidly disappearing because of low visitation and high maintenance costs, that women (though often nameless) were highlighted. As domestics or as upper-class doyennes, the portrayal of women's history at such museums has tended to underscore the myth of women's confinement in the domestic sphere while passing up on opportunities to interpret the history of women in the more public arenas of the paid labour force and in the wider community.[20]

In western Canada, women's history has enjoyed a somewhat greater visibility in relation to heritage place at the restored historic homes of well-known women writers, artists, politicians, and community activists. While these particular house museums are useful for relating individual stories, they provide little contextual material about the larger social, cultural, economic, political, and religious stories of women in western Canada. Here it is crucial to claim new space for women in the built environment, in cultural landscapes, in urban settings, and in rural locations. That history must be explored at places of work, at places of leisure, at places of religious practice, and at places of protest. A central Canadian example is the 1998 national designation of the Hersey Pavilion, an early nurses' residence at the Royal Victoria Hospital in Montreal, where the themes of the professionalization of nursing and medical culture are commemorated and interpreted.[21] In Manitoba similar themes are commemorated at the St. Boniface Hospital Nurses' Residence, built in 1928 and commemorated in 1997 to mark the "growing recognition of nursing as a profession and . . . to commemorate the contribution of nurses to medicine and the role of women as health care professionals."[22] Other sites include Miss Davis's School, built in 1866 and renamed Twin Oaks; Maison Gabrielle-Roy, designated in 2008 to commemorate the life and writings of the well-known St. Boniface author; and the Grey Nuns Convent in St. Boniface, a large

Red River frame mission house built in 1851 and now the St. Boniface Museum. Another site is the Ukrainian Labour Temple in Winnipeg, built in 1919 and commemorated by the HSMBC in 2009, a long-time centre of Ukrainian culture in the city and a gathering place for strikers, many of whom were women, and their families during the Winnipeg General Strike of 1919. In fact, it was women who began the Winnipeg general sympathetic strike. At 7:00 a.m. on the morning of Thursday, 15 May 1919, 500 telephone operators left at the end of their shifts. No other workers came in to replace them.[23]

In its interpretive programming, Riel House NHS in Winnipeg does mention the women in Louis Riel's life, although again primarily within a domestic capacity. Aside from a focus on the political role of Riel himself, much of the interpretation encourages visitors to "explore a traditional Métis way of life in the mid-1880s."[24] In Saskatchewan, national historic sites that look at aspects of women's history include a number of early farmsteads, places such as Seeger Wheeler's Maple Grove Farm and Motherwell Homestead NHS (discussed in Chapter 3).

For the most part, however, the places mentioned above, while commemorating aspects of women's history in the West, offer little in the way of interactive interpretation and certainly far less in interpretive resources than do the major (and older) historic sites. Settler colonial sites, for instance, might include a domesticized interpretation of women's lives, but the overarching theme at such sites is one of pioneer authenticity, claim to place, and the influence of "founding father" narratives. Along with settler sites, the commemorative emphasis in Manitoba and Saskatchewan includes early fur trade and Northwest Resistance sites as well as heritage buildings commemorated for their architectural value. What these western provinces lack, for example, is a later industrial site that could commemorate and interpret the role of working-class women in the workforce in the twentieth century, a site such as the Gulf of Georgia Cannery in British Columbia, where women worked on the line processing and canning the products of the west-coast fishery. In *Working Girls in the West: Representations of Wage-Earning Women*, Lindsey McMaster describes how, in the early twentieth century, "working girls" were seen as representative of the angst of modern life through sensitivities around the suffrage movement, the perceived disintegration of the family, and male anxieties about the independence of women.[25] Such themes—particularly themes regarding working women and urban life—are little recognized in the Western catalogue of historic places. Urban places rarely focus on such modernist tropes, as Canadian heritage agencies have historically preferred those origin story sites that are related to the fur trade and settler colonialism.

If, in western Canada, there have been difficulties with relating women's stories beyond the superficial, heritage preservationists in the United States have looked to urban landscapes to explore issues around the history of working women, especially women of colour. The Power of Place project in Los Angeles, for instance, has, since the 1980s, established three sites that interpret the experiences of African-American, Latina, and Japanese-American women in a variety of commercial enterprises from the late nineteenth and early twentieth centuries. These include the establishment of interpretive public art at an African-American midwife's home from the nineteenth century, the interpretation of a surviving union hall where Latina women helped organize female garment workers in the 1930s, and the preservation of commercial flower fields run by Japanese-American families in the 1890s.[26] As Dolores Hayden, a professor of American Studies at Yale University and the founder of the Power of Place project, has written: "Finding the stories of diverse working women, and inscribing them in public space, is one small part of creating a public, political culture that can carry the North American city into the next century."[27]

Finding Her Indigenous Place

Critical to an analysis of women and place in the heritage of western Canada is the inclusion of Indigenous women and their stories at historic places. In earlier chapters of this book I touch on the topics of women situated in pre-contact and early post-contact Indigenous cultural landscapes, women at fur trade sites, and women at settler sites. In the West, initiatives to recognize Indigenous women's history in the public realm (with the exception of Wanuskewin) have been minimal, again because such programs have been pursued within the current limited commemorations at historic places. At Lower Fort Garry, the site's "Native Encampment" is staffed predominantly by female interpreters. The camp has been allotted limited resources over the years—one or two archetypal canvas teepees remain the focal point; the Anishinaabe bark-covered structures that were historically common in that region and in the 1850s time period are considered too expensive to construct. While the mostly young, university-age interpreters impart some information to visitors about the nineteenth-century lives of Indigenous women in southern Manitoba, their interpretation focuses largely upon material culture. Historian Laura Peers, who conducted extensive research on the interpretation of Indigenous peoples at fur trade sites in both Canada and the U.S., describes the encampment at Lower Fort Garry:

> Interpreters sit on low folding camp chairs that are covered by trade blankets, and engage in beadwork and other crafts. A *tikinagan* (baby carrier), a wooden trunk with cooking and domestic items, and some obviously Aboriginal objects . . . are laid out for visitors to see and touch. . . . Interpreters greet visitors in the cooking area outside, and then after initial discussion explain the contents of the trunk, and then invite the visitors to come into the [canvas] tipi with them . . . all the interpreters were young adults. Most were women from the Winnipeg area . . . [and] one of the female interpreters was Filipino.[28]

Although the interpretation of Indigenous life at the Lower Fort Garry encampment emphasizes the material culture of women's domestic lives in the mid-nineteenth century (beadwork and crafts), this "outside the palisades" interpretation, an approach common to most fur trade restorations or reconstructions, reinforces the view of Indigenous people, especially women, as apart, as almost foreigners in their own land. And, as Peers points out, the "administrative burden" at Lower Fort Garry is so cumbersome that little or no interpretive instruction is provided. The one week of training for the young interpreters is taken up, for the most part, by talks related to fire drills, transportation to the site, and pensions.[29] (I can add from personal experience that the week also included much time devoted to how to wear one's costume, and the time and location of the end-of-training-week party.) Though historical manuals have been prepared, site supervisors spend little time encouraging summer staff to actually read these manuals.[30]

Beyond the staged, prop-centred interpretation of some historic sites, more recent sources might assist in incorporating Indigenous women's history into historic places. Because of the scarcity of written records pertaining to the early history of Indigenous women, most especially women outside of the domestic life of nineteenth-century fur trade posts, their commemoration, whether individually or as a community, has relied increasingly upon oral history. When available, the oral record allows for a direct voice that presents the social and cultural history of life experiences and everyday events. Oral history can reveal how historical reality—where Indigenous women lived, worked, and made sense of the world around them—is multivocal. Julie Cruikshank's *Life Lived Like a Story*, which explores the lives of three women Elders from southern Yukon; Freda Ahenakew's and H.C. Wolfart's *Our Grandmothers' Lives as Told in Their Own Words*, which describes the daily lives and beliefs of Cree women in the West; and Regina Flannery's *Ellen Smallboy: Glimpses of a Cree Woman's Life*, which tells about one person's life in a Cree community, all centre the daily lives and stories of Indigenous women in place and its importance to the individual and to the community. My own involvement in collecting and editing the early twentieth-century stories of Indigenous women from the York Factory region with Muskego Cree historian Flora Beardy revealed (for me anyway) the strong role of place for women as part of lives lived, steeped in tradition and culture. As daughters, wives, sisters, mothers, grandmothers, hunters, country provision processers, and post workers, they were critical to the strength and survival of Cree culture and society in the North during a particularly challenging economic time period.[31] These are historic places of meaning. They will not have plaques or interpretive centres, and their boundaries will remain indistinct, but they are as much a part of the heritage of their regions as those places chosen by the HSMBC or by the Historic Sites Advisory Board of Manitoba, or by Parks, Culture and Sport in Saskatchewan.

The commemoration of women and gender at heritage places can benefit as well from genealogical connection and kinship investigation. The concept of "prosopography," or the application of genealogical reconstruction and the knowledge of naming practices found in primary documents, can be employed to reconstruct not only kinship patterns and socio-political alliances but also the historical identity of specific Indigenous women in specific families. Their lives, their actions, their kinship ties can be used to expand the definition of space and place as well as their individual and collective historical significance beyond the traditional narratives of the heritage discourse.

These spaces and places are critical to telling the stories of the lives of Indigenous women in the West and how they interacted with colonial society. Linking this discussion with the previous section, one can cite the work of Sarah Carter, who noted in her book *Capturing Women: The Manipulation of Cultural Imagery in Canada's Prairie West* how the arrival of white women on the prairies in the late nineteenth and early twentieth centuries coincided with treaty making and the growth of ranching and farming, which helped to "consolidate the new order—and spacially separated the newcomers from the Indigenous peoples of the region."[32] Here she quotes from the 1870s correspondence of Mary Inderwick, an early female settler in the West who believed that Indigenous women should be "isolated in the mountains," which would lead to their eventual "extinction."[33] Though often rejected as farmers, as Carter writes in *Imperial Plots*, British female immigrants nevertheless contributed to the "spadework of the Empire" and remained a part of the colonialist project. Citing the American feminist scholar Anne McClintock, Carter notes that colonial women were "ambiguously complicit," being both privileged and restricted. Like their male counterparts they sought the bounty of Indigenous land, but in the process they faced gendered roadblocks and barriers.[34]

Ambiguous as well is our awareness of Indigenous women's heritage, and indeed the heritage of all Indigenous peoples in the West that has tended to concentrate on older landscapes and remote traditional communities considered in historical terms as pre-modern. More recent scholarship on Indigenous history has moved away from some of these older representations and has repositioned heritage place within the urban landscape. Postwar examples of Indigenous women working as nurses and in other areas of community health, as service industry workers, and in education bring concepts of First Nations and Métis women and place into modern landscapes or cityscapes, their everyday lives as much a part of their community's history as their grandmothers'.[35] And like Dolores Hayden's Power of Place initiatives, the physical recognition of these stories of adaptation, perseverance, and activism in the face of prejudice can expand our awareness of Indigenous heritage, and in fact all of heritage.

A Queer-Eye View of Heritage Place

Recognizing and commemorating women's history in relation to place on a broad scale can help bring heritage into the twenty-first century. Critical to modernizing heritage designation, as well as helping to promote a greater sense of inclusion within the wider community, is the recognition of sites related to gay and lesbian history. The subtitle for this section, particularly the term "Queer-Eye," is based on historian Valerie Korinek's article "A Queer-Eye View of the Prairies: Reorienting Western Canadian Histories." For those customarily involved in heritage advocacy, there has been a reluctance to support such themes with protection and commemoration of place usually reserved for traditional themes related to nation building and what I have earlier called "founding father" narratives. Of course, concepts that we define as nation building are not restricted to the eighteenth- and nineteenth-century themes of Indigenous history, fur trade life, exploration, settler colonialism, and struggles over land and corporate rights related to language and custom. Yet, for the most part, governments have stayed away from gay and lesbian commemorations as part of the history of community formation. Bureaucracies, traditionally conservative in their approaches, have feared alienating the mainstream, especially those groups that have been the most vocal supporters of heritage conservation. Commemorating those places associated with gay and lesbian history in western Canada is not an initiative that comes readily to mind for historical societies and other preservationist groups.

But there is a need to write the LGBTQ population into our collective history and into the preservation movement, as individuals, as communities, and as part of those places that have helped shape the social fabric of this country. Such initiatives will not happen without individuals, groups, and governments all taking an active role. It is a generalization, and perhaps a sweeping one, but there will be push-back, as heritage advocates can often be conservative in their views.[36] However, the kind of change that might see existing landmarks reinterpreted and new ones selected will not come about without strong advocacy. The heritage movement of the twenty-first century deserves nothing less.

In the U.S., author Gail Lee Dubrow has discussed initiatives such as the Queer Spaces project in New York that identifies nine sites related to gay and lesbian history throughout the city, and gay sites in

San Francisco, the first gay-related historic sites to be mentioned in the National Trust's *Preservation* magazine.[37] Dubrow also discusses those sites that have already been designated as landmarks as the first place to begin correcting the omissions and misrepresentations in the presentation of gay and lesbian history. There are, for instance, the many historic houses associated with famous individuals who were gay. In reinterpreting the houses of such people, Dubrow concedes that such an initiative raises ethical questions around private lives and public accomplishments, "outing" historical figures who may have wished to remain "closeted," and what she labels as "the fluidity of people's sexuality over a lifetime."[38] Dubrow goes on to discuss the "pressing need to preserve and interpret places associated with the emergence of homosexual community and identity," such as early gay bars and bathhouses, public open spaces where gay men met, parts of public beaches, and even the early havens of the homophile movement, such as the First Universalist Church in Los Angeles.[39] One could add the later establishment of gay bookstores and newspapers, as well as clubs, to this list. More currently, in June 2013 former U.S. president Barack Obama proclaimed the Stonewall Inn, an early gay bar in New York, to be a national monument.[40]

In Canada there have been similar attempts, although on the federal level these initiatives have been less than successful. Earlier in this work (see Introduction) I describe the 1981 raid on a group of Toronto bathhouses that culminated in a massive demonstration against police that was held the next day, a demonstration that, according to author Ed Jackson, "marked a seismic eruption of queer visibility into public space in Toronto, and launched a new chapter in the LGBTQ community's relationship with the police."[41] Some have portrayed these events as the beginning of the gay liberation movement in the country. However, commemoration of gay history in Toronto began prior to the 1981 raids with the establishment in the 1970s of gay and lesbian newspapers, bookstores, support organizations, churches, communes, and protest demonstrations.[42]

Queer places and communities, or "an imagined gay geography," have been mapped in some cities, identifying the enclaves and sanctuaries where gay people historically could escape examination by the police.[43] As noted earlier, Patrizia Gentile has looked at similar geographies in Cold War Ottawa, remarking that gay sanctuaries in the 1950s and 1960s in a government town like Ottawa were less secure. Yet, as Gentile suggests, the stories and memories of Ottawa's queer spaces provide a "critical archives" of where place and memory interconnect and where queer pasts are documented.[44] Researching and mapping such places and such history can be more than an archive, however. Recognizing these spaces as part of the socio-cultural history of the community and the country brings queer history into the mainstream, enlarging our conception of heritage beyond the conventional and the long-established themes of commemoration.

Turning to western Canada, Valerie Korinek, in her article "A Queer-Eye View of the Prairies," begins to historicize the later emergence of gay and lesbian communities in the West.[45] Although much has been written in more recent times on gender and sexuality in the West during the fur trade and settlement eras,[46] Korinek's work studies what it was like to be gay and lesbian on the prairies in the postwar era, how queer people came to form political and cultural organizations, and whether there was, in fact, what American anthropologist Kath Weston called, the "great gay migration of the seventies and eighties" to cities, a migration that in the case of the prairie West, according to Korinek, is a mythology. Korinek's 2018 work *Prairie Fairies* relates the queer history of five urban centres in the West, including Winnipeg, Saskatoon, Regina, Edmonton, and Calgary. Looking at the early formation of gay clubs and associations in these cities, Korinek explores how the leading activists from these urban centres in the West helped to create national gay liberation debates in Canada. But have queer histories been integrated into the commemoration of private and public space in the West? For the most part, no, although it is worth noting the growing collection of these histories at prairie universities and at such repositories as the Saskatchewan Archives Board, and the 2013 launch of the Manitoba Gay and Lesbian Society Archives at the University of Manitoba Archives and Special Collections.[47] But while gay and lesbian histories have found their way into mainstream historical and archival collections in the West and are emerging as an essential part of prairie historiography, their individual and collective histories have a ways to go to be completely integrated into public heritage and the language of place.[48]

Yet, just as gay and lesbian history in Canada has increasingly become a part of historical research in the academy, it can become as well a part of public history and how governments approach the topics of commemoration. Advocacy can start outside the typical heritage circles, the usual groups that lobby governments for the recognition and protection of this settler site, or that community forefather. LGBTQ groups have much to concern themselves with in gaining cultural and political acceptance within modern societies, so traditionally have had little time to look at the past as a reification of present realities. Yet, to help establish a past that brings out the realities of sexuality and gender, from places associated with the gay rights movement, to broader interpretations of social and intimate interactions in commemorated venues, to the historical figures who were lesbian, gay, or two-spirited would enlarge our cultural concept of heritage and its role in shaping the present and future. Advocacy from within public history can start with the researchers and planners who often craft the look of heritage from the ground up. More than some people might realize, it is at these levels that new ideas and new ways of thinking often emerge. Ultimately, however, it is at the senior levels of the heritage bureaucracy, in particular the HSMBC and provincial heritage boards, that such initiatives can be brought forward and acted upon. Just as heritage commemoration moved away from older colonial themes to such topics as Indigenous history, the history of women, and the history of immigration, so too can the history of sexuality become an integral part of the heritage vocabulary.

Like fur trade or settler colonial sites, the historic places that deal with women's history or the history of sexuality in prairie Canada are not based upon a significance that is innate; they are in fact cultural processes that provide a perspective on history and history making. If such themes, and indeed places, are often part of an imagined past, they take on a meaning that is defined by modern perceptions and, in terms of place, a landscape of aestheticized space. As with all heritage, charting the evolution of interpretation and changing versions of the past, how narratives are developed and how they come to be challenged, defended, authenticated, or oftentimes disassembled helps us to think about and define how issues around gender and sexuality can bring the past into the present.

History, Memory, and the Heritage Discourse

Identity is local and regional, rooted in the imagination and in works of culture.

Northrop Frye, *The Bush Garden:*
Essays on the Canadian Imagination

To the above quote from Northrop Frye one might add that identity and imagination are found not only in the "works of culture" but also in the works of nature and in how each intersects with the other. A particular landscape can also represent the imagined pasts of the viewer, its sense of place rendered authentic by meanings that are largely subjective. Place can have a broad language, which imprints our imagination with a meaning to which we readily respond. As the nineteenth-century English novelist Thomas Hardy once wrote of Egdon Heath in Wessex, "It was a spot which returned upon the memory of those who loved it with an aspect of peculiar and kindly congruity."[1]

This broad language of place, whether familiar or foreign, is much influenced by modern cultural processes that often express contemporary and changing views of heritage. At the places we have labelled as "heritage," we can often see an imagined past, a history we might view through the lens of modern perception and a cultural landscape created as aestheticized space. Although interpreting the past in the present can promote a dominant heritage discourse, at the same time challenges to that discourse can gain purchase as modern issues are re-examined through the lens of historical interpretation. Contemporary views around such things as class, gender, sexuality, and race can function outside hegemonic authority. Or they can come to influence that authority, bringing new ideas and new interpretations to the table.

For some writers, the classification of what is heritage and what is not, or more generally how we think about heritage, is the result of the victory of history over memory, a viewpoint put forward by the French historian Pierre Nora. Canadian historian Cecilia Morgan agrees with Nora's argument, suggesting that "the forces of modernization—urbanization, industrialization, the rise of secularism and the nation state, all modernist characteristics—have replaced memory with history, a form of knowledge that differs from memory by its reliance on written texts, linear chronology, rationality, logic, and above all its insistence that the present and past constitute different worlds."[2] With memory and history, however, we are not trapped between Scylla and Charybdis with dangers on both sides. In fact, some historians do not agree that history has triumphed over memory, or that they are in fact mutually exclusive. The increasing use of oral history, for example, rather than written documents, or the object, or the place itself—as with cultural landscapes—would suggest otherwise. Once considered unreliable and a poor substitute for the historical record, oral history has found new purchase as a record of the past (including in legal and academic forums), and if memory is sometimes selective, as critics of oral history might suggest, so too are written documents where issues around their production, who produces them and what material survives, can often be contested. Rather than oppositional, over time memory and history have become complementary, and while an authorized heritage discourse still predominates in the macro sense, it is often in memory that history can survive at the community and family levels.

The theme of Indigenous roles and rights and the interpretation of Indigenous histories are critical to how heritage agencies and community groups present the past, or at least their version of the past. In Chapter 1, I explore Indigenous cultural landscapes, and in Chapter 4 I look at those sites in Manitoba and Saskatchewan, traditionally viewed as places of early settlement, as sites of resistance in the colonialist story. If largely considered as the extension of the Canadian nation-state in the West, in a post-colonial world such places also provide the means to challenge hegemonic views of the past. These narratives can underscore the distinctions between traditional government narratives and those of non-governmental groups such as some community organizations, academics, and Indigenous publics. It is at such contested spaces that Indigenous perceptions of the past can confront the conventions of

settler-colonial history and where fluid cultural perspectives and historiographies can help define the shifting ground of heritage place.

The commemorations of Indigenous cultural landscapes such as
Wanuskewin, Seahorse Gully, Linear Mounds, and the sacred petroforms of Whiteshell Provincial Park tell the story of ancient land use,
including the economic, cultural, and religious themes that give them
their resonance and character. Today, these places are not simply relics
but living landscapes that demonstrate an old, continuous, and complex
relationship with the land. Traditional Indigenous knowledge locates
these associations through narratives, place names, sacred sites, rituals,
and long-established resource use. Just as these sites reveal an ancient
language of place, the contested places of a more modern era—the nineteenth century—provide a new language, the language of contentious
and claimed space and the exposure of the colonial discourse. Looking
at these historic sites and how they were commemorated and interpreted
from a new perspective has challenged the traditional heritage messages
found at many sites throughout the prairies, particularly the Northwest
Resistance sites of Batoche and Fort Battleford in Saskatchewan.
Changing this heritage discourse can change modern cultural relations
and power structures and reshape modern perceptions around land,
space, sovereignty, and economic rights.

Much can be said about the early themes behind the creation of various fur trade sites in the West. In particular, this includes considerable
detail about the history of Lower Fort Garry as a national historic site,
its research and physical development, and the way its interpretation has
evolved over the years. I refer to the lower fort as an "attraction," using
that word in a mostly pejorative sense, and describe its living history
program as a largely contrived portrayal of the past. While sites such as
York Factory, and to a lesser degree Prince of Wales Fort at Churchill,
retain integrity as heritage resources, their interpretation puts the focus on specific time periods or specific, and traditional, geographical
places. In these instances we might ask whose voice dictates the preferred narratives of history, the prominence of European stories over
Indigenous voices, and why the impoverishment of the York Factory
Muskego people in the later decades of the nineteenth century is not
a central part of that post's interpretation as a national historic site. It
does, after all, characterize colonialism and the consequences for those
who are colonized. For Indigenous history, being "outside the palisades"

describes more than trade protocol and practice; it represents much of the heritage legacy of the fur trade.

In the discussion in Chapter 3 of "constructing authenticity," the focus is on how the commemoration of settler colonialism in the West has built upon the celebration of nation building and how, with "pioneer" places, history quickly became heritage. The historic sites examined, from River Road Provincial Park, to ethnoreligious settlements, to Motherwell Homestead NHS, are examples of the commemorated settlement heritage of western Canada. As heritage sites they demonstrate how land and the real and imagined histories of community are celebrated, and how memory is both cherished and invented. Whether it is the Motherwell Homestead, River Road, Veregin, Mennonite Heritage Village, or Neubergthal Street Village, they commemorate how landscapes were reformed as colonial topographies and how "founding father" narratives came to define place as cultural legacy.

Chapter 5 moves away from the commemorative history and interpretation of specific sites and touches on how modernity has impacted an emerging preservationist movement, most particularly in regards to gender and sexuality. While all human cultures have had some form of relationship to places, objects, and rituals that carry importance within particular communities for understanding the past, modern societies, especially Western cultures, have developed characteristic ways of experiencing that past. As a more or less recent idea, "heritage" over the last few centuries has developed ever more complex methods of collection, organization, classification, and prioritization to commemorate the past and protect its representations, especially the representation of place.

Place and public space have always been part of a culture's view of itself. In more contemporary times, however, we have created more comprehensive public spheres, assigning a superior value to those stories that have formed the nucleus of "official" history. But in western Canada many historic sites continue to reflect the illiberalism of past perspectives, still interpreting the oftentimes tired stories that come with colonial history, founding narratives, and the fanciful descriptions of history as we have imagined it or wished it to be. For instance, the traditional dearth of women's history, especially the histories of Indigenous women, and the absence of the stories relating to sexuality, have skewed our understanding of the past. It is these stories—individual and collective—that must be reflected in heritage spaces to create a public, political culture that reflects the past in a twenty-first-century reality.

Throughout this study I have attempted to show how the authenticity of place in western Canada is not intrinsic or elemental but cultural. Doing so can illustrate how memory (or its lack), modern cultural processes, contemporary perspectives, and bureaucratic objectives have defined or redefined the heritage of many historic sites. At a number of the places in prairie Canada discussed in this study, we see examples of an imagined past, a heritage that is often prejudiced by modern experiences and a landscape fashioned as aestheticized space. The idea of collective memory is critical to how heritage is understood or perhaps misunderstood. Some historians, such as Rodney Harrison, believe that collective memory in the twenty-first century faces a "crisis of accumulation" of the past in the present, a crisis, he claims, that will undermine the role of collective memory by "overwhelming societies with disparate traces of heterogeneous pasts and distracting us from the active process of forming collective memories in the present."[3] Although Harrison's perspective might have value, one can also make the argument that the commemoration of pasts is not, and should not be, about simply establishing a collective memory. With the role of the state and the hegemony of a largely homogeneous memory, there will be no crisis of accumulation when one looks at recent trends in the commemoration of places, objects, architecture, and intangible cultural heritage. Though government has been the key driver in heritage commemoration, it has not come without the support and participation (though perhaps uneven) of community organizations. As Bruce Dawson, the director of cultural policy for the Saskatchewan government, noted in 2010, governments, including provincial governments, have become what he calls "the key author[s] of heritage with a diverse range of support from regional and community groups."[4] Writing in the late 1990s, historian, university director, and former heritage manager Frits Pannekoek suggested that the rise of state-controlled heritage policy and development has been due in large part to what he referred to as "the rise of the heritage priesthood," or that period between roughly 1965 and 1990 that witnessed the growth of heritage agencies and their bureaucracies of heritage managers, policy specialists, and public professionals such as historians, archaeologists, and curators.[5] The "priesthood" also came to include the professional interpreter, a trained communicator whose job was to repackage profes-sional work for public consumption.[6] However, the continuing influence of government in the world of heritage, the survival of certain "founding father" narratives, and arguably the decline of public memory in the face of present-centred culture will more than likely curtail the survival of what Harrison called the "disparate traces of heterogeneous pasts." Instead, authorized pasts will become collective pasts.

This study has looked at heritage as it relates to place in western Canada, examining how heritage value is established, how com-memoration reflects social and cultural perspectives, and how and why perceptions of a public past are often modified over time. The specific places studied, including built heritage, settler-colonial sites, cultural and ethnoreligious topographies, and Indigenous spiritual and contest-ed landscapes, illustrate the process of commemoration of some critical themes in western Canadian history. By balancing official themes with alternative community-based views of the past, we might find a middle way. If some form of authorized heritage has come to dominate the way we see past and place, we might also see community values and perceptions echoed in the official histories of the state. National and regional identities are historical constructions that are regularly chal-lenged, modified, and reformed.[7] The cultural pluralism that can come from the diversity of histories and the perceptions of those histories by others, while often butting up against the comforting narratives of a national mythology, can allow for different discourses. For the Indigenous Elders who visited York Factory in 2002, the far-reaching colonial and economic history of that place was for them a much less significant part of the collective and individual memories that make that former community such a critical part of Muskego heritage.

Heritage can play a vital role in the health of the state, yet it need not be one that is regressive in the sense that a country must be reliant upon homogeneous and conformist national traditions. Incorporating new stories, new meanings, and new ways of looking at the past at historic places can bring vitality to the well-being of civic life. By viewing heritage as less a depiction of the past in the present but rather the persistence of the past in the present, the language of place can be confident and progressive. With new commemorations and new stories we can replace rear-window nationalism with forward-looking ideas and narratives. Yet, to look ahead we must also remember.

ACKNOWLEDGEMENTS

I am grateful to a number of people who have helped me realize this work. After thirty-two years as a public historian with Parks Canada, I came to the University of Manitoba in 2013 where later this study would begin life as a dissertation. My advisor at the time, Dr. Adele Perry, provided a great deal of assistance. Adele is kind, patient, understanding, and above all intuitive and intelligent, and I benefitted enormously from her wise counsel. I benefitted as well from conversations with fellow students and faculty, especially Dr. Sarah Elvins, both in the History Department and at St. John's College, where I was a research fellow. A number of friends provided encouragement throughout this process, and in particular I want to thank Graham MacDonald for his supportive and always stimulating conversations. The breadth and depth of his work have been truly inspiring. A University of Manitoba doctoral fellowship, an award from the University of Manitoba Research Grants Program, and the J.W. Dafoe writing prize assisted my research travels.

   I owe thanks as well to staff at Library and Archives Canada in Ottawa and Winnipeg, the Archives of Saskatchewan, the Archives of Manitoba, and the Legislative Library of Manitoba for guiding me through the many collections relevant to this study. In particular, I would like to thank Parks Canada for permission to consult their internal Winnipeg files and for permission to use a number of the photographs that appear in this book. I owe Parks Canada a great deal of thanks for providing me the opportunity over the many years of my career to visit historic places in various (and often remote) parts of Canada. These travels were the highlight of my tenure with Parks and helped nurture a sense of curiosity that one does not always encounter in the records of government archives. As I explain in more detail in the Introduction, my visits to historic sites across the West and North have greatly influenced the way I have approached this topic. My criticisms of Parks Canada in this study do not preclude my genuine admiration for the important work that agency has done over a number of decades.

I would be remiss if I did not thank the anonymous reviewers who offered very helpful advice, along with the staff at the University of Manitoba Press. Director David Carr and especially Managing Editor Glenn Bergen provided considerable guidance and I would like to thank them for their patience and support throughout this project. As well, I would like to thank Jill McConkey and David Larsen of the press, along with copy editor Patricia Sanders, who smoothed out the oftentimes rough prose of the original text.

On a personal note, I want to thank my family: my daughters Lauren, Kathleen, and Emily, and especially my wife, Catherine, for their love and support, and their encouragement to reach for a goal even when the bloom of youth has long vanished.

Robert Coutts
Winnipeg

NOTES

Introduction: Landscapes of Memory in Prairie Canada

1 Hargrave, *Letters of Letitia Hargrave*, 246.

2 Ballantyne, *Hudson's Bay*, 140.

3 Smith, *Uses of Heritage*, 1.

4 Ibid.

5 Schama, *Landscape and Memory*, 24.

6 Friesen, *The West*, v–vii.

7 Ashley and Terry, "Introduction: Critical Heritage Studies," 1.

8 Schama, *Landscape and Memory*, 24.

9 See Payment, *The Free People*. Payment's work was the culmination of decades of oral and archival research and of spending considerable time in the Métis communities of the South Saskatchewan district.

10 Smith, *Uses of Heritage*, 6–7.

11 Lisbeth Haas, back cover promotional praise for Elizabeth Kryder-Reid, *California Mission Landscape*, n.p.

12 Smith, *Uses of Heritage*, 40–41.

13 The historic Indigenous sites near Churchill are discussed in more detail in Chapter 1.

14 At York Factory, for example, bank erosion has been a feature of the post since its founding in 1684 and has contributed to its relocation on two occasions. That problem persists to this day and has impacted a good deal of the historic place and its resources. See Lunn, "York Factory."

15 Foucault, *Language, Counter-Memory*.

16 See Gillis, *Commemorations*, 3.

17 Harrison, *Heritage: Critical Approaches*, 5, 14.

18 Tuan, *Space and Place*, 3.

19 Ibid., 17–18.

20 Relph, *Place and Placelessness*, 43–45.

21 See Cresswell, *Place: An Introduction*, 1–21.

22 Ibid., 121.

23 McKay and Bates, *In the Province of History*, 130, 369–80.

24 Opp and Walsh, *Placing Memory*, 16.

25 Schama, *Landscape and Memory*, 3–19. See also Cresswell, *Place: An Introduction*, 17–18.

26 Wolfe, "Settler Colonialism," 388–89.

27 Lowenthal, "Natural and Cultural Heritage."

28 Glassberg, *Sense of History*, 8.

29 Lowenthal, *Heritage Crusade*.

30 See Smith, *Uses of Heritage*, 29–34, 42.

31 Ibid., 42.

32 Ibid., 29.

33 For information regarding how Parks Canada defines "commemorative intent," see https://www.pc.gc.ca/en/docs/pc/guide/guide/commemorative_glossary_1/commemorative_glossary_6. In more recent decades the concepts of "designation" and "designated place" have been interpreted more liberally and have moved away from the restrictive definitions of earlier times. For instance, see the writings of architectural historian Christina Cameron, which include "Spirit of Place" and a later work, "Finding the Spirit of Place." At one time Cameron was the director general of National Historic Sites for Parks Canada, and her later work depicts a broader understanding of historic place as opposed to her earlier and more restrictive comments about historic site and commemorative intent, which are explored in more detail throughout this study.

34 See https://www.pc.gc.ca/en/docs/r/on/rideau/pd-mp/page_A-02.

35 The modern view of architecture and heritage can be traced to the writings of John Ruskin, whose 1849 book *The Seven Lamps of Architecture* argued against the practice of restoration as then practised in favour of a "conserve as found" approach to the preservation of important buildings.

36 Coutts, "Stone Symbols of Dominance," 5.

37 Morgan, *Commemorating Canada*, 131.

38 Opp and Walsh, *Placing Memory*, 16.

39 See "The Barracks," http://www.queerstory.ca/2013/10/11/the-barracks/, 11 October 2013 (accessed 12 December 2017). Other examples of alternative heritage and place memory can be found in Patrizia Gentile's "Capital Queers." Gentile looks at queer spaces of surveillance and cultural formation, and how these spaces functioned beside and within Ottawa's sites of political power.

40 For information about the International African American Museum at Gadsden's Wharf, see https://iaamuseum.org/about/inside-the-museum/ (accessed 9 July 2019).

41 Lowenthal, *Heritage Crusade*, 78.

42 High, "Placing the Displaced Worker," 181.

43 Urry and Larsen, *Tourist Gaze, 3.0.*

44 Harrison, *Heritage: Critical Approaches*, 1.

45 Lowenthal, *Heritage Crusade*, 128.

46 Ibid., 137.

47 Ibid., 156.

48 Harrison, *Heritage: Critical Approaches*, 3.

49 Ibid., 47.

50 Parks Canada, *Canada's Historic Places Initiative,* 1.

51 Ibid., 2.

52 See *Guidelines for the Conservation of Historic Places in Canada,* https://www.canadianarchitect.com/features/guidelines-for-the-conservation-of-historic-places-in-canada/ (accessed 14 December 2017).

53 In England, the Heritage List includes nearly 400,000 of the most important historic places in the country. The list includes buildings, battlefields, monuments, parks, gardens, shipwrecks, and more. See *Historic England,* https://historicengland.org.uk/ (accessed 14 December 2017).

54 Harrison, *Heritage: Critical Approaches,* 5.

55 Lowenthal, *Heritage Crusade,* x.

56 Eric Hobsbawm, "Introduction: Inventing Traditions," in Hobsbawm and Ranger, *Invention of Tradition,* 1.

57 "Heritage" now includes "intangible cultural practices"; there are now almost 500 listed on UNESCO's register of Intangible Cultural Practices from 117 countries. These generally describe such things as traditional folk dances and music, art forms, and traditional craftsmanship. Cuisine has also become part of the list: recently the art of Neapolitan pizza making was added to UNESCO's inventory of recognized cultural practices. See https://ich.unesco.org/en/lists (accessed 10 May 2018).

58 Foucault, *Language, Counter-Memory,* 115–16.

59 Marx, *Eighteenth Brumaire,* 3.

60 Smith, *Uses of Heritage,* 75.

61 Creates, *Places of Presence,* as cited in Opp and Walsh, *Placing Memory,* 3.

62 Nora, "Between Memory and History."

63 Ibid., 12.

64 Ibid., 8–9.

65 Opp and Walsh, *Placing Memory,* 5.

66 Ibid.

67 See Crane, "Writing the Individual Back," 1375.

68 Nietzsche, "On the Utility and Liability," 131–35.

69 Butler, "Victims of Communism Memorial."

70 U.S. National Parks Service, "The Wall that Heals," https://www.nps.gov/vive/index.htm (accessed 18 December 2017).

71 See Young, "Memory and Counter-Memory."

72 Smith, *Uses of Heritage,* 83.

73 Ricketts, "Cultural Selection," 23–24.

74 Ibid., 24.

75 Swyripa, *Storied Landscapes,* 9.

76 Ibid., 5.

77 See Parks Canada, *Guide to the Preparation of Commemorative Integrity Statements: Developing the Statement of Commemorative Intent.*

78 Smith, *Uses of Heritage,* 300.

Chapter 1: Memory Hooks: Commemorating Indigenous Cultural Landscapes

1   Andrews and Zoe, "The Idaa Trail," 160–77.

2   See Hanks, "Ancient Knowledge," 178.

3   Nunn, *Edge of Memory*, 23–24.

4   The Historic Sites and Monuments Board of Canada was established by the federal government in 1919 to recommend candidate historic places, people, and events for national commemoration to the Department of the Interior headed by James Harkin. In his 1990 history of the Board, C.J. Taylor describes how fiscal restraint, along with the dual nature of the heritage program—preservation and commemoration—complicated the work of the Board's early members. Today, with representatives from each province and territory, the HSMBC still advises the minister regarding commemoration. See Taylor, *Negotiating the Past*, 32–34.

5   See Buggey, *Approach to Aboriginal Cultural Landscapes* (accessed 5 September 2017).

6   Canada, Privy Council Office, *Report of the Royal Commission*, vol. 4, 137, as quoted in ibid., 11.

7   TRC, *Calls to Action*, 83–84.

8   See Parks Canada, http://www.pc.gc.ca/leg/docs/r/pca-acl/sec4/index_e.asp (accessed 4 September 2017).

9   See Parks Canada, http://www.pc.gc.ca/leg/docs/r/pca-acl/sec1/index_e.asp (accessed 4 September 2017).

10 Lee, "Aboriginal Heritage Issues." Copy of paper in possession of the author.

11 For a description of Gitxsan territories and land rights, see: http://www.gitxsan.com/about/our-land/. For the Wet'suwet'en, see http://www.wetsuweten.com/territory/.

12 Among many examples see, for instance, the discussions regarding traditional relationships between people and the land in such books as Bullchild, *The Sun Came Down;* Ahenakew and Wolfart, *Our Grandmothers' Lives;* and Bussidor and Bilgen-Reinart, *Night Spirits.*

13 McBryde, "Those Truly Outstanding Examples."

14 Chambers and Blood, "Love Thy Neighbour."

15 Ibid., 259–60.

16 Ibid., 260. Ibid., 277.

17 Meyer, "Pre-Dorset Settlements," 1.

18 See Stoddard, *Seahorse Gully Site.*

19 Government of Manitoba, Historic Resources Branch, *Arctic Small Tool Tradition*, 8.

20 Ibid., 3–8.

21 Stoddard, *Seahorse Gully Site*, 3–5.

22 Prentiss, Walsh, and Foor, "Evolution of Early Thule."

23 See Canada's Historic Places, *Seahorse Gully Remains*, http://www.historicplaces.ca/en/rep-reg/place-lieu.aspx?id=18791 (accessed 13 February 2018).

24 Ibid.

25 See Coutts, Keith, and Stewart, *Kuugjuaq.* The word "*Kuugjuaq,*" meaning "Big River," is the Inuktitut term for the Churchill River.

26 For more on Parks Canada's policy of "commemorative intent" and its inherent conservatism, see the Introduction and the section entitled: "Decentring the Commemorative Narrative" in Chapter 4.

27 Hobsbawm and Ranger, *Invention of Tradition*, 1–14.

28 Parks Canada, Winnipeg Historical Collection, Linear Mounds, Management Plan, 1.

29 Ibid., 3–4.

30 Canada's Historic Places, *Linear Mounds* (accessed 14 February 2018).

31 Parks Canada, Winnipeg Historical Collection, Linear Mounds, Management Plan, 4.

32 Sharon Thomson, Parks Canada archaeologist, Winnipeg, personal communication, 15 February 2018.

33 Parks Canada, Winnipeg Historical Collection, Linear Mounds, Management Plan, 5.

34 Ibid., 6–7.

35 Ibid., 9.

36 Kives, "Linear Mounds."

37 Petroforms differ from petroglyphs, which are carvings on a rock face, and from pictographs, in which red ochre is used to paint on stone surfaces.

38 Pettipas, "Petroform Phenomenon" (accessed 15 February 2018).

39 Ibid., 6–10.

40 Steinbring, "Dating Rock Art." Steinbring considers the petroform builders to be "pre-tribal," predating the Cree, Siouian speakers, and later Anishanaabe (including the Ojibwa) of the region.

41 Buchner, "Archaeo-Astronomical Investigation," 96.

42 According to a *Winnipeg Free Press* interview with Sagkeeng First Nation member Dave Courchene, an annual "Ignite the Fire" gathering is held each September at Bannock Point, the most accessible petroform site in the park. See "Whiteshell's Sacred Stones," *Winnipeg Free Press*, 30 July 2011.

43 See "Ancient Petroform in Manitoba's Whiteshell Park Destroyed," CBC News, 30 June 2017.

44 Under the Manitoba Provincial Parks Act, restrictions on park use include prohibitions on mining or the development of oil, petroleum, natural gas, or hydroelectric power, as well as activities that compromise wilderness, backcountry, or heritage land use categories. The petroform sites in the park fall under this latter category. See the Manitoba Provincial Parks Act, http://web2.gov.mb.ca/laws/statutes/ccsm/p020e.php (accessed 1 March 2018).

45 One example, with which I was involved, was a late 1990s case where a long-time, non-Indigenous resident of the York Factory area and a former custodian of the national historic site there removed remains of the historic Anglican church located on provincial land adjacent to the site. Rather than being prosecuted under the Act for destroying these resources, he was in fact thanked by the provincial Historic Resources Branch for his interest in heritage.

46 Anonymous, e-mail to author dated 17 October 2018. Used with permission.

47 Saunders, "At the Mouth," 172.

48 See Keegan, *Pueblo People*. Keegan studied and photographed the ancient cliff dwellings of Colorado, Arizona, and New Mexico, and also the more contemporary Pueblo villages and people of that region.

49 Provincial Archives of Saskatchewan (hereinafter PAS), Wanuskewin Heritage Park. file HB 89.04.03.01.

50 Ibid.

51   See Canada's Historic Places, *Wanuskewin National Historic Site*.

52   Library and Archives Canada (hereinafter LAC), RG 37-F, Minutes of the Historic Sites and Monuments Board of Canada, June 1986.

53   Ibid.

54   PAS, Meewasin Valley Authority, Wanuskewin Heritage Park, file 401.8.4.

55   Ibid.

56   Thomas Symons to W.G. Bolstad, Executive Director, Meewasin Valley Authority, 2 December 1987, PAS, Meewasin Valley Authority, Wanuskewin Heritage Park, Federal Funding, file 401.8.2.

57   PAS, Meewasin Valley Authority, Wanuskewin Heritage Park, file 401.8.4.1.

58   Ibid.

59   Ibid.

60   Fred Heal, Meewasin Valley Authority, to Tom Young, Provincial Department of Economic Development and Tourism, 9 March 1989, PAS, Meewasin Valley Authority, Wanuskewin Heritage Park, Legislation, file 401.8.4. The word "Provincial" was also dropped from the title of the Act so as not to confuse Wanuskewin with provincial park status. See Colin Maxwell, Provincial Minister of Parks, Recreation and Culture to Joan Duncan, Provincial Minister of Economic Development and Tourism, 31 January 1989, in ibid. The 1989 Act creating the WHPA was amended in 1997. See http://www.publications.gov.sk.ca/freelaw/documents/English/Statutes/Statutes/W1-3.pdf (accessed 5 March 2018).

61   Ibid., 1997.

62   PAS, Wanuskewin Heritage Park, file HB 91.04.02.01, June 1989. WIHI claims to represent all five Indigenous language groups in Saskatchewan including the Dene, Cree, Dakota, Nakota, and Saulteaux.

63   Ibid.

64   Fred Heal, Meewasin Valley Authority to Tom Young, Saskatchewan Department of Economic Development and Tourism, 15 March 1989, PAS, Meewasin Valley Authority, Wanuskewin Heritage Park, Legislation, file 401.8.4.1.

65   PAS, Meewasin Valley Authority, Wanuskewin Heritage Park, Legislation, file 401.8.4.1.

66   PAS, Meewasin Valley Authority, Wanuskewin: The Beginnings of a World Class Heritage Attraction, Saskatchewan Report, November 1989, file 401.8.4.

67   See https://wanuskewin.com/.

68   PAS, *Wanuskewin Heritage Park: Visitor Services Program Final Report*, Kanata Heritage Research, November 1986, section 7.5.4, Meewasin Valley Authority, Wanuskewin Heritage Park, file 401.8.4.1.

69   PAS, Meewasin Valley Authority, Wanuskewin Heritage Park, *Wanuskewin Pre-design Document*, Aldrich Pears, 10 November 1989, 31. Throughout much of the documentation that relates to the development of Wanuskewin Heritage Park, the traditional term "Indians" is used rather than more contemporary terms. This no doubt relates to the Saskatchewan First Nations organization then known as the Federation of Saskatchewan Indian Nations. In 2016 the name was changed to the Federation of Sovereign Indigenous Nations of Saskatchewan.

70   Ibid.

71   See https://wanuskewin.com/visit/exhibitions/ (accessed 12 March 2018).

72 See https://wanuskewin.com/isl/uploads/2017/12/Campaign-Update-Dec-2017-Complete-sm.pdf (accessed 12 March 2018).

73 See https://www.theglobeandmail.com/news/national/canada-adds-eight-sites-to-list-of-candidates-for-unesco-world-heritage-status/article374 (accessed 13 March 2018).

Chapter 2: National Dreams: Commemorating the Fur Trade in Manitoba

1 Peers, *Playing Ourselves*, 169–80.

2 Ibid.

3 Payne and Taylor, "Western Canadian Fur Trade," 2. While I frequently use the acronym HSMBC for the Historic Sites and Monuments Board of Canada, I also employ the shortened phrase "the Board" as well.

4 Innis, *Fur Trade in Canada*, 393.

5 Prince of Wales Fort was one of the earliest national historic sites to be designated in Western Canada, being commemorated in 1920, not long after the founding of the HSMBC. Fort Langley was designated in 1923. See LAC, RG 37-F, Minutes and Correspondence of the Historic Sites and Monuments Board of Canada.

6 Upper Fort Garry (along with forts Rouge and Gibraltar) were designated by the HSMBC in 1924, Rocky Mountain House in 1926, York Factory in 1936, and Fort Edmonton in 1959. See LAC, RG 37-F, Minutes and Correspondence of the Historic Sites and Monuments Board of Canada.

7 See LAC, RG 37-F, Minutes and Correspondence of the Historic Sites and Monuments Board of Canada, 19 May 1925.

8 The Hudson's Bay Company gifted the fort to the federal government in 1950. By federal Order-in-Council Lower Fort Garry was declared a "National Historic Park" on 17 January 1951.

9 University of Manitoba Archives and Special Collections, *Winnipeg Evening Tribune*, 16 May 1931.

10 See Campbell, *Century of Parks Canada*, 2. After the Department of the Interior was disbanded in 1936, the Parks Branch came under a variety of departments including Mines and Resources, Indian and Northern Affairs, Canadian Heritage, and Environment Canada. See ibid., 7. The National Historic Sites Division (NHSD) was part of the Parks Branch. See also http://www.pc.gc.ca/apps/dfhd/page_nhs_eng.aspx?id=12876 (accessed 19 December 2017).

11 See Taylor, *Negotiating the Past*, 3–31.

12 In 1942 Lower Fort Garry hosted "If Day," a mock invasion of "German troops" designed to boost the sale of war bonds. The premier, lieutenant-governor, mayor, and various city officials were "imprisoned" at the fort. See Newman, "February 19, 1942."

13 LAC, RG84, Parks Canada Records, vol. 1071, FG2, "Lease Between His Majesty the King and the Motor Country Club," 1 January 1951.

14 See *Winnipeg Tribune*, 14 July 1956, as cited in ibid, RG84, vol. 7, 1956.

15 LAC, RG84, Parks Canada Records, vol. 1072, FG28, 1962. Properties north and south of the fort walls were purchased by the provincial government in the hope of developing a "sympathetic heritage development." See ibid., vol. 1077, FG56, 1962.

16 LAC, RG 37-F, Minutes and Correspondence of the Historic Sites and Monuments Board of Canada, 19 May 1925.

17   LAC, RG84, Parks Canada Records, vol. 1070, FG2. F.W. Howay to J.B. Harkin, 17 June 1929.

18   Ibid.

19   HSMBC, Plaque Text, "Indian Treaty Number One," Lower Fort Garry National Historic Site.

20   See Craft, *Breathing Life,* 102–6. For a discussion of how provincial conservation measures abrogated treaty rights in Manitoba after 1880, see Friesen, "Grant Me Wherewith."

21   *Winnipeg Free Press,* 4 August, 2020, A4. On a recent visit to the fort in August of 2020 it was noted that the 1970s Treaty 1 plaque had been removed from the exterior of the fort's west wall and located near the temporary entrance to the site. A welcoming staff member provided a brief overview of the history of the fort beginning with a short history of the treaty.

22   LAC, RG 37-F, Minutes and Correspondence of the Historic Sites and Monuments Board of Canada, 1 June 1950.

23   Ibid., February 1950. See also Lower Fort Garry Commemorative Integrity Statement, 1999, at http://www.historicplaces.ca/en/rep-reg/place-lieu. aspx?id=4224 (accessed 22 December 2017).

24   In Chapter 3, I discuss Mennonite Heritage Village near Steinbach, Manitoba. Comprised of relocated heritage structures and reconstructions set in a contrived village setting, the village portrays the traditional perspective that a built environment is crucial to the heritage "experience."

25   Bradley, *British Columbia by the Road,* 230–32.

26   Payne and Taylor, "Western Canadian Fur Trade." 3.

27   Ibid.

28   LAC, Parks Canada Records, RG84, vol. 1076, FG2, vol. 8, J.E. Wilkins to G.L. Scott, 19 December 1956, 1–30.

29   Ibid., 28.

30   See, for instance, Watson, *Lower Fort Garry;* and McKay, *Stone Fort,*

31   LAC, Parks Canada Records, RG84, vol. 1076, FG28, vol. 2, Barbara Johnstone to Jack Herbert, 15 October 1959.

32   LAC, RG84, vol. 1076, FG28, vol. 2, 1965.

33   As cited in Coutts and Pettipas, "'Mere Curiosities,'" 14.

34   For a history of the HBC Collection, see ibid., 13–19. While the HBC continued to own the collection, Parks Canada conserved, curated, and displayed the materials for thirty years at the lower fort and even devoted a full-time curator to the care and maintenance of the collection. The Manitoba Museum does not mention these years of federal stewardship in its current literature. See https://manitobamuseum. ca/main/visit/museum-galleries/hbc-gallery/ (accessed 3 January 2018).

35   Taylor, *Negotiating the Past.*

36   LAC, Parks Canada Records, RG84, vol. 1076, FG2, 1962.

37   Ibid., FG56, 1965.

38   Parks Canada, Winnipeg Historical Collection, Lower Fort Garry Files, "Summary of Restoration Work at the Big House," n.p, n.d.

39   LAC, Parks Canada Records, RG84, FG56, vol. 3, 1968.

40   Much of the research on the Saleshop/Furloft was carried out by Parks Canada historian George Ingram, whose 1967 report *Lower Fort Garry: The Saleshop:*

Structure and Function provided the division with considerable information on the building's look and function in the 1850s. See Ingram, *Lower Fort Garry*.

41 See Thomas, *Men's House*.

42 Parks Canada, Winnipeg Historical Collection, Lower Fort Garry Files, file 8441/L3-6, 11 April 1975.

43 Thomas, Lower Fort Garry, Warehouse Building.

44 In the 1860s the Engineer's Cottage was home to E.R. Abell and his family. Abell managed the "industrial complex" located along the creek south of the fort.

45 Parks Canada, Winnipeg Historical Collection, Lower Fort Garry Files, file 8559/L9, July 1998.

46 LAC, Parks Canada Records, RG84, FG56, vol. 6, 1970.

47 Parks Canada, Winnipeg Historical Collection, Lower Fort Garry Files, May 1971.

48 Elder, *Survey Report*, 1974.

49 See "Cultural Resource Management Policy," in Parks Canada, *Guiding Principles*, 114.

50 It appears as if the approach of large capital investment rather than ongoing maintenance continues. Further wall restoration is under way at Lower Fort Garry, first proposed in the 2017–18 federal government infrastructure program. A total of $4.6 million will be spent to "Repair the perimeter limestone walls surrounding Lower Fort Garry to ensure the stability of this structure over a long lifecycle and to sustain meaningful visitor experience." The work at Lower Fort Garry is part of a $2.6 billion Parks Canada infrastructure rehabilitation across the agency. How this repair work at the fort will be carried out is not explained. It is hoped that the amount of the expenditure does not suggest an approach similar to the "restoration" program of the 1980s and 1990s. See https://www.pc.gc.ca/en/lhn-nhs/mb/fortgarry/visit/infrastructure (accessed 16 July 2019).

51 See Taylor, *Negotiating the Past*, 169–90.

52 Among many reports, see, for example, Canadian Historic Sites, *Occasional Papers*, no. 4; and Livermore, *Lower Fort Garry*.

53 Parks Canada, Winnipeg Historical Collection, Lower Fort Garry Files. Currently, both this plaque and the Treaty 1 plaque are located at the site.

54 As cited in *Lower Fort Garry National Historic Site*, Management Plan, Parks Canada, October 2007. http://publications.gc.ca/collections/collection_2016/pc/R64-105-59-2007-eng.pdf (accessed 7 January 2018).

55 See http://www.historicplaces.ca/en/rep-reg/place-lieu.aspx?id=4224 (accessed 8 January 2018).

56 For information on the farm at Lower Fort Garry see *Occasional Papers in Archaeology and History*. No. 4, 44–92.

57 For a much lengthier discussion of how Indigenous histories are interpreted at historic sites, see Peers, *Playing Ourselves*. See also Peers and Coutts, "Aboriginal History and Historic Sites, 274–94.

58 See https://www.pc.gc.ca/en/lhn-nhs/mb/fortgarry/info/gestion-management-2018 (accessed 16 July 2019).

59 Ibid.

60 Ibid.

61 Ibid.

62   Andersen, "More than the Sum," 630.

63   Kirshenblatt-Gimblett, "Theorizing Heritage," 375.

64   See http://publications.gc.ca/collections/collection_2016/pc/R64-105-59-2007-eng.pdf (accessed 12 January 2018). According to site sources there has been an uptick in visitation in recent years as 2017 saw 45,000 people visit the fort. Information courtesy of email to author from lfg.info@pc.gc.ca, 15 January 2018. Contrast attendance at Lower Fort Garry with a site such as Sovereign Hill in Australia. Sovereign Hill is a reconstructed 1850s gold rush town. In 2015 well over half a million people visited the site (as did I in November of 2018). See https://www.sovereignhill.com.au/media/uploads/SovHill_AnnualReport_2014-15_Full_W.pdf.

65   See Coutts, "Prince of Wales Fort," 504.

66   The Fort Churchill site was also the wintering site (1619–20) of the Danish explorer Jens Munk, a short-lived HBC post in 1689, and the Churchill River post built by the HBC in 1717 and abandoned in 1740.

67   According to LAC documents, "by the order of the Governor General in Council on the 4th of February 1922, Prince of Wales Fort comprising an approximate area of 50 acres was set apart … as an historic memorial site and placed under the control of the Commissioner of Dominion Parks." LAC, RG84, Parks Canada Records, A-2-a, reel T-11295.

68   LAC, RG 37-F, Minutes of the Historic Sites and Monuments Board of Canada, February 1931.

69   The English-based Muscovy Company chartered in 1555 and the Dutch East India Company formed in 1602 were among the first transnational "corporations."

70   See Coutts, "Prince of Wales Fort," 504.

71   LAC, RG 37-F, Minutes of the Historic Sites and Monuments Board of Canada, 27 May 1933.

72   LAC, RG84, Parks Canada Records, A-2-a, reel T-11295, Chief Engineer, Department of Railways and Canals to Major A.A. Pinard, National Parks Branch, Department of the Interior, 7 November 1929. Vandalism reported at the fort site included the theft of artifacts, mostly by workers employed in building the Churchill port facilities across the river. The deep-water port of Churchill opened in 1931 and shipped grain to Europe brought from the prairies to the port via the Hudson Bay Railway.

73   Chief Engineer, Department of Railways and Canals, to J.B. Harkin, Dominion Parks Branch, 3 December 1931, ibid. In 2010 E.J. Hart published a lengthy biography of Harkin, the first commissioner of the Dominion Parks Branch. It is entitled *J.B. Harkin: Father of Canada's National Parks*. While Harkin remained a force for many years in the creation and conservation of many of Canada's national parks, he was also a key player in historic site preservation and the early development of tourism at parks and sites.

74   Ibid., F.L. Farley to J.B. Harkin, 5 July 1931.

75   See Hucker, *Prince of Wales Fort*. Much of Hucker's work relied upon a photogrammetrical analysis of the exterior walls, a process whereby modern photographs are compared with photographs of the walls prior to, during, and after restoration. The restoration of the Cape Merry battery, completed in 1960, was also part of the restoration of the site. Weekly journals recorded the progress of the work, although most were from the 1950s.

76 For a more lengthy description of the fort's character-defining elements, see *Prince of Wales Fort National Historic Site* in Canada's Historic Places, http://www. historicplaces.ca/en/rep-reg/place-lieu.aspx?id=7760 (accessed 22 January 2018).

77 Seahorse Gully NHS is examined in greater detail in Chapter 1.

78 Parks Canada, *Guide to the Preparation of Commemorative Integrity Statements: Developing the Statement of Commemorative Intent*, http://www.pc.gc.ca/eng/docs/ pc/guide/guide/sec3/commemorative (accessed 24 January 2018).

79 For a copy of the 2000 Parks Canada System Plan, see https://www.pc.gc.ca/en/ lhn-nhs/plan (accessed 12 January 2018).

80 See Pannekoek, "Who Matters?," 207.

81 See http://www.pc.gc.ca/en/lhn-nhs/mb/yorkfactory/decouvrir-discover/ commemoration (accessed 12 November 2017).

82 Colpitts, *Pemmican Empire*.

83 For a discussion of the impacts of York Factory's decline, see Tough, *"As Their Natural Resources,"* 63–74; and Coutts, "'We See Hard Times.'"

84 For discussions regarding the decline of Subarctic fur trade communities in the late nineteenth and early twentieth centuries, see McCormack, *Fort Chipewyan;* Tough, *"As Their Natural Resources";* and Ray, *Canadian Fur Trade*.

85 LAC, RG84, Parks Canada Records, York Factory NHS, A-2-a, microfilm reel T-11470.

86 Ibid.

87 See Beardy and Coutts, *Voices from Hudson Bay*, xxi.

88 LAC, RG84, Parks Canada Records, York Factory NHS, A-2-a, microfilm reel T-14170. A.R. Huband, Executive Assistant, Hudson's Bay Company, Winnipeg, to J.D. Herbert, National Historic Sites Division, 12 January 1960. Later, when the federal government acquired York, Bland's application to continue operation of his hunting lodge was rejected because of the negative impacts on the game resources of the area, an important source of subsistence for the Indigenous people who had returned to the area. See *Winnipeg Tribune*, 13 May 1968.

89 The present site of York Factory (known as York Factory III, 1788 to 1957) dates from the late eighteenth century. Earlier locations, approximately three kilometres downstream, include York Factory I (1684 to 1714) and York Factory II (1714 to 1788), which were abandoned because of riverbank erosion and flooding.

90 LAC, RG84, A-2-a, Parks Canada Records, York Factory NHS, reel T-14170, T.C. Fenton to Chief Engineer Gordon Scott, National Historic Sites Division, 18 September 1959. However, an earlier memorandum to the minister from Assistant Deputy Minister E.A. Cote recommended that the department not go beyond the "moth-balling stage [at York Factory] for some years to come." Ibid., E.A. Cote to Minister, file 01340, 24 August 1959.

91 LAC, RG84, A-2-a, Parks Canada Records, York Factory NHS, reel T-14170, Willis A. Richford, Executive Director, HBRS, to Alvin Hamilton, Minister of Northern Affairs and Natural Resources, 17 January 1958.

92 In 1961 Northern Affairs Minister Walter Dinsdale wrote to Derek Bedson, the clerk of the provincial Executive Council in Manitoba, stating, "I can now say that the Department has decided against preserving the remaining building [at York Factory] for the present, our emphasis has to be on Lower Fort Garry and Prince of Wales' Fort to carry the story of the Fur Trade as far as Manitoba is concerned."

LAC, RG84, A-2-a, Parks Canada Records, York Factory NHS, reel T-14170, Walter Dinsdale to Derek Bedson, 6 March 1961.

93 LAC, RG84, A-2-a, Parks Canada Records, York Factory NHS, reel T-14170, Walter Dinsdale to Robert Simpson, Member of Parliament for Churchill, 3 March 1961.

94 LAC, RG84, A-2-a, Parks Canada Records, York Factory NHS, reel T-14170.

95 LAC, RG84, A-2-a, Parks Canada Records, York Factory NHS, reel T-14170, Sterling Lyon to Arthur Laing, 5 January 1967.

96 See Hunter, *Depot and Library Buildings,* 11, Parks Canada, Winnipeg Historical Collection, York Factory files.

97 LAC, RG84, A-2-a, Parks Canada Records, York Factory NHS, reel T-14170, Peter Bennett to John Rick, NHSD, 6 November 1967.

98 Board minutes indicate that opposition to the move was unanimous, and the Board recommended strongly "that the site of York Factory be acquired [and] that steps be undertaken towards stabilization...." LAC, RG84, Minutes and Correspondence of the Historic Sites and Monuments Board of Canada, vol. 1179, HS-1, vol. 26, 4, 1967.

99 Ibid., vol. 1179, HS-1, vol. 29, 2. Coming on the heels of the election of Pierre Trudeau and his federal Liberal government in June of 1968, Chrétien's comments about York echoed the new government's commitment to the policy of bilingualism and biculturalism.

100 See Parks Canada Attendance, 2006–2012, http://publications.gc.ca/collections/collection_2017/pc/R61-107-2012-eng.pdf (accessed 30 January 2018).

101 Morgan, *Commemorating Canada,* 131.

Chapter 3: "We Came. We Toiled. God Blessed.": Settler Colonialism and Constructing Authenticity

1 See O'Brien, *Firsting and Lasting.*

2 Swyripa, *Storied Landscapes,* 79.

3 Ibid., 74.

4 Dick, "Prairie Settlement Patterns," 365.

5 Spry, "Tragedy of the Loss," 203.

6 See https://www.pc.gc.ca/en/lhn-nhs/plan (accessed 21 March 2018).

·7 The Pasts Collective, *Canadians and Their Pasts,* 105. See also Mandel, "Images of Prairie Man," 206.

8 Gerald Friesen, as quoted in Payne, "Commemorating Ethno-cultural Communities," 13.

9 For descriptions of agriculture and the river lot system in Red River, see Hall, "Red River Farming." See also Coutts, "St. Andrew's," 131–52.

10 Jean Friesen and Gerald Friesen, "River Road," in Friesen, *River Road,* 4.

11 Archives of Manitoba, River Road Heritage Parkway, 1977, 1, Howard Pawley fonds, 1977-162, M-93-7-17, file 5.

12 Legislative Library of Manitoba (hereinafter LLM), Red River Master Development Plan.

13 LLM, River Road Heritage Parkway: Concept Plan, 1.

14 Campbell, *Nature, Place, and Story,* 92–93. Beyond the 3.6-hectare Parks Canada land at The Forks, the site lacks the green space once promised by developers. Housing has also been on the agenda for the site but has yet to be realized. In *Nature,*

Place, and Story, Campbell endeavours to rewrite "public history as environmental history," with The Forks, she argues, having been made "useful again." Though a site reclaimed, The Forks does little to interpret public history, since environmental history as its riverside focus is for the most part overwhelmed by the kind of urban development found in most communities looking for a mix of retail, commercial, and entertainment attractions. The federal government's 1990s Green Plan, once heavily publicized for The Forks, is for the most part a forgotten objective, essentially lost under the pressure for continuing financial investment in the built environment. For more on Campbell's study of The Forks development, see Chapter 4 of this study. The nearby Upper Fort Garry Heritage Park on Main Street does contain green space with gardens, identified building locations, and a sound and light heritage wall, as well as physical, online, and smart phone QR code interpretation. The park's deliberate low-key development, though criticized by some people, does go some way in creating a heritage urban oasis.

15 LLM, Manitoba ARC Authority Inc., River Road Heritage Parkway: Concept Plan, 1982, 1.

16 Ibid., 3. The Concept Plan did recognize the increasing negative impacts of "development pressures" and that the project represented "a last chance opportunity," ibid., 4. According to the site analysis contained in the 1982 River Road Parkway: Proposed Project Plan, the landscapes of the River Road area "have been created and manipulated over time by the natural processes of a slow river meandering through a fairly restricted flood plain. The resulting landform, vegetation, and river configuration have contributed to the land-use patterns that we see today [1982]. River Road itself has evolved as an integral part of this land use pattern, historically linking its components to each other, to the river, and to larger urban centres. This evolutionary process continues as new pressures for housing, recreation, and leisure activities increase." LLM, Manitoba ARC Authority Inc., River Road Parkway: Proposed Project Plan, 12.

17 Ibid., 1.

18 Ibid., 8.

19 Around that same time, Parks Canada restored Riel House, the surviving 19th-century home of the Riel family and a national historic site located in St. Vital in the south of the city. An opportunity to purchase and preserve the old river lot associated with the house was declined by the federal government and that land too was then predictably altered by modern urban development.

20 LLM, Manitoba ARC Authority Inc., River Road Heritage Parkway: Concept Plan, 1982, 9. Kennedy House was closed in the spring of 2015 because of structural issues. Closing with it was the Maple Grove Tea Room, a popular tourist destination. The elaborate gardens adjacent to Kennedy House were developed in the 1920s.

21 Parks Canada, Winnipeg Historical Collection, St. Andrew's Rectory National Historic Site, Management Plan, 1980. A second management plan was published in 2003 although it added little to the existing scope and interpretation of the Rectory. See http://publications.gc.ca/site/eng/98469/publication.html (accessed 13 April 2018).

22 Anglican Church of Canada, Diocese of Rupert's Land Archives, St. Andrews-on-the Red, http://www.rupertsland.ca/about/archives/ (accessed 13 April 2018).

23 Parks Canada, Winnipeg Historical Collection, St. Andrew's-on-the-Red, Historical and Architectural Survey and Rededication Service, May 1995.

24   As riverbank erosion has been a problem for some time along River Road, stone riprap was added in the 1990s at key points along the riverbank.

25   LLM, Manitoba ARC Authority Inc., River Road Heritage Parkway: Proposed Project Plan, 1982, 64.

26   Ibid., 64–72.

27   The new signage was developed by Sherry Dangerfield Interpretive Planning. It won Interpretation Canada's Gold Award of Excellence in 2007.

28   Manitoba Parks, River Road Provincial Park: Draft Management Plan, Spring 2013, 7. See http://www.gov.mb.ca/sd/parks/consult/pdf/june_18/river_road_dmp.pdf (accessed 16 April 2018).

29   Archives Manitoba, River Road Heritage Parkway, Zoning and Acquisition Proposals, 1973, Schedule AG 0002A, A2.

30   Ibid.

31   Ibid.

32   Swyripa, *Storied Landscapes*, 200–201.

33   Ibid., 201.

34   Much of the impetus for the creation of Upper Canada Village was the construction of the St. Lawrence Seaway and the destruction of surviving mid-nineteenth-century structures in the region. Some of the buildings from that area were moved to the new heritage attraction beginning in 1958.

35   See Gabert, "Locating Identity," 55.

36   LLM, Manitoba Department of Tourism, Recreation, and Cultural Affairs, A Survey of the Mennonite Village Museum, Winnipeg, 1975, 10.

37   LLM, Manitoba Multicultural Museums Committee, Ethno-cultural Museums and Historical Societies, 4.

38   Ibid., 45.

39   Ibid., 46.

40   LLM, Mennonite Heritage Village, The Mennonite Heritage Village Story, 1975 (updated 1990), 8–21. See also David McInnis, Historic Resources Officer, to Donna Dul, Director, Historic Resources Branch, AM, CH0007A, file D-9-8-12.

41   See https://mennoniteheritagevillage.com/ (accessed 23 April 2018).

42   Ibid.

43   Gordon, *Time Travel*, 268–69.

44   Lowenthal, *Past Is a Foreign Country*, 25.

45   LLM, Manitoba Department of Tourism, Recreation, and Cultural Affairs, Survey of the Mennonite Village Museum, 28–47.

46   Gabert, "Locating Identity," 55.

47   Margruite Krahn, *Pembina Valley Online*, 2 March 2015, https://www.pembinavalleyonline.com/ (accessed 24 April 2018).

48   Lowenthal, *Past Is a Foreign Country*, 4.

49   Friesen, "Heritage," 209.

50   Parks Canada, Winnipeg Historical Collection, Neubergthal Street Village National Historic Site, Commemorative Integrity Statement, 1998, 6.

51   Ibid., 3.

52   Ibid. The Board also noted that the particular forms of land use that accompanied ethnic settlement on the prairies, in particular the Mormon settlement at Stirling

in Alberta and the Ukrainian "Four Corner" settlement at Gardenton, Manitoba, should be commemorated as well. For an analysis of early Ukrainian settlement patterns in the West, see Lehr, "Landscape of Ukrainian Settlement." The commemoration of Gardenton was later withdrawn by the Board.

53 The name of the settlement near Altona has seen a variety of spellings over the years. The name "Neubergthal" originated with the Mennonite village of Bergthal in southern Russia. In 1994 the Canadian *Gazeteer* officially changed the name from New Bergthal to its original Neubergthal.

54 Parks Canada, Winnipeg Historical Collection, Neubergthal Street Village National Historic Site, Commemorative Integrity Statement, 1998, 4.

55 Ibid., 7.

56 See http://www.neubergthalheritagefoundation.com/ (accessed 4 May 2018).

57 Canada's Historic Places, *Doukhobors at Veregin National Historic Site of Canada*. See http://www.historicplaces.ca/en/rep-reg/place-lieu.aspx?id=12783 (accessed 7 May 2018).

58 Ibid. Although the settlement took its name from Doukhobor leader Peter Verigin, it was incorporated under the spelling "Veregin." The community recognizes both spellings as legitimate. See Coutts, *Doukhobor Village*.

59 Koozma Tarasoff, "Doukhobors," in *Encyclopedia of Canada's Peoples*, ed. Paul Magosci (Toronto: University of Toronto Press, 1999), 422, as cited in Coutts, ibid., 1971.

60 Decisions regarding land tenure were made on behalf of the collective by village Elders. For a discussion of the differing views with government, see Adelman, "Early Doukhobor Experience," 111–13.

61 Coutts, *Doukhobor Village*.

62 Ibid.

63 As minister of the Interior, Oliver not only promoted a hard-line policy against the immigration of non-English-speaking peoples but facilitated the surrender and expropriation of Indigenous treaty lands in the West.

64 Canada's Historic Places, *Doukhobors at Veregin National Historic Site of Canada*, http://www.historicplaces.ca/en/rep-reg/place-lieu.aspx?id=12783 (accessed 8 May 2018).

65 Ibid.

66 Allen, *Region of the Mind*.

67 See, for example, Wardhaugh, *Towards Defining the Prairies*. Eyford's *White Settler Reserve* looks at one example of socially constituted space within the context of settler colonial history.

68 Schama, *Landscape and Memory*, 23–36.

69 Parks Canada, Winnipeg Historical Collection, Dick, "Prairie Settlement Patterns," 400.

70 Ibid.

71 Carter, "Review of Florence Miller's *Motherwell*," 117. As part of the federal government infrastructure program, $1.2 million was invested in 2017 in the rehabilitation of the site's Visitor Centre. See https://www.pc.gc.ca/en/lhn-nhs/sk/motherwell/visit/infrastructure (accessed 14 May 2018).

72 See http://www.historicplaces.ca/en/rep-reg/place-lieu.aspx?id=1209 (accessed 14 May 2018).

73   Ibid.

74   See Motherwell Homestead National Historic Site of Canada, https://www.pc.gc.ca/apps/dfhd/page_nhs_eng.aspx?id=730 (accessed 14 May 2018).

75   LAC, RG84-A-2a, Motherwell Homestead—Buildings Documentation, microfilm reel, T-14257, 1968.

76   Parks Canada, Winnipeg Historical Collection, Doull, "Motherwell Homestead," Federal Heritage Buildings Review Office, Ottawa, Building Report 88-14, 1988, 1.

77   Ibid.

78   Ibid., 2.

79   The best known of these studies is Dick's *Farmers "Making Good."* This is a revised edition of the original 1989 work published by Parks Canada, in which Dick employs a microhistorical analysis of settlement and land use in the Abernethy district of Saskatchewan between 1882 and 1920 when Ontarian settlers established social and economic structures in the prairie West.

80   See https://www.pc.gc.ca/en/lhn-nhs/sk/motherwell/culture/histoire-history (accessed 15 May 2018).

81   Ibid.

82   See http://publications.gc.ca/collections/collection_2011/pc/R61-56-2011-eng.pdf, 7.

83   Ibid., 10–11.

84   Mackey, "Tricky Myths," 314.

85   Ibid.

86   Ulrich, *Age of Homespun*, 250.

Chapter 4: Contested Space:
Commemorating Indigenous Places of Resistance

1   Studying the colonial process as it evolved in British Columbia between 1850 and 1938 as distinct from the rest of Canada, Cole Harris traces the struggle to both restrict and make Indigenous space over a century of confrontation, imperialism, jurisdictional disputes, resistance, and compromise. See Harris, *Making Native Space*, 265–92.

2   Devine, *People Who Own Themselves*. See also Devine, "Prosopographical Approaches," 361–86.

3   Cresswell, *Place: An Introduction*, 123.

4   Brown, *Civil War Canon*, 201–35.

5   *Globe and Mail*, 19 August 2017, A8–A9.

6   See, for instance, Shore, "Origins of Métis Nationalism," 81.

7   See Friesen, *Canadian Prairies*, 75–80.

8   The 1891 Seven Oaks monument was actually the first historic monument to be erected in Western Canada.

9   LAC, H3/701/1818, NMC 6069, Peter Fidler, *Map showing the area of Seven Oaks, 1816. A true copy, Wm. Sax, D.P. Surveyor, April, 1818.* See Warkentin and Ruggles, *Historical Atlas of Manitoba*, 186–89. The battlefield site is also in the general area of Seven Oaks House, the still extant 1853 home of John Inkster and Mary Sinclair. Inkster was a farmer and merchant in the Red River Settlement. In 1891 the Inkster family donated the small parcel of land upon which sits the Seven Oaks monument.

10   Dick, "Seven Oaks Incident," 93.

11   Ibid., 92.

12   See, for example, Barkwell, *Battle of Seven Oaks*. Interestingly, while Barkwell provides an admirably detailed account of the events of Seven Oaks from a Métis perspective, the cover of his publication is illustrated with C.W. Jefferys's painting *Battle of Seven Oaks, 1816*, a completely inaccurate portrayal of the battle in which mounted Métis and Indians are depicted charging a ragtag group of "settlers," most of whom are on foot. It is this illustration that for many years graced the book covers, school literature, and interpretive panels of the dominant plot.

13   "An Account of the Affair of Seven Oaks: The Circumstances That Led up to it; a Description of the Contestants; the Events of the Conflict, including the Death of Governor Semple and his Followers; and a Report of Proceedings of the Gathering for the 'Unveiling of the Seven Oaks Monument,' June 19th, 1891 by George Bryce and Charles N. Bell," Manitoba Historical Society, *Transactions*, Series 1, No. 43, 19 June 1891, Winnipeg. The *Transactions* series was published between 1879 and 1909, between 1926 and 1936, and from 1944 until 1980.

14   LAC, RG84, Minutes and Correspondence of the Historic Sites and Monuments Board of Canada, Minutes, 30 January 1920.

15   Ibid.

16   Ibid., 18 May 1920.

17   Ibid., May–June 1951.

18   Letter from A.J.H. Richardson to Rev. Antoine D'Eschambault, 18 September 1956, and Rev. D'Eschambault to Richardson, 25 September 1956, LAC, RG84, Minutes and Correspondence of the Historic Sites and Monuments Board of Canada, Correspondence, vol. 1384, file HS 10-4, part 2.

19   Canada's Historic Places, *Battle of Seven Oaks, Statement of Commemorative Intent and Designated Place*, Historic Sites and Monuments Board of Canada, Parks Canada report number 2009-CED-SDC-027. See also http://www.pc.gc.ca/apps/ dfhd/page_nhs_eng.aspx?id=149. According to the document's "Description of Historic Place," the designation "refers to the plot of land, located in the northeast corner of Main Street and Rupert's Land Boulevard in the City of Winnipeg."

20   Proclaimed in 1814 by Red River Governor Miles Macdonell, the Pemmican Proclamation forbade the export of pemmican and other supplies from the District of Assiniboia, the large colonial district set up by the HBC with the establishment of the Red River Colony. Intended by Macdonell to retain foodstuffs for the settlers, the Act severely restricted Métis commerce in the region.

21   MacLeod and Morton, *Cuthbert Grant of Grantown*, 49.

22   Historian George Stanley's views on the 1885 Resistance are relevant here when he argued the "inevitable disorganization which is produced among primitive people when they are suddenly brought into contact with a more complex civilization." See Stanley, *Birth of Western Canada*, 179.

23   In his description of the battle of Seven Oaks, Giraud uses the word "massacre" repeatedly. See Giraud, *Métis in the Canadian West*, 458–64. MacLeod and Morton in *Cuthbert Grant of Grantown* employ the terms "collision" and "massacre" to describe Seven Oaks; see pp. 38–72.

24   See Dick, "Seven Oaks Incident," 1–30.

25   See, for instance, Newman, *Caesars of the Wilderness*, 173–75. See also Joseph Martin, who, in "Conflict at Red River," concludes that the battle was a "massacre." Martin's

article repeated his earlier conclusion from a 1965 piece entitled "The 150th Anniversary of Seven Oaks," in Manitoba Historical Society, *Transactions,* Series 3, no. 22, 1965.

26 These organizations included Parks Canada, the Province of Manitoba Community Places Program, the Winnipeg Foundation, the City of Winnipeg, the Manitoba Métis Federation, the Manitoba Historical Society, the Anglican Church of Canada, and the Seven Oaks School Division.

27 LaRocque, "For the Love of Place," 179.

28 Dick, "Seven Oaks Incident," 104.

29 Bryce, "Old Settlers of Red River," Manitoba Historical Society, *Transactions* Series 1, no. 19, 1885, http://www.mhs.mb.ca/docs/transactions/1/settlers.shtml.

30 Payment, *Native Society and Economy,* 55–56.

31 Parks Canada, Directory of Federal Heritage Designations, *Forts Rouge, Garry and Gibraltar National Historic Site of Canada, Winnipeg, Manitoba,* http://www.pc.gc.ca/apps/dfhd/page_nhs_eng.aspx?id=1728.

32 Parks Canada, Directory of Federal Heritage Designations, *The Forks National Historic Site of Canada,* http://www.pc.gc.ca/apps/dfhd/page_nhs_eng.aspx?id=151.

33 See The Forks North Portage Partnership website: http://www.theforks.com/business/the-forks-north-portage-partnership/mission-mandate-vision.

34 Campbell, *Nature, Place, and Story,* 100.

35 See Friends of Upper Fort Garry, http://www.upperfortgarry.com/.

36 Ibid.

37 In a 2014 article in the *Winnipeg Free Press,* Friends of Upper Fort Garry Chair Jerry Gray stated, "There's all kinds of stories that come out of that fort and the reason we're doing this one right now is it's so significant to our history with the signing of the papers of 1870 for Confederation. The focus on that is the reason we're saving this fort." See *Winnipeg Free Press,* 18 October 2014, https://www.winnipegfreepress.com/local/friends-of-upper-fort-garry-defend-reasoning-279655462.html.

38 At a 2014 ceremony at the upper fort park, Manitoba Métis Federation President David Chartrand told the gathering that the park's primary significance was as a Métis location. "Upper Fort Garry is the birthplace of the Métis Nation," Chartrand said. "It's here in 1869 that the Métis introduced what's been described as the first bill of rights . . . this will be the site to showcase the Métis national heritage centre." See https://www.winnipegfreepress.com/local/park-to-celebrate-upper-fort-garry-279699702.html. Not all agreed with Chartrand's perspective or the interpretive focus at the park. The Scottish Heritage Council expressed their disagreement with the de-emphasis on the traditional Scottish history of the upper fort in favour of a greater Indigenous perspective. See "Scots Slam Perceived Snub," *Winnipeg Free Press,* 17 October 2014.

39 Urry, *Consuming Places,* 129–40.

40 Ibid., 131–32.

41 McRae, "Remembering What We Forget." For a more in-depth study of Indigenous memories of 1885, see McRae, "Remembering Rebellion," especially pp. 176–93 for a summary of HSMBC and Parks Canada treatments of the 1885 sites and what McRae calls the "Battle for Batoche."

42 Foote, *Shadowed Ground,* 208.

43 Hildebrandt, *Views from Fort Battleford,* 103.

44 Parks Canada, Fort Battleford National Historic Site of Canada, http://pc.gc.ca/en/lhn-nhs/sk/battleford/info.

45 Taylor, *Negotiating the Past*, 145.

46 LAC, RG84, vol. 1382, HS 10-3-6.

47 See McCullough, "Parks Canada and the 1885 Rebellion," 167.

48 See Fort Battleford Statement of Commemorative Intent. See http://pc.gc.ca/en/lhn-nhs/sk/battleford/decouvrir-discover.

49 See "Cree Win War of Words over 'Siege' of Fort Battleford 125 Years Ago," *Globe and Mail*, 21 October 2010.

50 McCullough, "Parks Canada and the 1885 Rebellion," 163.

51 Fort Battleford NHS Statement of Commemorative Intent.

52 See the full Batoche plaque text further down page 173.

53 LAC, RG84, vol. 1380, HS-10-3-2, Part 1.

54 LAC, RG84, vol. 979, BA2, Part 1.

55 McCullough, "Parks Canada and the 1885 Rebellion," 171.

56 Ibid., 170.

57 LAC, RG84, vol. 979, BA2, Part 2.

58 McCullough, "Parks Canada and the 1885 Rebellion," 173.

59 Parks Canada, Directory of Federal Heritage Designations, *Batoche National Historic Site of Canada*, http://www.pc.gc.ca/apps/dfhd/page_nhs_eng.aspx?id=731.

60 Parks Canada, Batoche Management Plan, 1972, RG84, Parks Canada file 8400/B3.

61 See Payment, *Structural and Settlement History*. While Payment's later book, *The Free People/Li Gens Libres: A History of the Métis Community of Batoche Saskatchewan*, published in 2009, builds extensively upon earlier themes in her work, it was in her 1977 report for Parks Canada that she first developed the history of Batoche to include the post-1885 period. Walter Hildebrandt's book *The Battle of Batoche: British Small Warfare and the Entrenched Métis* is a revised edition of his earlier work for Parks Canada and tells the story of the detailed strategies of both sides during the four-day siege of the settlement.

62 Bennett, "Commemorative Integrity."

63 Cameron, "Commemoration: A Moving Target?," 29.

64 Parks Canada, Winnipeg Historical Collection, Batoche National Historic Site of Canada, Commemorative Integrity Statement, March 1997, Parks Canada Winnipeg Office, 2.

65 Ibid., 10–11.

66 Ibid., "Historic Place," 4–7.

67 Parks Canada, Directory of Federal Heritage Designations, *Batoche National Historic Site of Canada*, http://www.pc.gc.ca/apps/dfhd/page_nhs_eng.aspx?id=731.

68 See Parks Canada, Directory of Federal Heritage Designations, "Description of Historic Place," *Battle of Cut Knife Hill National Historic Site of Canada*, http://www.pc.gc.ca/apps/dfhd/page_nhs_eng.aspx?id=737.

69 Canada's Historic Places, *Battle of Duck Lake National Historic Site of Canada*, http://www.historicplaces.ca/en/rep-reg/place-lieu.aspx?id=12916.

70 Parks Canada, Winnipeg Historical Collection, Battle of Tourand's Coulee/Fish Creek National Historic Site of Canada, Management Plan, 2007, 4. The 2000 Statement of Commemorative Intent for the site is fairly straightforward, stating

that Fish Creek was designated a national historic site because "at this place occurred a military engagement of the North West Rebellion /Métis Resistance between Middleton's North West Field Force and Gabriel Dumont's Métis and First Nations forces." No mention is made, however, of who actually won the battle. See ibid., 4.

71 See Klippenstein, "On a New Approach," 3–4.

72 Ibid.

73 Andersen, "More than the Sum," 620.

74 See Peers, *Playing Ourselves*, 169–80.

75 Andersen, "More than the Sum," 630.

76 Ashworth and Tunbridge, *Dissonant Heritage*, 21.

77 Smith, *Uses of Heritage*, 282.

Chapter 5: Heritage Place: The Function of Modernity, Gender, and Sexuality

1   See Berman, *All That Is Solid*, 15–20.

2   Foucault, *Discipline and Punish*.

3   Harrison, *Heritage: Critical Approaches*, 68.

4   Virginia Woolf, *A Room of One's Own; Three Guineas* (London: Penguin Books, 1993), 51. Actually, Woolf's famous passage is a misquote of her line, "I would venture to guess that Anon, who wrote so many poems without signing them, was often a woman."

5   Huyck, "Proceeding from Here," 364.

6   See Parks Canada, National Historic Sites System Plan, 1991, https://www.google.ca/search?q=Parks+Canada+System+Plan+1991&rlz=1C5CHFA_enCA503CA503&tbm=isch&tbo=u&source=univ&sa=X&ved=0a (accessed 4 June 2018).

7   Dodd, "Canadian Historic Sites." Dodd writes that in 2008, of the 126 designations relating to Canadian women (or 6 percent of the total number of HSMBC designations since 1919), the largest number, 66, related to individuals, 33 to events, and only 27 to sites. Virtually all of these sites are simply plaqued sites without active interpretation and, as discussed later in this chapter, that number declines in Manitoba and Saskatchewan.

8   McCullough, "Parks Canada and Women's History," 339.

9   Dodd, "Canadian Historic Sites," 32.

10 See Dodd., ibid., n9.

11 See Parks Canada, "Heritage Value," Butchart Gardens National Historic Site of Canada, https://www.pc.gc.ca/apps/dfhd/page_nhs_eng.aspx?id=10910 (accessed 25 October 2019).

12 These budget cuts, which began in the late 1990s, were capped by massive reductions (at least federally) to heritage programs in the spring of 2012. See "Federal Budget 2012: Parks Canada Feels the Pinch as Harper Government Makes More Cuts," *Toronto Star*, 30 April 2012.

13 I want to note that this last comment refers to the superficial way women are often portrayed at fur trade sites like Lower Fort Garry and is not intended to characterize a more general interpretation of women in the history of the fur trade. Since the groundbreaking work of Sylvia Van Kirk in 1980, the changing views of race and gender and the social and cultural roles of Indigenous women have greatly influenced the course of fur trade social studies over the last forty years. Van Kirk studied the processes by which Indigenous women gained agency in the fur trade

primarily through their relationships with HBC men, particularly officers. But as Adele Perry suggests, Van Kirk's *Many Tender Ties* is an example of a type of feminism where heterosexual relationships are set within a liberal interpretation of the western Canadian fur trade, a "consensual possibility" and "positivist naiveté" that Perry says do not readily fit "the messy context of the colonial archive" as it came to be understood by feminist scholars working in the 1990s and 2000s. For such writers, agency, she argues, does not sit so comfortably with the "enduring legacies" of colonialism and sexuality. See Perry, "Historiography that Breaks Your Heart," 85, 92. See also Van Kirk, *Many Tender Ties*. While the focus of gender studies in regard to the fur trade has evolved in recent years, at historic sites in the West such nuances have only scratched the surface of their programming.

14   Sangster, "Beyond Dichotomies," 109.

15   Carter, *Imperial Plots*, 4.

16   Ibid., 327, 376.

17   Graham, Ashworth, and Tunbridge, *Geography of Heritage*, 44. See also Felski, "Gender of Modernity," 146. Uma Kothari and Tim Edensor, in "Masculinization of Stirling's Heritage," 115–34, argue that the artifacts from the past that have been valued as heritage have been largely selected from a masculine perspective.

18   Parks Canada's policy on Commemorative Intent is explored earlier in this work. See Chapter 4.

19   Dubrow, "Restoring Women's History," 2.

20   Ibid., 7. See also West, "Uncovering and Interpreting Women's History."

21   Adams, "Rooms of Their Own."

22   See https://en.wikipedia.org/wiki/List_of_Natrional_Historic_Sites_of_Canada_in_Manitoba (accessed 5 June 2018).

23   Horodyski, "Women and the Winnipeg General Strike of 1919," 1.

24   See https://www.pc.gc.ca/en/lhn-nhs/mb/riel (accessed 20 August 2018).

25   McMaster, *Working Girls in the West*.

26   Hayden, "Power of Place."

27   Ibid., 76.

28   Peers, *Playing Ourselves*, 6–7.

29   Ibid., 7–8.

30   Over the years that I participated in staff training at Lower Fort Garry, my contribution as a historian was usually restricted to a couple of hours with the interpretive staff. On the other hand, the full week of training included up to a half-day of information regarding fire drills.

31   Beardy and Coutts, *Voices from Hudson Bay*, 44–48.

32   Carter, *Capturing Women*, 159.

33   Ibid., 158.

34   Carter, *Imperial Plots*, 17.

35   See McCallum, *Indigenous Women, Work, and History*.

36   I base this assertion upon my thirty-two-year career in heritage, my extensive and ongoing involvement with groups such as the Manitoba Historical Society, and my time serving on heritage boards such as the Manitoba Historic Sites Advisory Board and the City of Winnipeg's Heritage Buildings Committee.

37   Dubrow, "Blazing Trails with Pink Triangles," 284–85.

38   Ibid., 287.

39   Ibid., 291.

40   See http://spacing.ca/toronto/2017/06/15/making-places-torontos-queer-history/ (accessed 18 June 2018).

41   Quoted in "Making Places for Toronto's Queer History," ibid.

42   Ibid.

43   See Churchill, "Mother Goose's Map," 830, as quoted in Gentile, "Capital Queers," 188.

44   Gentile, "Capital Queers," 209.

45   Korinek, "A Queer-Eye View," 239–53.

46   See, for instance, Lyle Dick's articles "Heterohegemonic Discourse," and "Male Homosexuality." See also Duder, *Awfully Devoted Women.*

47   According to its archival website, the Manitoba Gay and Lesbian Archives is "a symbolic culmination of Lesbian, Gay, Bisexual, Transgendered, Two-spirited, and Queer individuals and organizations recording people's history . . . dating back to the 1920s." See http://umanitoba.ca/libraries/units/archives/digital/gay_lesbian/ (accessed 18 June 2018). The fact that the launch of the archival website was announced on the Manitoba Historical Society's *Historical News* website in 2013 might indicate some progress within traditional heritage communities. See http://www.mhs.mb.ca/news/archive05.shtml (accessed 18 June 2018).

48   In 2005 Parks Canada and the Department of Canadian Heritage put out a brochure entitled *Out and About: Towards a Better Understanding of Gay, Lesbian, Bisexual and Transgendered Persons in the Workplace.* However, as the title suggests, the booklet is not about sexuality and heritage but rather a twenty-eight-page guide for LGBTQ individuals in the workplace. See http://hrcouncil.ca/hr-toolkit/documents/CH37-4-9-2005E.pdf (accessed 19 June 2018).

Conclusion: History, Memory, and the Heritage Discourse

1   Hardy, *Return of the Native,* 2.

2   Morgan, *Commemorating Canada,* 9.

3   Harrison, *Heritage: Critical Approaches,* 166.

4   Dawson, "'It's a Landmark,'" 407.

5   Pannekoek, "Rise of the Heritage Priesthood." It is perhaps curious that Pannekoek, a former and long-time heritage manager for both Parks Canada and the Government of Alberta, warns of the increased influence of the professional heritage manager, as much of his career was devoted to hiring and managing heritage professionals and making sure that their work was considered authoritative in historic site preservation and interpretation.

6   Many interpretive specialists are members of Interpretation Canada, an organization founded in 1977 to represent and promote the work of interpretive specialists across the country. According to its website, the organization's members "enrich the experience of visitors to museums, historic sites, parks, farms, nature centres, Indigenous cultural sites, zoos, aquaria, botanical gardens, and a host of other heritage sites and wilderness locations." See https://interpretationcanada. wildapricot.org/ (accessed 3 July 2018).

7   Osborne, "Landscapes, Memory, Monuments," 77.

BIBLIOGRAPHY

My argument is that history is made by men and women, just as it can also be unmade and rewritten, always with various silences and elisions, always with shapes imposed and disfigurements tolerated.

Edward Said, *Orientalism*, 1978

Primary Sources

Library and Archives Canada

RG 37-F, RG84, Minutes and Correspondence of the Historic Sites and Monuments Board of Canada.

RG84, Parks Canada Records.

Fort Battleford National Historic Site of Canada, Microfilm: T-11977.

Batoche National Historic Site of Canada, Microfilm: T-11019, T-11020, T-11113, T-11114.

Lower Fort Garry National Historic Site of Canada, Microfilm: T-11208, T-11209, T-11210, T-11260, T-11261, T-11262, T-11271.

Motherwell Homestead—Buildings Documentation, 1968, Microfilm: T-14257.

Prince of Wales Fort National Historic Site of Canada, Microfilm: T-11294, T-11295, T-11296.

York Factory National Historic Site of Canada, Microfilm: T-14170, T-14171.

Archives of Manitoba

River Road Heritage Parkway. Howard Pawley fonds, 1977.

———. Zoning and Acquisition Proposals, 1973.

Legislative Library of Manitoba

Manitoba ARC Authority. Red River Master Development Plan, 1981.

———. River Road Heritage Parkway, Concept Plan, 1982.

———. River Road Heritage Parkway, Proposed Project Plan, 1982.

Manitoba Department of Tourism, Recreation, and Cultural Affairs. A Survey of the Mennonite Village Museum, Winnipeg, 1975.

Mennonite Heritage Village. The Mennonite Heritage Village Story, 1975.

Manitoba Multicultural Museums Committee. Ethno-cultural Museums and Historical Societies in Manitoba, 1983.

Parks Canada, Winnipeg Historical Collection

Batoche National Historic Site of Canada. Commemorative Integrity Statement, March 1997.

_____. Miscellaneous files.

Battle of Tourand's Coulee/Fish Creek National Historic Site of Canada. Management Plan, 2007.

Dick, Lyle. "Prairie Settlement Patterns: Preliminary Report," 1984.

Doull, Ian. "Motherwell Homestead National Historic Park, Abernethy, Saskatchewan," Federal Heritage Buildings Review Office, Ottawa, Building Report 88-14, 1988.

Fort Battleford National Historic Site of Canada. Miscellaneous files.

Hunter, Robert. Architectural History Branch, Federal Heritage Review Office Building Report 88-72, Depot and Library Buildings, York Factory, Manitoba. York Factory files.

Linear Mounds National Historic Site of Canada. Management Plan, 2007.

Lower Fort Garry National Historic Site of Canada. Management Plan, 2007.

_____. Miscellaneous files, Summary of Restoration Work at the Big House and Fur Loft/Saleshop.

Neubergthal Street Village National Historic Site of Canada. Commemorative Integrity Statement, 1998.

Prince of Wales Fort National Historic Site of Canada. Miscellaneous files.

St. Andrew's Rectory National Historic Site of Canada. Management Plan, 1980.

St. Andrew's-on-the-Red. Historical and Architectural Survey and Re-dedication Service, May 1995.

York Factory National Historic Site of Canada. Miscellaneous files.

Provincial Archives of Saskatchewan

Meewasin Valley Authority. Wanuskewin Heritage Park, file 401.8.4.

Wanuskewin Heritage Park, file HB 89.04.03.01.

University of Manitoba Archives and Special Collections

Winnipeg Evening Tribune.

Government Publications

Government of Canada

Buggey, Susan. *An Approach to Aboriginal Cultural Landscapes.* March 1999. http://www.
pc.gc.ca/leg/docs/r/pca-acl/images/Aboriginal_Cultural_Landscapes_e.pdf.

Canada, Privy Council Office. *Report of the Royal Commission on Aboriginal Peoples.* Vol.
4, *Perspectives and Realities.* Ottawa: Canada, Privy Council Office, 1996.

Canadian Historic Sites. *Occasional Papers in Archaeology and History.* No. 4, *Lower Fort
Garry.* Ottawa: Department of Indian and Northern Affairs, 1972.

Coutts, Robert. *Batoche National Historic Site: A Period Landscape Study.* Ottawa: Parks
Canada, Manuscript Report Series, no. 404, 1980.

_____. *Doukhobor Village, Veregin, Saskatchewan.* Ottawa: Historic Sites and
Monuments Board of Canada, October 2003.

_____. *On the Edge of a Frozen Sea: Prince of Wales Fort, York Factory and the Fur Trade
of Western Hudson Bay.* Winnipeg: Parks Canada, 1997.

Coutts, Robert, Darren Keith, and Andrew Stewart. *Kuugjuaq: Memories of Inuit Life in
Churchill.* Winnipeg: Parks Canada, 1996.

"Cultural Resource Management Policy." In Parks Canada, *Guiding Principles and
Operational Policies.* Ottawa: Minister of Supply and Services, 1994.

Elder, Ken. *Survey Report and Maintenance Program, Perimeter Walls, Lower Fort Garry.*
Ottawa: Parks Canada, 1973.

Hucker, Jacqueline. *Prince of Wales Fort: A History, Documentation and Analysis of the
20th Century Repairs to the Outer Walls.* Ottawa: Architectural Division, National
Historic Sites Directorate, Parks Canada, 1994.

Ingram, George. *Lower Fort Garry: The Saleshop Structure and Function.* Parks Canada,
Manuscript Report Series, no. 148. Ottawa: National Historic Parks and Sites,
1967.

Klippenstein, Frieda. "On a New Approach to Heritage Presentation at National
Historic Sites." Parks Canada, *Research Links* (Summer/Autumn 1999): 3–4.

Livermore, Carol. *Lower Fort Garry, the Fur Trade and the Settlement at Red River.* Parks
Canada, Manuscript Report Series, no. 202. Ottawa: National Historic Parks and
Sites, 1976.

Parks Canada. *Canada's Historic Places Initiative: Overview of the Conservation Tools.*
Ottawa: Government of Canada, 2004.

Payment, Diane. *Native Society and Economy in Transition at the Forks, 1850–1900.* Parks
Canada, Microfiche Report Series 383, 1988.

_____. *A Structural and Settlement History of Batoche Village.* Parks Canada, Manuscript
Report Series no. 248, 1977.

Stoddard, N. *The Seahorse Gully Site.* Ottawa: Historic Sites and Monuments Board of
Canada, 22 September 1969.

Thomas, Gregory. *The Men's House, Lower Fort Garry: Its Furnishings and Place Within
the Hudson's Bay Company Post Environment.* Parks Canada, Manuscript Report
Series, no. 246. Ottawa: National Historic Parks and Sites, 1978.

_____. *Lower Fort Garry, Warehouse Building: Structural and Use History.* Ottawa: Parks
Canada, 1977.

Truth and Reconciliation Commission of Canada. *Truth and Reconciliation Commission of Canada: Calls to Action.* Winnipeg: National Centre for Truth and Reconciliation, 2015.

Government of Manitoba

Historic Resources Branch. *The Arctic Small Tool Tradition in Manitoba.* Winnipeg: Historic Resources Branch, 1990.

Pettipas, Katherine. *Towards a Working Paper to Establish Guidelines for the Identification, Documentation, Protection and Commemoration of Native Heritage and Sacred Sites.* Winnipeg: Manitoba Historic Sites Advisory Board, 1991.

Websites

General

Anglican Church of Canada. Diocese of Rupert's Land Archives, St. Andrews-on-the Red. http://www.rupertsland.ca/about/archives/.

The Barracks. http://www.queerstory.ca/2013/10/11/the-barracks/, 11 October 2013.

Forks North Portage Partnership. http://www.theforks.com/business/the-forks-north-portage-partnership/mission-mandate-vision.

Friends of Upper Fort Garry. http://www.upperfortgarry.com/.

Historic England. https://historicengland.org.uk/.

Interpretation Canada. https://interpretationcanada.wildapricot.org/.

Manitoba Museum. https://manitobamuseum.ca/main/visit/museum-galleries/hbc-gallery/.

Mennonite Heritage Village. https://mennoniteheritagevillage.com/.

Neubergthal Heritage Foundation. http://www.neubergthalheritagefoundation.com/.

Pembina Valley Online, 2 March 2015. https://www.pembinavalleyonline.com/.

Pettipas, Leo. "The Petroform Phenomenon of Southeastern Manitoba and Its Significance," 2004. http://rockpiles.blogspot.com/2012/03/petroform-phenomenon-of-southeastern.html.

United Nations Economic, Social and Cultural Organization (UNESCO). "Recognized Cultural Practices." https://ich.unesco.org/en/lists.

Government of Canada

Canada's Historic Places. *Doukhobors at Veregin National Historic Site of Canada.* http://www.historicplaces.ca/en/rep-reg/place-lieu.aspx?id=12783.

———. *Linear Mounds National Historic Site of Canada.* http://historicplaces.ca/en/rep-reg/place-lieu.aspx?id=10475.

———. *Lower Fort Garry National Historic Site of Canada.* http://www.historicplaces.ca/en/rep-reg/place-lieu.aspx?id=4224.

———. *Prince of Wales Fort National Historic Site of Canada.* http://www.historicplaces.ca/en/rep-reg/place-lieu.aspx?id=7760.

———. *Seahorse Gully Remains National Historic Site of Canada.* http://www. historicplaces.ca/en/rep-reg/place-lieu.aspx?id=18791.

———. *Wanuskewin National Historic Site of Canada.* http://www.historicplaces.ca/en/ rep-reg/place-lieu.aspx?id=15685&pid=0.

Parks Canada. *An Approach to Aboriginal Cultural Landscapes: Definition of Aboriginal Cultural Landscapes.* http://www.pc.gc.ca/leg/docs/r/pca-acl/sec4/index_e.asp.

———. *An Approach to Aboriginal Cultural Landscapes: Aboriginal World Views.* http:// www.pc.gc.ca/leg/docs/r/pca-acl/sec1/index_e.asp.

———. *Battle of Seven Oaks, Statement of Commemorative Intent and Designated Place.* http://www.pc.gc.ca/apps/dfhd/page_nhs_eng.aspx?id=149.

Parks Canada. Directory of Federal Heritage Designations. *Batoche National Historic Site of Canada.* http://www.pc.gc.ca/apps/dfhd/page_nhs_eng.aspx?id=731.

———. *Battle of Cut Knife Hill National Historic Site of Canada.* http://www.pc.gc.ca/ apps/dfhd/page_nhs_eng.aspx?id=737.

———. *Battle of Duck Lake National Historic Site of Canada.* http://www.historicplaces. ca/en/rep-reg/place-lieu.aspx?id=12916.

———. *The Forks National Historic Site of Canada.* http://www.pc.gc.ca/apps/dfhd/ page_nhs_eng.aspx?id=151.

———. *Fort Battleford National Historic Site of Canada.* http://pc.gc.ca/en/lhn-nhs/sk/ battleford/info.

———. *Fort Battleford, National Historic Site of Canada.* Commemorative Intent Statement. http://pc.gc.ca/en/lhn-nhs/sk/battleford/decouvrir-discover.

———. *Forts Rouge, Garry and Gibraltar National Historic Site of Canada, Winnipeg, Manitoba.* http://www.pc.gc.ca/apps/dfhd/page_nhs_eng.aspx?id=1728.

———. *Lower Fort Garry National Historic Site of Canada.* Management Plan, October 2007. http://publications.gc.ca/collections/collection_2016/pc/R64-105-59-2007-eng.pdf.

———. *Motherwell National Historic Site of Canada.* https://www.pc.gc.ca/apps/dfhd/ page_nhs_eng.aspx?id=730.

———. *Motherwell National Historic Site of Canada.* History. https://www.pc.gc.ca/en/ lhn-nhs/sk/motherwell/culture/histoire-history.

———. *Motherwell National Historic Site of Canada.* Infrastructure Program. https:// www.pc.gc.ca/en/lhn-nhs/sk/motherwell/visit/infrastructure.

———. *Motherwell National Historic Site of Canada.* Management Plan 2011. http:// publications.gc.ca/collections/collection_2011/pc/R61-56-2011-eng.pdf.

———. *National Historic Sites Systems Plan.* Ottawa, 1991. https://www.google.ca/sear ch?q=Parks+Canada+System+Plan+1991&rlz=1C5CHFA_enCA503CA503&t bm=isch&tbo=u&source=univ&sa=X&ved=0a.

———. *Out and About: Towards a Better Understanding of Gay, Lesbian, Bisexual and Transgendered Persons in the Workplace.* http://hrcouncil.ca/hr-toolkit/documents/ CH37-4-9-2005E.pdf. 2005.

———. *St. Andrew's Rectory National Historic Site of Canada.* Management Plan, 2003. http://publications.gc.ca/site/eng/98469/publication.html.

Government of Manitoba

The Manitoba Provincial Parks Act. http://web2.gov.mb.ca/laws/statutes/ccsm/p020e.php.

Government of Saskatchewan

Wanuskewin Heritage Park. https://wanuskewin.com/visit/exhibitions/.

Government of the United States

U.S. National Parks Service. https://www.nps.gov/vive/index.htm.

Theses

McRae, Matthew. "Remembering Rebellion, Remembering Resistance: Collective Memory, Identity, and the Veterans of 1869–70 and 1885." PhD diss., University of Western Ontario, 2018.

Meyer, David A. "Pre-Dorset Settlements at the Seahorse Gully Site." Master's thesis, University of Manitoba, 1970.

Newspapers

New York Times

"Is Charleston Coming to Terms with the Past?" *New York Times*, 20 November 2016. https://www.nytimes.com/2016/11/20/travel/charleston-south-carolina-past-slave-trade-history.html.

Ottawa Citizen

Butler, Don. "Victims of Communism Memorial to Be Moved, Joly Announces." *Ottawa Citizen*, 17 December 2015. https://ottawacitizen.com/news/local-news/joly-announces-next-steps-for-victims-of-communism-memorial.

Winnipeg Free Press

"Friends of Upper Fort Garry Defend Reasoning." *Winnipeg Free Press*, 18 October 2014. https://www.winnipegfreepress.com/local/friends-of-upper-fort-garry-defend-reasoning-279655462.html.

Kives, Bartley. "Linear Mounds One of Manitoba's Best-Kept Archaeological Secrets: Many Want to Keep It That Way." *Winnipeg Free Press*, 21 September 2013. https://www.winnipegfreepress.com/local/sacred-grounds-224681602.html.

Piche, Gabrielle. "Celebrating a Partnership: 149th anniversary of Treaty 1 marked at Lower Fort Garry," *Winnipeg Free Press*, 4 August, 2020.

"Scots Slam Perceived Snub," *Winnipeg Free Press*, 17 October 2014. https://www.winnipegfreepress.com/local/scots-slam-perceived-snub-279533302.html.

"Whiteshell's Sacred Stones." *Winnipeg Free Press*, 30 July 2011.

The Globe and Mail

"Canada Adds Eight Sites to List of Candidates for UNESCO World Heritage Status." *Globe and Mail*, 20 December, 2017. https://www.theglobeandmail.com/news/national/canada-adds-eight-sites-to-list-of-candidates-for-unesco-world-heritage-status/article374.

"Cree Win War of Words over 'Siege' of Fort Battleford 125 Years Ago." *Globe and Mail*, 21 October 2010. https://beta.theglobeandmail.com/news/national/cree-win-war-of-words-over-siege-of-fort-battleford-125-yearsago/article1461558/?ref=http://www.theglobeandmail.com&.

Published Sources

Adams, Annmarie. "Rooms of Their Own: The Nurses Residence at Montreal's Royal Victoria Hospital." In *Restoring Women's History Through Historic Preservation*, edited by Gail Lee Dubrow and Jennifer B. Goodman, 131–44. Baltimore: The Johns Hopkins University Press, 2003.

Adelman, Jeremy. "Early Doukhobor Experience on the Canadian Prairies." *Journal of Canadian Studies* 25, no. 4 (Winter 1990–91): 111–28.

Ahenakew, Freda, and H.C. Wolfart. *Our Grandmothers' Lives as Told in Their Own Words*. Regina: University of Regina Press, 1998.

Allen, Richard, ed. *A Region of the Mind: Interpreting the Western Canadian Plains*. Regina: Canadian Plains Studies Center, 1973.

Andersen, Chris. "More than the Sum of Our Rebellions: Métis Histories Beyond Batoche." *Ethnohistory* 61, no. 4 (Autumn 2014): 619–33.

Andrews, Thomas D., and John B. Zoe. "The Idaa Trail: Archaeology and the Dogrib Cultural Landscape." In *At a Crossroads: Archaeology and First Peoples in Canada*, edited by George P. Nicholas and Thomas D. Andrews, 160–77. Burnaby: SFU Archaeology Press, 1997.

Androsoff, Ashleigh. "A Larger Frame: 'Redressing' the Image of Doukhobor-Canadian Women in the Twentieth Century." *Journal of the Canadian Historical Association* 18, no. 1 (2007): 81–105.

———. "The Trouble with Teamwork: Doukhobor Women's Plow Pulling in Western Canada, 1899." *Canadian Historical Review* 100, no. 4 (December 2019): 540–63.

Appadurai, Arjun. *Modernity at Large: Cultural Dimensions of Globalization*. Minneapolis: University of Minnesota Press, 1996.

Ashley, Susan L.T., and Andrea Terry. "Introduction: Critical Heritage Studies in Canada." *Journal of Canadian Studies* 52, no. 1 (Winter 2018): 1–10.

Ashworth, Gregory, Brian Graham, and John Tunbridge. *Pluralising Pasts: Heritage Identity and Place in Multicultural Societies*. London: Pluto Press, 2007.

Ashworth, Gregory, and John Tunbridge. *Dissonant Heritage: The Management of the Past as a Resource in Conflict*. Chichester: John Wiley and Sons, 1996.

Ballantyne, Robert M. *Hudson's Bay or Every-day Life in the Wilds of North America*. London: Thomas Nelson, 1902.

Barkwell, Lawrence. *The Battle of Seven Oaks: A Métis Perspective*. Winnipeg: Louis Riel Institute, 2015.

Beardy, Flora, and Robert Coutts. *Voices from Hudson Bay: Cree Stories from York Factory*. Montreal: McGill-Queen's University Press, 2017.

Bennett, Gordon. "Commemorative Integrity: Monitoring the State of Canada's National Historic Sites." *Momentum* 4, no. 3, ICOMOS Canada (1995): n.p.

Berman, Marshall. *All That Is Solid Melts into Air: The Experience of Modernity.* New York: Penguin Books, 1988.

Bradley, Ben. *British Columbia by the Road: Car Culture and the Making of the Modern Landscape.* Vancouver: University of British Columbia Press, 2017.

Brown, Thomas. *Civil War Canon: Sites of Confederate Memory in South Carolina.* Chapel Hill: University of North Carolina Press, 2015.

Bryce, George. "The Old Settlers of Red River." Manitoba Historical Society, *Transactions*, Series 1, no. 19, 1885.

Buchner, Anthony. "Archaeo-Astronomical Investigation of the Petroform Phenomenon of Southeastern Manitoba." In *Directions in Manitoba Prehistory*, edited by Leo Pettipas, 1–23. Winnipeg: Association of Manitoba Archaeologists and Manitoba Archaeological Association, 1980.

Bullchild, Percy. *The Sun Came Down: The History of the World as My Blackfeet Elders Told It.* Lincoln: University of Nebraska Press Bison Books, 2005.

Bussidor, Ila, and Üstün Bilgen-Reinart. *Night Spirits: The Story of the Relocation of the Sayisi Dene.* Winnipeg: University of Manitoba Press, 1997.

Cameron, Christina. "Commemoration: A Moving Target?" In *The Place of History: Commemorating Canada's Past*, edited by Thomas Symons, 27–39. Ottawa: The Royal Society of Canada, 1997.

———. "Finding the Spirit of Place: A World Heritage Perspective." In *Spirit of Place: Between Tangible and Intangible Heritage*, edited by Laurier Turgeon, 15–22. Québec: Laval University Press, 2009.

———. "The Spirit of Place: The Physical Memory of Canada." *Journal of Canadian Studies* 35, no. 1 (2000): 77–94.

Campbell, Claire Elizabeth, ed. *A Century of Parks Canada, 1911–2011.* Calgary: University of Calgary Press, 2011.

———. *Nature, Place, and Story: Rethinking Historic Sites in Canada.* Montreal: McGill-Queen's University Press, 2017.

Carlson, Keith Thor. *The Power of Place, the Problem of Time: Aboriginal Identity and Historical Consciousness in the Cauldron of Colonialism.* Toronto: University of Toronto Press, 2010.

Carter, Sarah. *Capturing Women: The Manipulation of Cultural Imagery in Canada's Prairie West.* Montreal: McGill-Queen's University Press, 1997.

———. *Imperial Plots: Women, Land, and the Spadework of British Colonialism on the Canadian Prairies.* Winnipeg: University of Manitoba Press, 2016.

———. Review of Florence Miller's *Motherwell National Historic Site of Canada. The Public Historian* 31, no. 1 (Winter 2009): 117–20.

Chambers, Cynthia M., and Narcisse J. Blood. "Love Thy Neighbour: Repatriating Precarious Blackfoot Sites." *International Journal of Canadian Studies* 39–40 (2009): 253–79.

Churchill, David. "Mother Goose's Map: Tabloid Geographies and Gay Male Experiences in 1950s Toronto." *Journal of Urban History* 30, no. 6 (September 2004): 826–52.

Colpitts, George. *Pemmican Empire: Food, Trade, and the Last Bison Hunts in the North American Plains, 1780–1882.* Cambridge: Cambridge University Press, 2014.

Coutts, Robert. "Prince of Wales Fort." In *The Oxford Companion to Canadian History*, edited by Gerald Hallowell, 504. Toronto: Oxford University Press, 2004.

———. "St. Andrew's and the Agricultural Economy." In *The Road to the Rapids: Nineteenth Century Church and Society in St. Andrew's Parish, Red River*, 131–52. Calgary: University of Calgary Press, 2000.

———. "Stone Symbols of Dominance: The River Road Heritage Parkway and the Bias of Architectural Commemoration." *NeWest Review* (March 1988): 3–5.

———. "'We See Hard Times Ahead of Us': York Factory and Indigenous Life in the Western Hudson Region, 1880–1925." *Journal of Canadian Studies* 51, no. 2 (Spring 2017): 434–60.

Coutts, Robert, and Katherine Pettipas. "'Mere Curiosities Are Not Required': The Story of the HBC Museum Collection." *The Beaver* 74, no. 3 (June/July 1994): 13–19.

Craft, Aimee. *Breathing Life into the Stone Fort Treaty: An Anishinaabe Understanding of Treaty One.* Saskatoon: Purich Publishing, 2013.

Crane, Susan A. "Writing the Individual Back into Collective Memory." *American Historical Review Forum* 102, no. 5 (December 1997): 1372–85.

Creates, Marlene. *Places of Presence: Newfoundland Kin and Ancestral Land, Newfoundland, 1989–1991.* St. John's: Killick Press, 1997.

Cresswell, Tim. *Place: An Introduction.* Chichester, West Sussex: John Wiley and Sons, 2015.

Cruikshank, Julie. *Life Lived Like a Story.* Lincoln: University of Nebraska Press, 1990.

Dawson, Bruce. "'It's a Landmark in the Community': The Conservation of Historic Places in Saskatchewan, 1911–2009." In *The West and Beyond: New Perspectives on an Imagined Region*, edited by Alvin Finkel, Sarah Carter, and Peter Fortna, 397–416. Edmonton: Athabasca University Press, 2010.

Devine, Heather. *The People Who Own Themselves: Aboriginal Ethnogenesis in a Canadian Family.* Calgary: University of Calgary Press, 2004.

———. "Prosopographical Approaches in Canadian Native History." In *Prosopographical Approaches and Applications: A Handbook*, edited by K.S.B. Keats-Rohan, 361–86. Oxford: Oxford University Press, 2007.

Dick, Lyle. *Farmers "Making Good": The Development of Abernethy District, Saskatchewan, 1880–1920.* Calgary: University of Calgary Press, 2008.

———. "Heterohegemonic Discourse and Homosexual Acts: The Case of Saskatchewan in the Settlement Era." Sex and State History Conference, Toronto, July 1985.

———. "Male Homosexuality in Saskatchewan's Settlement Era: The 1895 Case of Regina's 'Oscar Wilde.'" Paper presented at the Canadian Historical Association Conference, York University, Toronto, 30 May 2006.

———. "The Seven Oaks Incident and the Construction of a Historical Tradition." *Journal of the Canadian Historical Association* 2 (1991): 91–113.

Dodd, Dianne. "Canadian Historic Sites and Plaques: Heroines, Trailblazers, the Famous Five." *CRM: The Journal of Heritage Stewardship* 6, no. 2 (Summer 2009): 29–66.

Domicelj, Joan, and Serge Domicelj, eds. *A Sense of Place: A Conversation in Three Cultures.* Canberra: Australian Heritage Commission, 1990.

Dubrow, Gail Lee. "Blazing Trails with Pink Triangles and Rainbow Flags: Improving the Preservation of Gay and Lesbian History." In *Restoring Women's History Through Historic Preservation,* edited by Gail Lee Dubrow and Jennifer Goodman, 281–300. Baltimore: The Johns Hopkins University Press, 2003.

———. "Restoring Women's History Through Historic Preservation: Recent Developments in Scholarship and Public Historical Practice." In *Restoring Women's History Through Historic Preservation,* edited by Gail Lee Dubrow and Jennifer B. Goodman, 1–14. Baltimore: The Johns Hopkins University Press, 2003.

Duder, Cameron. *Awfully Devoted Women: Lesbian Lives in Canada, 1900–1965.* Vancouver: University of British Columbia Press, 2011.

Eyford, Ryan. *White Settler Reserve: New Iceland and the Colonization of the Canadian West.* Vancouver: University of British Columbia Press, 2017.

Fawcett, Jane. *The Future of the Past: Attitudes to Conservation, 1174–1974.* London: Thames and Hudson, 1976.

Felski, Rita. "The Gender of Modernity." In *Political Gender: Texts and Contexts,* edited by S. Ledger, J. MacDonagh, and J. Spencer, 144–55. New York: Harvester Wheatsheaf, 1994.

Flannery, Regina. *Ellen Smallboy: Glimpses of a Cree Woman's Life.* Montreal: McGill-Queen's University Press, 1995.

Foote, Kenneth. *Shadowed Ground: America's Landscapes of Violence and Tragedy.* Austin: University of Texas Press, 1997.

Foucault, Michel. *Discipline and Punish: The Growth of the Prison.* New York: Vintage Books, 1977.

———. *Language, Counter-Memory, Practice: Selected Essays and Interviews.* Ithaca: Cornell University Press, 1977.

Friesen, Gerald. *The Canadian Prairies: A History.* Toronto: University of Toronto Press, 1984.

———. *River Road: Essays on Manitoba and Prairie History.* Winnipeg: University of Manitoba Press, 1996.

———. *The West: Regional Ambitions, National Debates, Global Age.* Toronto: Penguin Books, 1999.

Friesen, Jean. "Grant Me Wherewith to Make My Living." In *Aboriginal Resource Use in Canada: Historical and Legal Aspects,* edited by Kerry Abel and Jean Friesen, 141–55. Winnipeg: University of Manitoba Press, 1991.

———. "Heritage: The Manitoba Experience." *Prairie Forum* 15, no. 2 (1990): 199–220.

Gabert, Karen. "Locating Identity: The Ukrainian Cultural Heritage Village as a Public History Text." In *Re-imagining Ukrainian-Canadians: History, Politics, and Identity,* edited by R.L. Hinther and J. Mochoruk, 54–84. Toronto: University of Toronto Press, 2011.

Gardner, James, and Peter LaPaglia. *Public History: Essays from the Field.* Malabar, FL: Krieger Publishing Company, 2004.

Gentile, Patrizia. "Capital Queers: Social Memory and Queer Place(s) in Cold War Ottawa." In *Placing Memory and Remembering Place in Canada,* edited by James

Opp and John C. Walsh, 187–214. Vancouver: University of British Columbia Press, 2011.

Gillis, John, R., ed. *Commemorations: The Politics of National Identity.* Princeton: Princeton University Press, 1994.

Giraud, Marcel. *The Métis in the Canadian West.* Vol. 1. Edmonton: University of Alberta Press, 1986.

Glassberg, David. *Sense of History: The Place of the Past in American Life.* Amherst: University of Massachusetts Press, 2001.

Gordon, Alan. *Time Travel: Tourism and the Rise of the Living History Museum in Mid-Twentieth-Century Canada.* Vancouver: University of British Columbia Press, 2016.

Graham, Brian, Greg J. Ashworth, and John E. Tunbridge. *A Geography of Heritage: Power, Culture, and Economy.* New York: Routledge, 2000.

Halbwachs, Maurice. *La Mémoire Collective.* 2nd ed. Paris: Les Presses Univesitaires de France, 1950. Translated as *On Collective Memory.* Chicago: University of Chicago Press, 1992.

Hall, Norma. "Red River Farming." In *A Casualty of Colonialism: Métis Red River Farming 1810–1870.* https://casualtyofcolonialism.wordpress.com/bibliography/.

Hanks, Christopher C. "Ancient Knowledge of Ancient Sites: Tracing Dene Identity from the Late Pleistocene and Holocene." In *At a Crossroads: Archaeology and First Peoples in Canada,* edited by George P. Nicholas and Thomas D. Andrews, 178–89. Burnaby: SFU Archaeology Press, 1997.

Hardy, Thomas. *The Return of the Native.* New York: Mineola, 2003.

Hargrave, Letitia. *The Letters of Letitia Hargrave,* edited by Margaret MacLeod. Toronto: Champlain Society, 1947.

Harris, Cole. *Making Native Space: Colonialism, Resistance, and Reserves in British Columbia.* Vancouver: University of British Columbia Press, 2002.

Harrison, Rodney. *Heritage: Critical Approaches.* New York: Routledge, 2013.

———. *Understanding the Politics of Heritage.* Manchester: Manchester University Press, 2010.

Hart, E.J. (Ted). *J.B. Harkin: Father of Canada's National Parks.* Edmonton: University of Alberta Press, 2010.

Hayden, Dolores. "The Power of Place: Claiming Women's History in the Urban Landscape." In *The Place of History: Commemorating Canada's Past. Proceedings of the National Symposium held on the Occasion of the 75th Anniversary of the HSMBC.* Historic Sites and Monuments Board of Canada, 66–77. Ottawa: The Royal Society of Canada, 1997.

———. *The Power of Place: Urban Landscapes as Public History.* Cambridge: MIT Press, 1995.

High, Steven. "Placing the Displaced Worker: Narrating Place in De-industrializing Sturgeon Falls, Ontario." In James Opp and John C. Walsh, eds., *Placing Memory and Remembering Place in Canada,* 159–86. Vancouver: University of British Columbia Press, 2011.

Hildebrandt, Walter. *The Battle of Batoche: British Small Warfare and the Entrenched Métis.* 2nd ed. Vancouver: Talon Books, 2012.

————. *Views from Fort Battleford: Constructed Visions of an Anglo-Canadian West.* Regina: Canadian Plains Research Center, 1994.

Hillmer, Norman, and Adam Chapnick, eds. *Canadas of the Mind: The Making and Unmaking of Canadian Nationalism in the Twentieth Century.* Montreal: McGill-Queen's University Press, 2007.

Hobsbawm, Eric, and Terence Ranger, eds. *The Invention of Tradition.* Cambridge: Cambridge University Press, 1983.

Horodyski, Mary. "Women and the Winnipeg General Strike of 1919." *Manitoba History*, no. 11 (Spring, 1986).

Huyck, Heather. "Proceeding from Here." In *Restoring Women's History through Historic Preservation*, edited by Gail Lee Dubrow and Jennifer Goodman, 355–64. Baltimore: The Johns Hopkins University Press, 2003.

Innis, Harold. *The Fur Trade in Canada: An Introduction to Canadian Economic History.* Toronto: University of Toronto Press, 1970.

Jackson, John. *A Sense of Place, a Sense of Time.* New Haven: Yale University Press, 1994.

Keegan, Marcia. *Pueblo People: Ancient Traditions, Modern Lives.* Santa Fe: Clear Light Publishing, 1998.

Kirshenblatt-Gimblett, Barbara. "Theorizing Heritage." *Ethnomusicology* 39, no. 3 (1995): 367–80.

Korinek, Valerie. *Prairie Fairies: A History of Queer Communities and Peoples in Western Canada, 1930–1985.* Toronto: University of Toronto Press, 2018.

————. "A Queer-Eye View of the Prairies: Reorienting Western Canadian Histories." In *The West and Beyond: New Perspectives on an Imagined Region*, edited by Alvin Finkel, Sarah Carter, and Peter Fortna, 278–96. Edmonton: Athabasca University Press, 2010.

Kothari, Uma, and Tim Edensor. "The Masculinization of Stirling's Heritage." In *Tourism: A Gender Analysis*, edited by V. Kinnaird, 115–34. London: John Wiley, 1994.

Kryder-Reid, Elizabeth. *California Mission Landscapes: Race, Memory, and the Politics of Heritage.* Minneapolis: University of Minnesota Press, 2016.

LaRocque, Emma. "For the Love of Place—Not Just Any Place: Selected Métis Writings." In *Place and Replace: Essays on Western Canada*, edited by Adele Perry, Esyllt Jones, and Leah Morton, 179–85. Winnipeg: University of Manitoba Press, 2013.

Lee, Ellen. "Aboriginal Heritage Issues in Canadian Land Claims Negotiations." Paper presented at the Fulbright Symposium, "Aboriginal Cultures in an Interconnected World," Darwin, Australia, 1997.

Lehr, John C. "The Landscape of Ukrainian Settlement in the Canadian West." *Great Plains Quarterly* 2, no. 2 (Spring 1982): 94–105.

Loewen, James W. *Lies Across America: What Our Historic Sites Get Wrong.* New York: The New Press, 1999.

Lowenthal, David. *The Heritage Crusade and the Spoils of History.* Cambridge: Cambridge University Press, 1998.

————. "Natural and Cultural Heritage." *International Journal of Heritage Studies* 11, no. 1 (2005): 81–92.

———. *The Past Is a Foreign Country*. Cambridge: Cambridge University Press, 1985.

Lunn, Kevin. "York Factory National Historic Site of Canada: Planning the Future for a Place with a Momentous Past." *Manitoba History* 48 (Autumn/Winter 2004–05). http://www.mhs.mb.ca/docs/mb_history/48/yorkfactory.shtml.

McBryde, Isabel. "Those Truly Outstanding Examples: Kakadu in the Context of Australia's World Heritage Properties." In *A Sense of Place: A Conversation in Three Cultures*, edited by J. Domicelj and S. Domicelj, 15–19. Canberra: Australian Heritage Commission, 1990.

McCallum, Mary Jane Logan. *Indigenous Women, Work, and History, 1940–1980*. Winnipeg: University of Manitoba Press, 2014.

McCormack, Patricia. *Fort Chipewyan and the Shaping of Canadian History, 1788–1920s*. Vancouver: University of British Columbia Press, 2010.

McCullough, Alan. "Parks Canada and the 1885 Rebellion/Uprising/Resistance." *Prairie Forum* 27, no. 2 (Fall 2002): 161–98.

———. "Parks Canada and Women's History." In *Restoring Women's History through Historic Preservation*, edited by Gail Lee Dubrov and Jennifer Goodman, 337–54. Baltimore: The Johns Hopkins University Press, 2003.

McKay, Elsie. *The Stone Fort*. Selkirk: Enterprise Publishers, 1960.

McKay, Ian. *Quest of the Folk: Antimodernism and Cultural Selection in Twentieth-Century Nova Scotia*. Montreal: McGill-Queen's University Press, 1994.

McKay, Ian, and Robin Bates. *In the Province of History: The Making of the Public Past in Twentieth-Century Nova Scotia*. Montreal: McGill-Queen's University Press, 2010.

Mackey, Eva. "Tricky Myths: Settler Pasts and Landscapes of Innocence." In *Settling and Unsettling Memories: Essays in Canadian Public History*, edited by Nicole Neatby and Peter Hodgins, 310–39. Toronto: University of Toronto Press, 2012.

MacLeod, Margaret, and W.L. Morton. *Cuthbert Grant of Grantown*. 2nd. ed. Toronto: McClelland and Stewart, 1974.

McMaster, Lindsey. *Working Girls in the West: Representations of Wage-Earning Women*. Vancouver: University of British Columbia Press, 2008.

McRae, Matthew. "Remembering What We Forget: Memory, Commemoration and the 1885 Resistance." *Active History* (November 2019). http://activehistory.ca/2019/11/remembering-what-we-forget-memory-commemoration-and-the-1885-resistance/.

Marsh, John, and Bruce Hodgins, eds. *Changing Parks: The History, Future and Cultural Context of Parks and Heritage Landscapes*. Toronto: Natural Heritage, 1998.

Martin, Joseph. "Conflict at Red River: Collision at Seven Oaks." In *The Forks and the Battle of Seven Oaks in Manitoba History*, edited by Robert Coutts and Richard Stuart, 58–64. Winnipeg: Manitoba Historical Society, 1994.

Marx, Karl. *The Eighteenth Brumaire of Louis Bonaparte*. London: Origami Books, 2018.

Massey, Doreen. "Places and Their Pasts." *History Workshop Journal* 39, no. 1 (March 1995): 182–92.

Meinig, Donald W. "The Beholding Eye: Ten Versions of the Same Scene." In *The Interpretation of Ordinary Landscapes: Geographical Essays*, edited by Donald W. Meinig and John Brinckerhoff Jackson, 33–48. New York: Oxford University Press, 1979.

Misztal, Barbara. *Theories of Social Remembering*. Maidenhead, Berkshire: Open University Press, 2003.

Morgan, Cecilia. *Commemorating Canada: History, Heritage, and Memory, 1850s–1990s*. Toronto: University of Toronto Press, 2016.

———. *Creating Colonial Pasts: History, Memory, and Commemoration in Southern Ontario, 1860–1980*. Toronto: University of Toronto Press, 2015.

Neatby, Nicole, and Peter Hodgins. *Settling and Unsettling Memories: Essays in Canadian Public History*. Toronto: University of Toronto Press, 2012.

Nelles, Henry V. *The Art of Nation-Building: Pageantry and Spectacle at Quebec's Tercentenary*. Toronto: University of Toronto Press, 1999.

Neufeld, David. "Parks Canada, the Commemoration of Canada, and Northern Aboriginal Oral History." In *Oral History and Public Memories*, edited by Linda Shopes and Paula Hamilton, 7–30. Philadelphia: Temple University Press, 2008.

Newman, Michael. "February 19, 1942: If Day." *Manitoba History* (Spring 1987): 27–30.

Newman, Peter. *Caesars of the Wilderness*. Toronto: Penguin Books, 1989.

Nietzsche, Friedrich. "On the Utility and Liability of History for Life." In *The Nietzsche Reader*, edited by Keith Ansell Pearson and Duncan Large, 131–35. Oxford: Blackwell Press, 2006.

Nora, Pierre. "Between Memory and History: Les Lieux de Mémoire." *Representations* 26 (Spring 1989): 7–24.

Nunn, Patrick. *The Edge of Memory: Ancient Stories, Oral Tradition and the Post-Glacial World*. London: Bloomsbury Sigma, 2018.

Oakes, Jill, Rick Riewe, Yale Belanger, Sharon Blady, Kelly Legge, and Patsy Wiebe, eds. *Aboriginal Cultural Landscapes*. Winnipeg: Aboriginal Issues Press, 2004.

O'Brien, Jean. *Firsting and Lasting: Writing Indians out of Existence in New England*. Minneapolis: University of Minnesota Press, 2010.

Opp, James, and John C. Walsh. *Placing Memory and Remembering Place in Canada*. Vancouver: University of British Columbia Press, 2010.

Osborne, Brian S. "From Space to Place: Images of Nationhood." In *Reflections from the Prairies: Geographical Essays*, edited by H.J. Selwood and J.H. Lehr, 1–13. Winnipeg: Department of Geography, University of Winnipeg, 1992.

———. "Landscapes, Memory, Monuments, and Commemoration: Putting Identity in Its Place." *Canadian Ethnic Studies* 23, no. 3 (2001): 39–77.

Pannekoek, Frits. "The Rise of the Heritage Priesthood or the Decline of Community Based Heritage." *Historic Preservation Forum* 12, no. 3 (Spring 1998): 4–10.

———. "Who Matters? Public History and the Invention of the Canadian Past." *Acadiensis* 29, no. 2 (Spring 2000): 205–17.

Payment, Diane. *The Free People—Li Gens Libres: A History of the Métis Community of Batoche, Saskatchewan*. Calgary: University of Calgary Press, 2009.

Payne, Michael. "Commemorating Ethno-cultural Communities in Manitoba." *Manitoba History* 50 (October 2005). http://www.mhs.mb.ca/docs/mb_history/50/commemoration.shtml.

Payne, Michael, and C.J. Taylor. "Western Canadian Fur Trade Sites and the Iconography of Public Memory." *Manitoba History* 46 (Autumn/Winter 2003–04): 2–6.

Peers, Laura. *Playing Ourselves: Interpreting Native Histories at Historic Reconstructions.* Plymouth, UK: AltaMira Press, 2007.

Peers, Laura, and Robert Coutts. "Aboriginal History and Historic Sites: The Shifting Ground." In *Gathering Places: Aboriginal and Fur Trade Histories*, edited by Carolyn Prodruchny and Laura Peers, 274–94. Vancouver: University of British Columbia Press, 2010.

Perry, Adele. "Historiography that Breaks Your Heart: Van Kirk and the Writing of Feminist History." In *Finding a Way to the Heart: Feminist Writings on Aboriginal and Women's History in Canada*, edited by Robin Jarvis Brownlie and Valerie Korinek, 81–97. Winnipeg: University of Manitoba Press, 2012.

Prentiss, Anna Marie, Matthew J. Walsh, and Thomas A. Foor. "Evolution of Early Thule Material Culture: Cultural Transmission and Terrestrial Ecology." *Arctic Research Centre*, Aarhus University, 27 March 2018. Also published in *Human Ecology* 46 (2018): 633–50.

Rabinowitz, Richard. *Curating America: Journeys Through Storyscapes of the American Past.* Chapel Hill: University of North Carolina Press, 2016.

Ray, Arthur. *The Canadian Fur Trade in the Industrial Age.* Toronto: University of Toronto Press, 1990.

Relph, Edward. *Place and Placelessness.* London: Pion Ltd., 1976.

Ricketts, Shannon. "Cultural Selection and National Identity: Establishing Historic Sites in a National Framework, 1920–1939." *The Public Historian* 18, no. 3 (Summer 1996): 23–41.

Rosenzweig, Roy, and David Thelen. *The Presence of the Past: Popular Uses of History in American Life.* New York: Columbia University Press, 1998.

Said, Edward. *Orientalism.* New York: Random House, 1978.

Sangster, Joan. "Beyond Dichotomies: Re-Assessing Gender History and Women's History in Canada." *Left History* 3, no. 1 (Spring/Summer 1995): 109–21.

Saunders, Nicholas J. "At the Mouth of the Obsidian Cave: Deity and Place in Aztec Religion." In *Sacred Sites, Sacred Places*, edited by David Carmichael, 172–83. London: Routledge, 1994.

Schama, Simon. *Landscape and Memory.* New York: A.A. Knopf, 1995.

Shore, Fred. "The Origins of Métis Nationalism and the Pemmican Wars, 1780–1821." In *The Forks and the Battle of Seven Oaks in Manitoba History*, edited by Robert Coutts and Richard Stuart, 78–81. Winnipeg: Manitoba Historical Society, 1994.

Smith, Laurajane. *Uses of Heritage.* Abingdon: Routledge Publishing, 2006.

Spry, Irene M. "The Tragedy of the Loss of the Commons in Western Canada." In *As Long as the Sun Shines and the Water Flows: A Reader in Canadian Native Studies*, edited by A.L. Getty and Antoine Lussier, 203–28. Vancouver: University of British Columbia Press, 1983.

Stanley, George F.G. *The Birth of Western Canada.* Toronto: University of Toronto Press, 1936.

Stanton, Catherine. "The Past as a Public Good: The U.S. National Park Service and 'Cultural Repair' in Postindustrial Places." In *People and Their Pasts: Public History Today*, edited by Hilda Kean and Paul Ashton, 57–73. London: Palgrave Macmillan, 2008.

Steinbring, Jack H. "Dating Rock Art in the Northern Midcontinent." *American Indian Rock Art* 12 (1993): 15–29.

Steinbring, Jack H., and Anthony Buchner. "Cathedrals of Prehistory: Rock Art Sites of the Northern Plains." *American Indian Rock Art* 23 (1997): 73–84.

Swyripa, Frances. *Storied Landscapes: Ethno-Religious Identity and the Canadian Prairies.* Winnipeg: University of Manitoba Press, 2010.

Taylor, C.J. *Negotiating the Past: The Making of Canada's National Historic Parks and Sites.* Montreal: McGill-Queen's University Press, 1990.

Terry, Andrea. *Family Ties: Living History in Canadian House Museums.* Montreal: McGill-Queen's University Press, 2015.

The Pasts Collective. *Canadians and Their Pasts.* Toronto: University of Toronto Press, 2013.

Tough, Frank. *"As Their Natural Resources Fail": Native Peoples and the Economic History of Northern Manitoba, 1870–1930.* Vancouver: University of British Columbia Press, 1996.

Tuan, Yi-Fu. *Space and Place: The Perspective of Experience.* Minneapolis: University of Minnesota Press, 1977.

Ulrich, Laurel Thatcher. *The Age of Homespun: Objects and Stories in the Creation of an American Myth.* New York: A.A. Knopf, 2001.

Urry, John. *Consuming Places.* London: Routledge, 1995.

Urry, John, and Jonas Larsen. *The Tourist Gaze 3.0: Leisure and Travel in Contemporary Societies.* Thousand Oaks, CA: Sage Publications, 2011.

Van Kirk, Sylvia. *Many Tender Ties: Women in Fur Trade Society, 1670–1870.* Winnipeg: Watson and Dwyer Publishing, 1980.

Wardhaugh, Robert, ed. *Towards Defining the Prairies: Region, Culture, and History.* Winnipeg: University of Manitoba Press, 2001.

Warkentin, John, and Richard Ruggles. *Historical Atlas of Manitoba.* Winnipeg: Manitoba Historical Society, 1970.

Watson, Robert. *Lower Fort Garry: A History of the Stone Fort.* Winnipeg: Hudson's Bay Company, 1928.

West, Patricia. "Uncovering and Interpreting Women's History at Historic House Museums." In *Restoring Women's History Through Historic Preservation*, edited by Gail Lee Dubrow and Jennifer B. Goodman, 83–95. Baltimore: The Johns Hopkins University Press, 2003.

Wolfe, Patrick. "Settler Colonialism and the Elimination of the Native." *Journal of Genocide Research* 8, no. 4 (2006): 387–409.

Wright, Patrick. *On Living in an Old Country: The National Past in Contemporary Britain.* London: Verso Press, 1985.

Young, James E. "Memory and Counter-Memory." *Harvard Design Magazine* 9 (Fall 1999). http://partizaning.org/wp-content/uploads/2014/01/Memory-and-Counter-Memory.pdf.

INDEX